studies in jazz

Institute of Jazz Studies
Rutgers—The State University of New Jersey
General Editors: Dan Morgenstern and Edward Berger

25. BACK BEATS AND RIM SHOTS: The Johnny Blowers Story, *by Warren W. Vaché Sr., 1997*
26. DUKE ELLINGTON: A Listener's Guide, *by Eddie Lambert, 1998*
27. SERGE CHALOFF: A Musical Biography and Discography, *by Vladimir Simosko, 1998*
28. HOT JAZZ: From Harlem to Storyville, *by David Griffiths, 1998*
29. ARTIE SHAW: A Musical Biography and Discography, *by Vladimir Simosko, 2000*
30. JIMMY DORSEY: A Study in Contrasts, *by Robert L. Stockdale, 1998*
31. STRIDE!: Fats, Jimmy, Lion, Lamb and All the Other Ticklers, *by John L. Fell and Terkild Vinding, 1999*
32. GIANT STRIDES: The Legacy of Dick Wellstood, *by Edward N. Meyer, 1999*
33. JAZZ GENTRY: Aristocrats of the Music World, *by Warren W. Vaché Sr., 1999*
34. THE UNSUNG SONGWRITERS: America's Masters of Melody, *by Warren W. Vaché Sr., 2000*
35. THE MUSICAL WORLD OF J. J. JOHNSON, *by Joshua Berrett and Louis G. Bourgois, III, 1999*
36. THE LADIES WHO SING WITH THE BAND, *by Betty Bennett, 2000*
37. AN UNSUNG CAT: The Life and Music of Warne Marsh, *by Safford Chamberlain, 2000*
38. JAZZ IN NEW ORLEANS: The Postwar Years Through 1970, *by Charles Suhor, 2001*
39. THE YOUNG LOUIS ARMSTRONG ON RECORDS, *by Edward Brooks, 2001*
40. BENNY CARTER: A Life in American Music, Second Edition, *by Morroe Berger, Edward Berger, and James Patrick, 2 vols., 2002*

The *Annual Review of Jazz Studies* is published yearly by Scarecrow Press for the Institute of Jazz Studies at Rutgers, The State University of New Jersey.

Authors should address manuscripts and editorial correspondence to:

The Editors
Annual Review of Jazz Studies
Institute of Jazz Studies
Dana Library
Rutgers, The State University of New Jersey
Newark, New Jersey 07102

Review copies of books should be sent to this address by publishers and marked to the attention of the Book Review Editor.

Authors preparing manuscripts for consideration should follow *The Chicago Manual of Style*, 14th Edition. In particular: (1) manuscripts should be original typed or word-processed copies; (2) except for foreign-language quotations, manuscripts must be in English; (3) *all* material (text, quotations, endnotes, author's biographical note) must be neat, *double-spaced*, and with adequate margins; (4) notes must be grouped together on separate pages at the end of the manuscript and should be complete references following samples in *The Chicago Manual of Style;* (5) on a separate sheet, authors should provide a one- or two-sentence biographical note, including current affiliation; (6) musical samples must be on a separate sheet in camera-ready form, preferably computer-copied; (7) authors should take the size of the *ARJS* page into account in assembling their examples; (8) authors are required to submit a 3.5-inch computer diskette of their articles (Word or WordPerfect, Macintosh or PC); and (9) a cassette tape of any examples transcribed or reproduced from recordings must be included; this is to facilitate reading the paper and checking the accuracy of the transcriptions (a cassette is not necessary for printed music or examples composed by the author).

Authors alone are responsible for the contents of their article.

ANNUAL REVIEW OF JAZZ STUDIES 10
1999

Edited by
Edward Berger
David Cayer
Henry Martin
Dan Morgenstern

Institute of Jazz Studies
Rutgers—The State University
of New Jersey
and
The Scarecrow Press, Inc.
Lanham, Maryland, and London
2001

SCARECROW PRESS, INC.

Published in the United States of America
by Scarecrow Press, Inc.
4720 Boston Way
Lanham, Maryland 20706
www.scarecrowpress.com

4 Pleydell Gardens, Folkestone
Kent CT20 2DN, England

ISSN 0731-0641
ISBN 0-8108-4056-1

∞™ The paper used in this publication meets the minimum requirements
of American National Standard for Information Sciences—Permanence of
Paper for Printed Library Materials, ANSI/NISO Z39.48-1992.
Manufactured in the United States of America.

CONTENTS

PREFACE

Please note: If you have not already done so, please see the announcement of a new feature on the following page. We are grateful to Keith Waters and Jason R. Titus for volunteering as compilers of jazz-related bibliographic information from *nonjazz* journals, as provided by, and subsequently published for, all readers of future volumes of the *Annual Review.* We enlist your cooperation. As a related service, in this and future volumes, *ARJS* will list books recently received at the Rutgers Institute of Jazz Studies, as compiled by IJS Librarian Vincent Pelote.

The international span of jazz scholarship is evident in this tenth volume of *ARJS,* covering the year 1999, with three authors from Britain and one (our first) from Australia. This volume has a distinctly Monkish leaning. In addition to two musicological analyses centering on "Ruby, My Dear" and "Criss Cross," *ARJS* is happy to lead off with a most unusual and fascinating sonnet sequence in which six Monk compositions are blended in a marriage of musicology and Shakespearean poetry. A fourth contributor has reviewed three books on Monk.

Literature, this time prose fiction, makes another appearance with an overview essay on selected jazz fiction; *ARJS* expects to publish a formal bibliography of jazz fiction by the same author in a forthcoming issue. Two pianist-composers whose careers substantially overlapped Monk's receive extended treatments—McCoy Tyner and Bill Evans—and a recent book on Evans is reviewed.

This *ARJS* delves into earlier jazz in four very different formats. First, to celebrate Louis Armstrong's legendary birth in 1900 and his actual birth in 1901, Dan Morgenstern has contributed a very personal reminiscence of his friendship of almost a quarter century and, second, has helped assemble a Centennial Armstrong Photo Gallery from the archives of IJS. Third, we offer a survey of the early jazz and recording history of Hoagy Carmichael's "Stardust." Finally, biography and social history combine in a look back at the 1943 drug arrest of drummer Gene Krupa.

Charlie Parker and organist Jimmy Smith are also here. And discographers will find that an *ARJS* editor has addressed the highly contemporary mode of using the internet as a discographical source.

The Editors

A NEW FEATURE:

REQUEST FOR JAZZ BIBLIOGRAPHY ITEMS FROM NONJAZZ JOURNALS

There has been a tremendous expansion of serious jazz scholarship recently. This is reflected in the number of scholarly journals with articles that treat topics of jazz history, analysis, aesthetics, theory, and criticism. Some recent journals, such as the *Antioch Review* and *The Journal of Aesthetics and Art Criticism*, have devoted entire issues to jazz and improvisation.

In order to acknowledge this explosion of activity and to aid jazz researchers, the *Annual Review of Jazz Studies* will be including a bibliography of scholarly jazz articles in each of its subsequent issues. If you have references to scholarly jazz articles that have appeared in *nonjazz* journals within the past year, please e-mail Keith Waters (watersk@stripe. colorado.edu) and/or Jason R. Titus (jtitus@theory.esm.rochester.edu).

Please note that your suggestions should be academic articles, rather than opinion pieces or jazz journalism. Complete citations (date, volume and number, pages) would be appreciated.

MONKISHNESS
A SONNET SEQUENCE

Mark Haywood

Monkishness is a sequence of sonnets addressing various features of Thelonious Monk's style. The idea of presenting in a poetic form what could be described as a technical analysis might at first sight seem strange. However, our subject matter is Monk's music, which, like all music, is an expression of the spirit, appealing to aesthetic sensibilities. As such, the suitability of its inner workings for treatment by poetic means becomes more apparent.

But why choose the sonnet? The Shakespearean or English sonnet form demands of its writers a unique discipline. At its simplest level, it requires the expression of an idea through fourteen lines (three four-line quatrains plus a two-line couplet) of iambic pentameter (five short-long iambi per line) with an *abab-cdcd-efef-gg* rhyme scheme. At a more sophisticated level, though, the flow of thought can actually be expressed through the sonnet's own internal structure. For example, a description of something toppling over might involve a sentence which does not end, as one might logically expect, at the end of a quatrain, but itself topples over to end a short way into the next line; a description of conflict might be expressed using words whose pronunciation conflicts with their metrical stress (such as "*such* hos*tile* con*flict*"); particular rhythms might not only be described but actually "enacted" using the pentametric pulse of the line, and so forth. The medium of the sonnet is thus in fact an ideal vehicle for the exploration of the characteristics of Monk's multifaceted music, of "Monkishness."

The arguments voiced in this sonnet sequence stem originally from my article, "Rhythmic Readings in Thelonious Monk," which appeared in *ARJS* 7. To obviate the need to cross-refer to that article, each sonnet is fully annotated so that its theoretical, as well as its stylistic, content may be fully appreciated. Although this involves to a limited extent re-presenting theoretical ideas from "Rhythmic Readings," I hope that the sonnet sequence will not be felt to be a "repackaging" of material from that paper, but that it will be considered *per se* as an example of jazz poetry (or of a possibly new genre of "jazz-technical" poetry).

Enjoy!

1. *ON* WELL, YOU NEEDN'T *AND* MONK'S MOOD

Where Well, You Needn't*'s measurement is eight,*
Expected sounds premature seem, compared
Against a paradigm where, one beat late,
The selfsame form its sedes justly shared
With previous repetition. Thus bar seven   5
In triple time may audibly be read,
Chaotic hell restored to ordered heaven
And sounds divorced once more with pleasure wed.
Equivalent foreshortening reconciles
Monk's Mood*'s sixth tone with its just state, wherein*   10
It claims of three the strongest beat and piles
On common rhythm rhythm of other kin.
Or if we grant the foursquare time to reign,
Are not anacrustic the first notes twain?

Argument

In "Rhythmic Readings" an approach is developed whereby portions of
Monk's composed melodies which sound rhythmically dislocated or dis-
jointed (in a typically "Monkish" way) are actually reinterpreted or "re-
heard" by us in such a way that they make better "auditory sense." This approach is based on the idea that behind the tune as it is actually played by
Monk (which we will label "X") there is a simpler, more logical, paradigm
(which we will call "P"). The paradigm is the tune as played (X) but
stripped of the rhythmic complexities that make it sound dislocated.

The first eight lines of the sonnet address bars seven to eight of "Well,
You Needn't." Here, a phrase is repeated, but its second occurrence is a
rhythmic surprise, a "dislocation," because its position in the bar has
changed (see Example 1–1). This dislocation which we feel in X is removed in P, where the phrase's second sounding balances its first.

The final step in the process of making auditory sense of X is to adopt an
altered reading of X's time signature (shown beneath X), such that all its notes
occupy the rhythmic positions that they occupy in P. Thus, a subconscious
mental foreshortening of bar seven of X from 12/8 to 9/8 time allows the dislocated phrase to be "heard" in its more logical position—its P position.

In lines nine to twelve the sonnet moves on to discuss a similar situation
at the start of "Monk's Mood" (see Example 1–2), where the long G that

occupies bar two seems to come in one beat "early," dislocating the 4/4 pulse. Our paradigm again shows how X would look without this disconcerting effect, placing the G more logically on a first beat. Once again, we subconsciously reconcile X with P by foreshortening its first bar to 3/4 time. Hearing the opening bar in 3/4 makes more auditory sense than hearing the dislocated 4/4 pulse of X itself.

The final couplet suggests a totally different reading of X (see Example 1–3), which allows the 4/4 time to persist by using a new paradigm in which the first two notes form an upbeat or anacrusis.

Notes

1 measurement] Literally, its number of measures.

2] The "expected sound" is the repetition of the final phrase. The word "premature" evokes prematureness, its pronunciation being out of phase with the scansion.

3 one beat late] Late compared to its position in X.

4 *sedes*] Its rhythmic position in the bar.

7–8 Chaotic hell . . ./. . . wed] The chaos of X when heard in 12/8 time finally reconciled with P through use of 9/8.

9–14] The focus changes after the second quatrain, as often in the Shakespearean sonnet.

9 Equivalent foreshortening reconciles] The second of the three long words is itself metrically shortened to three syllables.

10 just] Its rightful reading, as in P.

11 of three the strongest beat] The first beat of a 3/4 bar.

12 On common rhythm rhythm of other kin] The first "rhythm" is scanned as two syllables, the second as one syllable, reflecting the sudden shortening of 4/4 to 3/4.

14 anacrustic] Scanned 'an*acrustic*' in conflict with its actual pronunciation, the word contains its own anacrusis.

Example 1–1: Well, You Needn't

Example 1–2: Monk's Mood

Example 1–3: Monk's Mood

2. *ON* HACKENSACK

Beneath the bridge of Hackensack *do flow*
The simplest of thematic bases, where
March onward whole note steps, doh-la-doh-sol-
Doh-la, which if we will but then compare
With their corruption, then we see a child   5
Deformed and limping, every other pace
Set down too early, mother's manner mild
And patient now an awkward, halting race.
This transmutation musicology
By amputation to have been performed   10
Might speculate, maternal constancy,
In common time embodied, rudely stormed
By filial gait wherein three meagre parts
Of that pure rhythm one foot sadly charts.

Argument

Example 2–1 shows the bridge section of *Hackensack*. Here the dislocation
felt in the tune as played (X) is caused by the apparently early arrival of the
D in bar one, the C in bar three, and the D in bar five. The paradigm (P)
"corrects" this by placing these notes on first beats, and it also simplifies
the tune's repeated notes to show the most basic underlying theme—six
dotted whole notes in succession.

In order to hear X in such a way that we feel the procession of these
whole notes, each one on a first beat, we mentally foreshorten bars one,
three, and five to 9/8 time.

Notes

1] The "bridge" is both musical and metaphorical. "Beneath the bridge"
flows the paradigm.

3–4] The notes are the long F-D-F-C-F-D of P.

5 their corruption] The tune as played (X).

5–8] The *enjambement* of phrases, whereby they straddle the lines, reflects the deformed and limping gait of X, the "child" of P.

9–11] Read as "Musicology might speculate this transmutation to have been performed by amputation."

11–12 maternal constancy,/. . . embodied] The original 12/8 pulse of X, which is effectively "common time," only swung.

13–14 three meagre parts] The three-beat 9/8 rhythm of the new reading.

14 one foot] Every odd-numbered bar (one, three, and five) is now reduced from 12/8 to 9/8; the other "foot" (each even-numbered bar) remains in 12/8 time.

Example 2–1: Hackensack

3. *ON* BOLIVAR BLUES

The undulation which the closing strain
Of Bolivar *evokes with constant pace*
Delights the ear and as a gilded chain
Boasts linkages of even-measured grace
And equidistant symmetry. Yet jars   5
Against this peaceful harmony, more pure
By far, a reading wherein single bars
Respectively each rising wave immure
And, all but for its very birth, enclose.
This paradise in which, two lovers wed,   10
Wherever content, there form also goes,
Seemed lost, yet should Balues-Are *so be read,*
Whereby quadruple triple time appears,
It is regained by him who this way hears.

Argument

This sonnet addresses the close of the main theme of "Bolivar Blues" (see
Example 3–1), and once again argues for a 9/8 reading of X, this time lasting two bars. Such a reading places each of the repetitions of the initial rising phrase in an identical rhythmic position, thus allowing the more logical
paradigm (P) to be felt.

Notes

5 yet jars] The intrusion of this new idea jars against the meter.

7–8] The 9/8 bars of the new reading which now each contain ("immure") an identical rising phrase.

9 all but for its very birth] All but for the very first B♭.

11] The very definition of paradigmatic readings, whereby the time signature (the "form") is chosen as the most logical match for the melody (the
"content").

12 seemed lost] That is, if we were just to hear the tune as written in X.

Balues-Are] An alternative title for the tune is *Balue-Bolivar-Balues-Are*.

13] Read as "Whereby quadruple (time) appears triple," *i.e.*, where 12/8
is converted to 9/8 time.

Example 3–1: Bolivar Blues

4. *ON* MONK'S DREAM

As in a sleep conflicting visions flock,
With one another vying, just so seem
Interpretations rhythmic each to block
Alternative construings as Monk's Dream,
Eponymous, concludes. For where there go   5
Two isolated couples, one wife yearns
Behind her spouse the door to close and so
More status to acquire, whilst sorely burns
The other her stronghold to find, removed
A little distance from her husband's sway: 10
By neither is the other's wish approved
And if the first by force her foe to pay
Compels then she will thereby also take
All power from him who follows in their wake.

Argument

Two possible rereadings of a portion of "Monk's Dream," each based on a
different paradigm, are set against each other in this sonnet. Each one, considered individually, seems eminently reasonable as a means of making better auditory sense of a particular note in X. However, each reading para-
doxically denies the validity of the other one. The notes below clarify this
theoretical argument further.

Notes

5 Eponymous] Living up to its title, in that it exemplifies the "conflicting visions" referred to in the initial dream imagery of the sonnet.

6 Two isolated couples] See Examples 4–1 and 4–2. In bar two of X, the
first couple (husband and wife) consists of the first two notes (E and A); the
second couple (husband and wife) consists of the next two notes (E and A♭).

6–8] The first wife's yearning is depicted in the reading (Example 4–1)
whereby she (the note A) is positioned at the beginning of an imagined 12/8
bar, her spouse (the immediately preceding E) being left stranded before the
barline.

8–10] The sore burning of the other wife is depicted by the other reading (Example 4–2) in which she (the A♭) occupies a strong beat in an imagined 11(5+6)/8 bar, thanks to the paradigm where she is rhythmically separated from her spouse (the immediately preceding E) by an eighth note ("A little distance") more than in X.

11] The two paradigmatic readings conflict with each other: the first reading gives rhythmic status to the first wife but denies it to the other, whereas the second reading does the opposite.

12–14] If in our minds the new 12/8 reading prevails over the 11/8 one, then the subsequent long E♭ ("him who follows") can no longer begin on a strong first beat, this "power" having been sapped by the duration of the 12/8 reading.

Example 4–1: Monk's Dream

Example 4–2: Monk's Dream

5. *ON* BRILLIANT CORNERS

The triplets which with joyful shout conclude
The line which Brilliant Corners *serves to end*
Contest their form, melodic grace accrued
By foursomes iterated which defend
Their right to independent stature. Fair   5
Appears their claim, a precedent to mime
The previous phrase conferring, wherein share
The measure fourstrong groupings twain. Thus rhyme
The triplets with their predecessors' law,
In new-found beauty revelling, the skin   10
Of formlessness cast off, yet they ignore
That all must pay who thus advantage win:
Which payment envious Time exacts, and so
Appears the music, instantly, to slow.

Argument

Example 5–1 shows the final four bars of the theme of "Brilliant Corners."
The sudden change in X from eighth notes to triplet quarter notes comes as
a surprise. The paradigm (P) shows how the ear would prefer to hear the
last two bars as a continuation of the run of eighth notes, given not only that
a momentum of eighth notes has been set up in bar two but also that the
triplets contain two balanced groups of four notes.

Now comes the problem of reconciling each of the triplets in X with its
own position in P. To do this using our familiar method of time signature
alteration would involve a separate reading to cater for each triplet note.
This is too much for the listener's brain to cope with, so instead it considers the phrase as a whole and simply hears it *as though* it consisted of
straight eighth notes. The cross-headed notes show how this interpretation
is mentally made. However, in hearing a series of notes which are in reality triplet quarter notes (six to a bar) as if they are eighth notes (eight to a
bar), the listener will experience the sensation that the tempo has suddenly
slowed down.

Notes

3 Contest their form] They belie their apparent status as triplets.

3–5 melodic grace . . ./. . . stature] The melodic structure of the triplets is that of two four-note groups. This structure thus claims its "independent stature" as bar three of P.

6–7] Read "the previous phrase conferring a precedent to mime," this phrase being the two sets of four eighth notes ("fourstrong groupings twain") in the second bar.

10–11] They were "formless" before, since (in X) their grouping was at odds with the bar structure.

Example 5–1: Brilliant Corners

6. *ON* BYE-YA

As customary ways of life a sense
Of reassurance give which patterns new
Destroy, the repetitious figures whence
Comes solace, as commences Bye-Ya, *cue*
A sudden stumbling whereby, premature,   5
The two expected hammer-blows arrive.
Security now rendered insecure,
To resurrect familiar things we strive
By sacrificing to that godly pair
A gift of time, to keep them in their thrones.   10
But then begins an ugly war, the share
Demanded by each deity met with groans
By his opponent who would then forego
That status which to be his right we know.

Argument

The opening of "Bye-Ya" presents us with an example of two conflicting rereadings of a passage, each of which derives from the same apparently sensible paradigm (see Example 6–1). In X, the initial phrase is repeated, leading the listener to expect any further repetition of it to be identical. However, on the third occurrence of the phrase the two "hammer-blows" (the repeated $B\flat$s) come unexpectedly early. The ear wants to place these notes in the positions that they have occupied twice already. The original rhythm of the phrase thus becomes a paradigm underlying the dislocated version that we hear in X.

Unfortunately however, the two $B\flat$s in X have been dislocated against their positions in P by different amounts. Consequently, the rereading of X that we must adopt in order to hear the first $B\flat$ in its paradigmatic position (a foreshortening of bar five of X to 11/8 time) does not allow the second $B\flat$ to be heard in its own P position. Similarly, the rereading that caters for the second $B\flat$ (involving a foreshortening of bar five of X to 9/8 time) deprives the first $B\flat$ of its paradigmatic position.

Notes

3 the repetitious figures] The rhythm of bar two, repeated in bar four.

5 A sudden stumbling] The rushing of this familiar rhythm on its third occurrence. The line itself stumbles along.

9–10] The sacrifice of time is the shortening of bar five of X to 11/8 and 9/8 time by the two new readings respectively.

11 ugly war] The mutual incompatibility of the two new readings.

14 That status] The status of occupying its paradigmatic position, the "throne" of line 10.

Example 6–1: Bye-Ya

JAZZ FICTION:
A BIBLIOGRAPHIC OVERVIEW[1]

David Rife

If the term *jazz fiction* is not as wildly oxymoronic as, say, *dance architecture* (to borrow an analogy from Thelonious Monk), it is nevertheless a problematic concept that resists facile definition. For instance: does the term refer to those stories and novels that employ a jazz setting and use the music as subject matter and vehicle for theme? Or should the term also embrace such works as the novels of Jack Kerouac, which are flecked with references to bebop artists within the mode of "jazzy" language? And what of a work like Alice Adams's haunting novel, *Listening to Billie* (New York: Knopf, 1978), in which the legendary singer Billie Holiday makes a brief, dramatic appearance at the beginning, disappears immediately from the narrative, and yet profoundly affects—through her physical presence as well as her music—the contingent life of the protagonist? To simplify matters, for this essay the term *jazz fiction* will simply denote those stories and novels in which jazz is somehow central to the narrative.

EARLY WORKS

Jazz fiction began auspiciously in 1912 with the publication of James Weldon Johnson's *The Autobiography of an Ex-Colored Man* (Boston: Sherman, French: 1912), the story of a light-skinned mulatto who achieves success when he applies his mastery of classical piano to ragtime. But instead of following his dream of making ragtime into respectable art, thus legitimating the African-American experience, he masquerades as a white and succumbs to a life of ease, nevertheless regretting that he had betrayed his race by selling his "birthright for a mess of pottage." This early work adumbrates certain elements that became increasingly persistent as both the music and its literature increased in popularity: the artist-patron association, the relationship between the races, the painful mystery of identity, and the potential of music to elevate not only the welfare of an individual but, indeed, a race.

But after this provocative start by Johnson, jazz fiction did little to distinguish itself over the next quarter-century, though scattered works of interest did occasionally appear. Two humorous pieces, the first by a black writer, the second by a white, are worth noting. Rudolph Fisher's "Common Meter" (*Baltimore Afro-American,* 8 and 15 February 1930) depicts a cutting contest between two bands in Harlem in the late 1920s; and Octavious Cohen's "Music Hath Charms" (*Dark Days and Black Knights,* New York: Dodd Mead, 1923) hinges on the comeuppance of a con man who claims to blow a mean horn but can neither read nor play a note. In another early short work, Hermann Deutsch's "Louis Armstrong" (*Esquire,* October 1935), the title character can play as many notes as his horn can handle. A vernacular account of Armstrong's rise from street kid to renowned musician, this story provides an early example in jazz fiction of a work that blurs the distinction between fact and fiction.

Certain popular writers also contributed to the genre at this time. In "Rhythm" *(The Love Nest and Other Stories,* New York: Scribner's, 1926), for example, Ring Lardner raises the question of whether it is morally reprehensible—or acceptable behavior—for jazz composers to "borrow" from classical sources for their ideas, and William Saroyan in "Jazz" (*Hairenik Daily* [Boston], 2 June 1934) likens the urban street sounds he hears to the "nervous noise" called jazz that was sweeping the country.

More substantial than these minor offerings were the works of two ranking black writers, Claude McKay and, more important, Langston Hughes. McKay uses jazz and the blues primarily as background in *Home to Harlem* (New York: Harper, 1928), but he makes the music integral to the novel. The same might be said of Hughes's *Not Without Laughter* (New York: Knopf, 1930), though Hughes more directly (especially in Chapter 8) addresses the issue of jazz in Black culture. Several of Hughes's shorter works are also centrally concerned with jazz, especially as it relates to cultural matters. For instance, in "The Blues I'm Playing" (*Scribner's,* May 1934), set during the Harlem Renaissance, Hughes explores the conflict between classical music and jazz and the disparate philosophies represented by these musical forms. This is dramatized through the conflict between Oceola Jones, a black pianist, and her wealthy white patron, Mrs. Ellsworth, reminding us of the cultural conundrum regarding the influence of white stewardship on black art. In "Bop" (*The Best of Simple,* New York: Hill and Wang, 1961), Hughes's series character, Simple, a lover of bebop, explains to the dubious narrator that the music is more than just nonsense syllables, that in fact its name derives from the sound made when cops hit blacks on the head with their billy clubs, thus creating an authentic "colored boys" music. "Jazz, Jive, and Jam" (*Simple Stakes a Claim,* New York: Holt, 1957) presents a more positive picture of the racial issue as Simple argues to his woman, who has been dragging him to talks on integration, that jazz would be far more effective in promoting racial harmony than any number of seminars on the topic because, since everyone loves jazz, blacks and whites would dance together to the music and racial differences would dissipate.

But the best-known work of jazz fiction's first quarter-century is Dorothy Baker's *Young Man With a Horn* (New York: Houghton Mifflin, 1938), whose lasting fame doubtless owes a considerable debt to a movie of the same name (1950). Inspired by the music but not the life of Bix Beiderbecke (so the author claims), *Young Man* is yet another portrait of the doomed artist as a young man, in this case, Rick Martin, an outsider who has neither family nor education to speak of. What Rick does have is a genuine feel for music and improvisation; in fact, a major conflict revolves around his powerful desire to improvise while being chained to Big Band charts. Rick is the prototype of the self-destructive jazz hero of the kind who achieves apotheosis a few years later in the life and legend of Charlie Parker, among others. Although *Young Man* is not a very good novel, it places the music center stage and in so doing opens the floodgates to jazz fiction.

THE 1940S AND 1950S

Jazz fiction proliferated in the decades following the publication of *Young Man With a Horn* and broadened its base of inquiry. Dale Curran contributed two novels in the 1940s. The lesser of these, *Dupree Blues* (New York: Knopf, 1948), tells the story of a jazzman whose cliché vices destine him for failure. Curran's other, more substantial work, *Piano in the Band* (New York: Reynal and Hitchcock, 1940), details the tedious on-the-road existence of a dance hall jazz band, the frustrations of rehearsals, and the stock conflict that arises when some band members want to create "real" music rather than follow the rigid routines of their leader. At the end the protagonist joins a predominantly black band where he will be free to create and, presumably, help to loosen the rigid color barrier.

Two other novels that challenge the color line are Clifton Cuthbert's *The Robbed Heart* (New York: L.B. Fischer, 1945) and Jack Baird's *Hot, Sweet and Blue* (New York: Gold Medal, 1956). In the first of these, well-born Denis Sloane is a music critic who takes jazz very seriously. His devotion to this music takes him frequently to Harlem where he meets and falls in love with the beautiful, intelligent, light-skinned Judy Foster, daughter of a prominent Harlem businessman. While the novel is primarily concerned with chronicling the complexities of an interracial relationship, it also makes significant reference to the dispiriting compromises musicians must make to ply their trade professionally; in fact, one of Sloane's black friends feels compelled to relinquish his trumpet in favor of dealing dope to survive. Baird's often embarrassingly stereotypical novel, on the other hand, concerns a white bandleader who falls in love with a black singer; unfortunately, the beautiful music—literal and metaphorical—they make together is not strong enough to overcome racial barriers.

As in *The Robbed Heart*, the theme of musical compromise is also important in Annemarie Ewing's *Little Gate* (New York: Rinehart, 1947) and Robert Sylvester's *Rough Sketch* (New York: Dial, 1948). Obsessed with jazz and accepted by blacks and other musicians, Ewing's Joe "Little Gate" Geddes leaves his small Midwestern town for the big city, where he establishes a reputation before being reduced to playing his sax in a band that does mostly novelty tunes, causing him to seek out the music he loves in Harlem, after hours. But after "Little Gate" forms a band of his own and makes a hit record, he discovers that he and his music have become a commodity over which he has no control. The section of *Rough Sketch* that concerns jazz (Part 2) also touches upon the economics of the music industry, as well as the rise of jazz in the 1920s and 1930s. The lead character in this book, Tony Fenner, had been a musicians' agent among other things, and this leads to considerable talk of the effects of the burgeoning music industry on the music itself.

Harold Sinclair's *Music Out of Dixie* (New York: Rinehart, 1952) is more concerned with the rise of jazz itself than the industry that formed around it. Growing up in the slums near New Orleans toward the turn of the century, Dade Tarrent is moved by music early in his life, learns to play the piano and then the clarinet, achieves success and then suffers defeat before becoming an artist-composer and heading to New York at the end. Jelly Roll Morton makes a brief but important appearance.

Several other novels of this period portray characters similar to Tarrent, but very few of these conclude on the note of qualified optimism offered by *Music Out of Dixie*. Jazz fiction—like the music itself—is riddled with tormented, self-destructive characters after the fashion of Dorothy Baker's Rick Martin. One of the more unusual of these is Virgil Jones from Stanford Whitmore's *Solo* (New York: Harcourt, Brace, 1955). Jones is reminiscent of Herman Melville's Bartleby ("Bartleby, the Scrivener") in his obduracy, his almost total disconnectedness, and his aura of mystery. Jones proclaims himself the last individual in the world and plays his piano and lives his life exclusively for himself. And the music he produced "was always new, always daring yet never tangled with badly conceived innovations, always a special brand of jazz that no one could imitate." When a manager and a music critic try to exploit Jones, he resists, always being true to his own peculiar nature and achieving whatever satisfaction that life has to offer by doing so.

James Updyke's Royal, in *It's Always Four O'Clock* (New York: Random House, 1956), is another eccentric, enigmatic pianist, but he is even more self-destructive than Virgil Jones. This novel is also interesting for its portrayal of serious musicians attempting to forge a new kind of jazz after World War II in the carnival atmosphere of a night club. George Lea's *Somewhere There's Music* (Philadelphia: Lippincott, 1958) is another postwar (Korean War) novel with a self-destructive musician. Saxophonist Mike Logan simply drifts through life without goal or direction, consuming drugs and alcohol as if they constituted his reason for being.

Several novels in the time-frame under examination, including some that have already been noted, dramatize the Big Band experience. Written for a juvenile audience, with a foreword by Benny Goodman, George T. Simon's *Don Watson Starts His Band* (New York: Dodd, Mead, 1941), for instance, focuses on a young hayseed who determines to become a professional band leader. Other juvenile novels that body forth this coming-of-age musical dilemma (though not all within the Big Band context) are Haskel Frankel's *Big Band* (Garden City, New York: Doubleday, 1965), James Lincoln Collier's *The Jazz Kid* (New York: Henry Holt, 1994), Nat Hentoff's *Jazz Country* (New York: Harper, 1965), and Richard Hill's *Riding Solo with the Golden Horde* (Athens, Georgia: University of Georgia Press, 1994). The last two titles also have much to do with the Civil Rights movement.

A short vertical step from the juvenile category is R. Pingank Malone's *Sound Your "A": The Story of Trumpeter Tom Stewart in Full-Length Novel Form*, a novel that was serialized in *Metronome* (September–December 1942, February 1943). Most of the characters are young musicians with jazz aspirations who are reduced to playing in a pit band. When one of them, Tom Stewart, gets a chance to fill in with a name band famous for its "tickety-tockety" style of music, the band leader falls in love with Tom's corny playing, unaware that Tom is making fun of the music. Two longer, more serious works concerned with Big Bands are Osborn Duke's *Sideman* (New York: Criterion, 1956) and Henry Steig's *Send Me Down* (New York: Knopf, 1941), both of which are very long and often windy but comprehensive in their explorations of the frustration of Big Band life.

Sideman offers a panoramic survey of the professional and personal lives of several members of a large post-Korean War dance band. The story centers on sideman Bernie Bell, who leaves college in Texas to play trombone in a band in Southern California, where he hopes to moonlight by composing "serious" music; in short, another portrait of the artist as a young man. *Send Me Down* also bears blockbuster heft but is valuable nevertheless for its realistic descriptions of the travails of travel, the economics of the music business, the conflict between art and entertainment, and the destructiveness of marijuana to the world of swing music. The plot revolves around two working-class brothers and a buddy growing up in New York City between the wars. At considerable sacrifice to their parents, the boys develop musical skill and become interested enough in jazz to pursue it as a career, disappointing their parents who, in keeping with the times, considered such music to be trash. The brothers soon go their own musical ways, one taking to the road with a small group, the other building a Big Band that eventually plays Carnegie Hall. In one telling exchange (for 1941), a black musician says to a white one that he supposes he ought to be grateful to be in music, to which the latter responds: "You certainly should. . . . In almost anything else where you had a chance at all, you'd have to be five times as good as a white man. In music you only have to be, say, twice as good."

This was also a fruitful time for short fiction. For instance, George Washington Lee wrote a series of stories that are collected in *Beale Street Sundown* (New York: House of Field, 1942), and jazz writer Leonard Feather, writing as Professor Snotty McSiegel, ran a series of jazz parodies in *Metronome*. A few titles will suffice to suggest their content: "Be-bop? I Was Pre-bop!" (December 1948), "Slide, Snotty, Slide" (December 1943), and "Bass Is Basic Basis of Basie" (April 1944). The comedian and pianist-composer Steve Allen produced a collection of *Bop Fables* (New York: Simon and Schuster, 1955) in which he retells familiar fairy tales in bopster language. And Martin Gardner wrote several humorous or parodic pieces, the first of which, "The Devil and the Trombone" (*The Record Changer*, October 1948), inspired *The Record Changer* to regularly open its pages to fiction. Other parodic stories are to be found in Charles Harvey's wide-ranging edited collection, *Jazz Parody (Anthology of Jazz Fiction)* (London: Spearman, 1948), notable as the first anthology of jazz fiction.

But the gemstones that could serve as bookends for the period are Eudora Welty's "Powerhouse" (*Atlantic*, June 1941) and James Baldwin's "Sonny's Blues" (*Partisan Review*, Summer 1957). "Powerhouse" is the story of a Black pianist (modeled after Fats Waller) of mythic stature doing a one-night gig at a white dance in Alligator, Mississippi. At the heart of this tale of alienation is an improvisational interpolated story that amounts to a verbal jam session. "Sonny's Blues" relates the story of two brothers, separated by age and outlook, who are poignantly brought together through the medium of music. The description of the music in the transcendent moment when this occurs could not be more effective; in fact, the whole final scene achieves the kind of purity and beauty that prose writers long to emulate when they are particularly moved by music.

Finally, if the short story seems to be slighted in this overview of jazz fiction, it is because two excellent anthologies of short fiction, with informed introductions and judicious selections, appeared in the 1990s: *Hot and Cool: Jazz Short Stories,* edited by Marcela Breton (New York: Plume, 1990) and *From Blues to Bop: A Collection of Jazz Fiction*, edited by Richard Albert (Baton Rouge: Louisiana State University Press, 1990). Albert also compiled *An Annotated Bibliography of Jazz Fiction and Jazz Criticism* (Westport, Connecticut: Greenwood, 1996). Aficionados of jazz fiction could not have a better starting point than these three books.

CHARLIE PARKER AND THE BEATS

Of all the jazz musicians who have influenced jazz fiction, no one has approached the impact of Charlie Parker. His life and his art are unquestionably the stuff of which legends are made. In novels and short stories, Parker occasionally makes a cameo appearance under his own name, as in Bart Schneider's *Blue Bossa* (New York: Viking, 1998). Sometimes a writer will attempt to evoke Parker's technique in his own prose while putting Parker and his music to symbolic use, like Thomas Pynchon in *Gravity's Rainbow* (New York: Viking, 1973). And at other times, as in James Baldwin's "Sonny's Blues" (*Partisan Review*, Summer 1957), among other works, Parker stands as the torchbearer for the revolutionary new music of bebop. But generally writers simply model characters after the groundbreaking musician and dramatize certain key events from his audacious life.

The earliest writer to do this was Elliott Grennard in his classic story, "Sparrow's Last Jump" (*Harper's Magazine*, May 1947), based on Parker's notorious "Lover Man" recording session, which the author, himself a music professional, had attended. The story emphasizes the Parker figure's (Sparrow's) disintegration from drugs and mental incapacity. Raymond Federman, in "Remembering Charlie Parker or how to get it out of your system" (*Take It or Leave It: An exaggerated second-hand tale to be read aloud either standing or sitting.* New York: Fiction Collective, 1976), also refers to a version of "Lover Man," but in concert rather than the recording studio. Federman is primarily interested in eulogizing Parker and in promoting the notion that blackness is essential to the making of jazz.

The clarinetist Tony Scott, who actually knew and played with Parker, discloses his deep admiration for his idol in his short, ironic "Destination K.C." in *The Jazz Word,* edited by Dom Ceruli, Burt Korall, and Mort Nasatir (New York: Ballantine, 1960). The record producer, Ross Russell, another writer who had a personal connection with Parker, wrote *The Sound* (New York: Dutton, 1961), a novel that recounts the story of Jewish piano player Bernie Rich. Rich is torn between joining the Big Band college circuit with its financial security and trying to make a go of it in the more vibrant but unstable Harlem scene in which Red Travers, the Parker figure, is transforming jazz from Big Band to bop. This often sensational work contains much about race, a preponderance of sex and drugs, and occasional stereotyping, as when Travers is described as having "an overpowering virile odor and primitive genital force." Nevertheless, *The Sound* feels authentic and contains much solid musical description.

John A. Williams's *Night Song* (New York: Farrar, Straus and Cudahy, 1961) provided another solid, extended treatment of the Parker legend and did so in a less sensational way than *The Sound. Night Song* is thick with jazz content, including how musicians are exploited by the music industry. But the novel is more deeply interested in race, culminating in a scene in which Richie Stokes (the Parker figure) is beaten by white cops while his white friend looks on. When Stokes—"The Eagle"—disintegrates and dies, he immediately becomes a folk hero, with graffiti proclaiming "Eagle Lives" and "The Eagle Still Soars" popping up everywhere, echoing the response to the real Charlie Parker's death. *Bird Lives!*, not incidentally, is the title of Bill Moody's fourth series novel featuring jazz-pianist-turned-sleuth, Evan Horne, who is called in on a case connected to the date on which Parker died (New York: Walker, 1999).

Argentine writer Julio Cortázar also based a serious extended piece, "The Pursuer" ["El Perseguida"] in *End of the Game and Other Stories,* translated by Paul Blackman (New York: Pantheon, 1967), on certain key events toward the end of Parker's life, but much of the novella's dramatic tension flows from the relationship between Bruno, a jazz critic, and his subject, Johnny Carter (the Parker figure). As Johnny says after reading Bruno's critical biography of him, "What you forgot to put in is me." Johnny is the pursuer of the title, a questor after the ineffable, but so is Bruno, a parasitic pursuer of Johnny and reflected glory.

Parker is a felt presence in much Beat literature, and he occupies center stage of John Clellon Holmes's *The Horn* (New York: Random House, 1958), a bible of the Beat Generation. In this novel, Edgar "The Horn" Pool (actually a composite of Parker and Lester Young) tries to regain his status as ranking saxophonist, but his skills, along with his psychological condition, have deteriorated too far. Other characters bear striking resemblances to actual jazz musicians, including a singer who must be patterned after Billie Holiday and a pianist whose name, "Junius Priest," evokes the figure of Thelonious Monk. This jazz-drenched novel frequently relates jazz artists to classic American romantic writers, especially those who promoted individualism, anti-materialism, racial equality, and art-as-religion. Holmes also describes the jazz scene in *Go!* (New York: Scribner's, 1952).

Another Beat writer, Jack Kerouac, who like James Baldwin expressed the desire to write in the same way that a jazz musician blows, never proceeds far without mentioning or doing something related to jazz. *Maggie Cassidy* (New York: Avon, 1959) refers to the Big Bands Kerouac listened to in the late 1930s. In *Town and the City* (New York: Harcourt Brace, 1950), he refers to bop and hipster musicians with their dark glasses and berets. *Desolation Angels* (New York: Coward-McCann, 1965) is sprinkled with references to Brew Moore. To an even greater extent, both the *Subterraneans* (New York: Grove, 1958) and, especially, *On the Road* (New York: Viking: 1957) have the spontaneity of jazz even as they refer to well known musicians of the day and describe the excitement of jazz performances. In *Visions of Cody* (New York: McGraw-Hill, 1973), Kerouac himself covertly pursues his hero, saxophonist Lee Konitz, across New York City. In an interesting twist, jazz singer Mark Murphy incorporates Kerouac's words in several of his own songs, including "Parker's Mood" (from *The Subterraneans)*, "San Francisco" (from *Big Sur)*, and "November in the Snow" and "All the Sad Young Men" (both from *On the Road*), bringing a tidy circularity to the Beats and jazz: whereas jazz once inspired their work, their work now inspires jazz.

THE INTERNATIONAL SCENE

Jazz fiction entered the international scene as early as 1927 in the German-born Swiss Hermann Hesse's *Der Steppenwolf* (Berlin: Fischer, 1927; translated by Basil Creighton as *Steppenwolf,* New York: Holt, 1929) in which a jazz saxophonist urges the introspective protagonist, Harry Haller, to abandon intellection and follow his instincts and emotions. Another pre–World

War II story, Belgian Maurice Roelants's "De Jazz-Speler" ["The Jazz
Player"] (Amsterdam: Salm, 1938; translated by Jo Mayo in *Harvest of the
Lowlands: An Anthology in English Translation of Creative Writing in the
Dutch Language,* edited by J. Greshoff, New York: Querido, 1945), high-
lights the transformative experience of a businessman whose life is changed
when he witnesses a black jazzman give an enraptured performance.

   But the most significant international contributions to jazz literature occurred after World War II when much of the Western world came under
American influence. The prolific German-born writer, Ernest Borneman
(who has written about jazz—among countless other topics—under the
name Cameron McCabe) published a Hitchcockian thriller, *Tremolo* (New
York and London: Harper, 1948), set in America. The epigraph quotes Jelly
Roll Morton on the relationship between tremolo and suspense, preparing
the reader for the mystery that is generated when inexplicable events begin
to disrupt the household serenity of a picture-perfect family. The protagonist is a former jazz musician who gave up the jazz life to design and man-
ufacture jazz instruments.

   The United Kingdom, predictably given its love of jazz, has also made
worthy contributions to the genre. Benny Green gives an insider's view of
struggling young musicians in the Brighton dancehall scene in *Fifty-Eight
Minutes to London* (London: MacGibbon & Kee, 1969), and Malcom
Lowry (author of the classic novel, *Under the Volcano*) wrote a story, "The
Forest Path to Spring" (*Hear Us O Lord From Heaven Thy Dwelling Place,*
Philadelphia: Lippincott, 1961), in which the narrator, a former jazz musician, decides to write a jazz symphony while trying to get his life together
in the Pacific Northwest. Another ranking British novelist, John Wain, in
Strike the Father Dead (London: Macmillan, 1962; New York: St. Martin's,
1962), underscores the barriers—philosophical, racial, emotional—that
separate people. When the young protagonist, Jeremy, commits himself to
jazz, he estranges himself from his classics professor father. Later, through
his association with a black American horn player, Jeremy comes to terms
with his music and his life. This novel nicely captures the moment when the
new post–World War II developments in jazz were filtering across the
ocean, often finding compatible accompaniment in French existentialism.
As in Wain's novel, Alan Pater's *Misterioso* (London: Methuen, 1987) involves the search for a father, in this case one whose life was enigmatically
connected to Thelonious Monk's tune, "Misterioso."

   One of the most compelling works to come out of Britain is Geoff Dyer's
But Beautiful (London: Jonathan Cape, 1991). The author calls this work
"imaginative criticism," explaining that he took many scenes from leg-

endary episodes in the lives of jazz musicians and created his own versions of them—improvising, as it were, in keeping with the subject matter. The book is a wondrously evocative combination of imaginative re-creation and reflection. Unfortunately, some knowledgeable readers will be offended by the emphasis on the pain, sadness, and neurosis of the jazz life; some such readers have put the book down in anger, knowing for instance that Dyer's Ben Webster barely resembles the original. Another intriguing work to come out of the UK is *Trumpet* by the self-described "Black Scottish Poet," Jackie Kay (London and Basingstoke: Picador, 1998); this novel dramatizes the life and death of jazz trumpeter Joss Moody, who is revealed to have been a woman despite his/her long-term marriage to Millie. The work resonates with questions concerning the indefinablity of gender and identity and the way in which these can be complicated and enriched through jazz.

France has always been congenial to American (especially African-American) expatriate musicians, but it has yet to produce a solid work of fiction on that or any other jazz-related phenomenon. In fact, the best that can be said about two contemporary works is that they have curiosity value. The first of these, Jacques de Loustal and Phillippe Paringaux's *Barney and the Blue Note* (translated by Frieda Leia Jacobowitz, Rijperman, 1988) could be considered a graphic (i.e., illustrated) novel or simply a comic book. Whatever it is, it exploits all of the worst myths and stereotypes of jazz life. The eponymous Barney had been the talk of the jazz world in the 1950s but the more famous he became, the more he retreated from the world—squandering his gift by shooting heroin and losing himself in a world of cigarettes, alcohol, hotel rooms, sex, and existential remoteness. An equally hackneyed French novel is Gerard Herzhaft's *Long Blues in A Minor* (translated by John Duval, Fayetteville and London: University of Arkansas Press, 1988) in which a young French boy grows up to discover, with the help of American blacks, that you don't have to be black to be blue.

The Argentine, Julio Cortázar, who has already been discussed in connection with Charlie Parker, also wrote an impressive novel that employs jazz technique and refers frequently and substantially to jazz matters, *HopScotch [Rayuela]* (translated by Gregory Rabassa, New York: Pantheon, 1966), and the Sri Lankan (now Canadian) writer, Michael Ondaatje, took the few known facts of one of jazz's "inventors," Buddy Bolden, and turned them into a stunning novel, *Coming Through Slaughter* (Toronto: House of Onansi, 1976). If this novel has more to say about aberrant behavior and modernist techniques than music, what it does say—and imply—about music-in-the-making is always provocative.

But if one writer can be said to dominate the international jazz scene, he is unquestionably the Czech (now Canadian) Joseph Škvorecký, who puts jazz to political use in several stories and novels. Three such works—"The Bass Saxophone" (*The Bass Saxophone: Two Novellas,* New York: Knopf, 1979), *The Cowards* (translated by Jeanne Nemcora, New York: Grove, 1970), and *The Swell Season: A Text on the Most Important Things* (translated by Paul Wilson: New York: Ecco, 1986)—form a trilogy set in Nazi- and later Russian-occupied Czechoslovakia near the end of World War II. The protagonist in these works is young Danny Smiricky, a saxophonist who finds solace from the pain and confusion of his chaotic world through jazz, which has been outlawed by the totalitarian regime. Although the many scattered references to jazz in these and Škvorecký's other jazz-related works do not form a coherent pattern, they are frequently related to the issues of freedom and slavery; in fact, for Danny in another work, *The Tenor Saxophonist's Story* (translated by Caleb Crane, Káca Poláčková-Henley, and Peter Kussi, Hopewell, New Jersey: Ecco, 1997), his tenor sax hitch counterbalances "the large, shining, five-point star" of Communism, reminding us of Thelonious Monk's statement that jazz means freedom. Another story, "Eine Kleine Jazzmusic" (translated by Alice Denesová in *The Literary Review,* Fall 1969), recounts the unsuccessful attempts by the government to suppress jazz, while "The Bebop of Richard Kambala" (translated by Káca Poláčková-Henley in *Rampike* 3, 1984–85) relates the story of the title character's suicide following an exhilarating jam session. Finally, the works of a variety of international writers, many of them little known, can be found in *B Flat, Bebop, Scat,* edited by Chris Parker (London: Quartet, 1986).

CONTEMPORARY WORK

As jazz and the fiction that flows from it approach their centennial, it is clear that only a few stories and no novels of the first rank have appeared; to be sure, such acclaimed works as Malcolm Lowry's *Under the Volcano* (New York: Reynal and Hitchcock, 1947; London: Jonathan Cape, 1947), Ralph Ellison's *Invisible Man* (New York: Random House, 1952), Julio Cortázar's *Hop-Scotch* [*Rayuela*] (translated by Gregory Rabassa, New York: Pantheon, 1966), and Thomas Pynchon's *Gravity's Rainbow* (New York: Viking, 1973) make substantive use of jazz, but the music is not at the center of these narratives. Nevertheless, jazz fiction seems to be gathering strength and momentum as it enters into the twenty-first century.

One genre that has demonstrated lasting power in jazz fiction is the mystery. A good early contemporary example is Malcolm Braly's *Shake Him Till He Rattles* (New York: Belmont, 1963), a noir novel set in San Francisco and containing solid descriptions of the Beat scene, including a cutting contest among three saxophonists. The plot features a bass saxophonist who is stalked by a narcotics cop; one notable theme—an enduring one in jazz literature—concerns the artist-musician in pursuit of some indefinable aesthetic or spiritual goal. Paul Pines's *The Tin Angel* (New York: William Morrow, 1983) also has narcotics at its center, but its chief interest may be its frequent references to and appearances by such jazz figures as Ted Curson and the Termini brothers and its realistic depiction regarding the challenges of operating a jazz club in New York's Lower East Side, where the author actually owned a jazz venue called The Tin Angel in the 1970s.

Two other mysteries have historical interest. The first of these, Harper Barnes's *Blue Monday* (St. Louis: Patrice, 1991), which is set in Kansas City in 1935, involves a young, idealistic, jazz-loving reporter who plays detective when he comes to suspect that Bennie Moten's death during an operation was really murder; the second, Jon Jackson's *A Man With an Axe* (New York: Atlantic Monthly, 1998), is laden with references to bop and free jazz and the musicians who matriculated in the "old" Detroit. As jazz-loving Detective "Fang" Mulheisen tries in this discursive story to solve the riddle of Jimmy Hoffa's disappearance, he encounters one important character who had played in Phil Woods's band, while another in a neat novelistic twist turns out to be the daughter of Albert Ayler.

At least four series mysteries also have jazz-loving protagonists. In the first of these, Dallas Murphy's wacky Artie Deemer sequence, the jazz content is not as great as the titles might suggest: *Lover Man* (New York: Scribner's, 1987), *Lush Life* (New York: Pocket Books, 1992), and *Don't Explain* (New York: Pocket Books, 1996), but the detective—and his jazz-loving dog Jellyroll—loves to listen to hard-driving, brain-blasting bebop when he needs to think, and when he goes to bed for the first time with his new sweetheart, Johnnie Hartman provides the background music, no doubt enabling the lovers' simultaneous orgasms. Charlotte Carter's sassy heroine, Nanette Hays, plays sax on the streets of New York when she's not solving crimes. In the first book, *Rhode Island Red* (London and New York: Serpent's Tale, 1997), she becomes involved in a mystery connected to one of Charlie Parker's saxophones; in the second, she goes to Paris where she teams up with an African-American jazz violinist who is passionately interested in the history of black American jazz expatriates in France. These novels are dense with jazz reference. In one book Nanette claims to be Django Reinhardt's illegitimate gypsy granddaughter; in the other she says she has accepted Thelonious Monk as her "personal savior" where jazz piano is concerned. A much more somber series is that of British writer John Harvey's Charley Resnick procedurals. In these ultraviolent novels (which number about ten to date), Resnik has four cats named after bop musicians and unwinds by reading about and listening to jazz; in *Still Waters* (New York: Holt, 1997), he tracks down a serial killer, accompanied by the music of Duke Ellington.

But the series that outstrips all others for jazz content is Bill Moody's Evan Horne mysteries. After jazz pianist Horne injured his hand in an accident, he turned to amateur sleuthing, first in *Solo Hand* (New York: Walker, 1994) in which he tries to disentangle two musicians from a career-threatening blackmail scam, and then in *The Death of a Tenor Man* (New York: Walker, 1995), where Horne leaves his home base in Los Angeles to help a friend in Las Vegas research the suspicious death of Wardell Gray in that city in 1955. *The Sound of the Trumpet* (New York: Walker, 1997) employs an interesting fictional technique to tell the story of an audio tape that may contain the last recording of legendary trumpeter Clifford Brown. The most recent number in the series, *Bird Lives!* (New York: Walker, 1999), concerns a case in the present connected to the death of Charlie Parker.

A significant number of more serious fictions, some of them of impressive quality, has also appeared in this period. Two early contemporary works still worth reading are Herbert Simmons's *Man Walking on Eggshells* (Boston: Houghton Mifflin, 1962) and William Melvin Kelley's *A Drop of Patience* (New York: Doubleday, 1965). *Man Walking* tells the story of black trumpeter and football player Raymond "Splib" Douglas, who represents the hope of the future for blacks but squanders his wonderful potential through drugs; this novel, which takes place primarily during prohibition in the St. Louis area and Harlem, contains substantial discussions of race and jazz, with much reference to "home boy" Miles Davis. *A Drop of Patience*, on the other hand, is an affecting portrait of a birth-blind horn player, Ludlow Washington, who leaves the South for New York and Chicago where he is finally recognized for his seminal role in shaping the new music—undoubtedly bebop. After being exploited and betrayed by commercialism and racism, Washington (already alienated by his color, blindness, and genius) suffers a breakdown but then recovers and sets out to find a place where he can exercise his gift of music.

Beginning in the 1970s, Don Asher (himself a jazz musician) wrote two diverting works. Dedicated to Hampton Hawes and Jaki Byard, the breezy novel, *The Electric Cotillion* (Garden City, New York: 1970), depicts the scruffy existence of the suggestively named Miles Davey, a pianist who wants to continue playing jazz in a world that has turned to rock-and-roll, forcing Davey to debase himself by playing for such events as a gay costume ball. Asher's story "The Barrier" (in *Angel on My Shoulder,* Santa Barbara, California: Capra, 1985) is more serious. It provides an account of a white piano player who catches the bebop bug in the 1950s and betakes himself to the black enclaves of New York and Boston, hoping to learn to swing; if he doesn't succeed in his aspiration, he nevertheless gains self-respect.

Ishmael Reed and Albert Murray also published notable books beginning in the 1970s. Reed's unclassifiable, hyperactive text, *Mumbo Jumbo* (New York: Atheneum, 1972), parodies the overlapping histories of voodoo and jazz within the framework of a metaphysical mystery. More serious—and comprehensive—by far is Albert Murray's trilogy focusing on the coming of age of young Black Scooter (later Schoolboy), who is learning to come to terms with a farcical reality. The sequence begins with *Train Whistle Guitar* (New York: McGraw-Hill, 1974) in which Scooter, a young boy in rural Alabama in the 1920s, falls under the powerful influence of a couple of bluesmen. Scooter matures in *The Spyglass Tree* (New York: Pantheon, 1991), where he is in college in the 1930s; the series ends—for the moment at least—with *The Seven League Boots* (New York: Pantheon, 1995) in which Schoolboy first becomes a bassist and then leaves the band to write music for the movies, after which he joins the expatriate colony in France. In these autobiographical works, Murray appropriates, in syntax and structure, certain stylistic devices associated with African-American music while referring frequently to jazz and the blues.

The 1980s and early 1990s also witnessed the appearance of a variety of jazz-dominated novels. In *Jazz Jazz Jazz* (New York: St. Martin's, 1981), Patrick Bruce Catling traces the stylistic history of jazz from its Storyville beginnings to the 1970s; Robert Oliphant, in *A Trumpet for Jackie* (Englewood Cliffs, New Jersey: Prentice-Hall, 1983), tells the story of Jackie Hayes, a jazz trumpeter who gives up performing to become successful in other endeavors, all the time retaining his love for jazz. Samuel Charters's *Jelly Roll Morton's Last Night at the Jungle Inn: An Imaginary Memoir by Samuel Charters* (New York: Marion Boyars, 1984) is a researched story that mixes fact and fiction as it details certain highlights from the life of the egotistical Jelly Roll Morton, who here credits himself with having invented jazz. Xam Wilson Cartiér contributed two novels in these years, *Be-Bop, Re-Bop* (New York: Ballantine, 1987) and *Muse-Echo Blues* (New York: Harmony, 1991), both of which employ female narrators who use rhythmic, alliterative language in the telling of their jazz-speckled narratives. Another woman writer, Jeane Westin, published *Swing Sisters* (New York: Scribner's, 1991), which takes place toward the end of the Great Depression and in over 500 pages dramatizes the hardships of a women's swing band, with considerable emphasis on alcohol and drugs. The title of Nobel Laureate Toni Morrison's *Jazz* (New York: Knopf, 1992) would seem to refer more to the novel's technique than the music. The story explores the lives of several African-Americans who live in Harlem in 1926 but have their roots in the South. The music announced by the title is associated with sex, violence, and chaos: it "made you do unwise disorderly things. Just having it was like violating the law."

In the second half of the 1990s, jazz fiction remained active. Walter Ellis's *Prince of Darkness: A Jazz Fiction Inspired by the Music of Miles Davis* (London: 20/20, 1998), unfortunately applies pop psychology to its subject, greatly diminishing Davis's complexity and stature while failing to make a convincing case for his being the prince of darkness. The jazz figures in Jon Hassler's *Rookery Blues* (New York: Ballantine, 1995), on the other hand, are all amateurs. This long campus novel focuses on five faculty members who fortunately find the companionship they crave by forming a jazz combo during the turbulent 1960s.

In contrast, David Huddle's *Tenorman* (San Francisco: Chronicle, 1995) is vastly shorter and draped around an unusual premise: seemingly at the end of the road, a black tenorman-composer is brought back to the U.S. from Sweden by the National Endowment for the Arts and provided with all the necessities of life on the condition that he allow every aspect of his daily existence to be recorded and studied; through this experiment, the lives of the researchers are changed in positive ways. Another short, resonant story is John Edgar Wideman's "The Silence of Thelonious Monk" (*Esquire,* November 1997), a story in the form of a meditation (or is it the other way around?) regarding the relationship between the silences in Monk's music and the speaker's yearning and sense of loss: "When it's time, when he [Monk] feels like it he'll play the note we've been waiting for. The note we thought was silence. And won't it be worth the wait." In the same year, coincidentally, Amiri Baraka published "A Monk Story" (*Brilliant Corners,* Summer 1997), in which the speaker encounters or thinks he encounters Monk after Monk's funeral.

Three novels in particular in this narrow but intense time-frame provide great hope for the future of jazz fiction. With a title from a Kenny Dorham tune and a dust jacket photo by William Claxton, Bart Schneider's *Blue Bossa* (New York: Viking, 1998) flaunts its jazz credentials. Framed by the

Patty Hearst kidnapping in 1970s San Francisco, this novel provides a rounded portrait of Ronnie Reboulet, a jazz trumpeter who, like Chet Baker, had once been famous both for his music and good looks. But at the height of his fame, he lost everything—his teeth, his looks, his lip—to drugs, and now he is trying, with the help of a strong woman, to get his life and career back together. The book contains excellent descriptions of music-making and frequent references to bop-era musicians.

Anthony Weller's *The Polish Lover* (New York: Marlowe, 1997) also contains solid jazz content, including an appearance by Adam Makowicz and analytical discussions of the harmonic ideas in John Coltrane's music, among other things. The plot involves a jazz clarinetist's globetrotting involvement with an enigmatic Polish woman and his reflection, a decade later, on the meaning of the relationship. The improvisational nature of jazz informs the structure, style, and theme of the novel. Weller, a jazz musician himself, may have produced a flawed novel, but he has provided an excellent jazz fiction.

Superior both as novel and jazz fiction, Rafi Zabor's epical *The Bear Comes Home* (New York and London: Norton, 1997) overflows with jazz-related energy and events. Several real jazz musicians, including Charlie Haden and Ornette Coleman, play small roles in this very long novel that vividly dramatizes the awesome challenges confronting the creative artist to be consistently spontaneous and innovative, and the joy—the grace, even—that can derive from meeting such challenges. The protagonist is a sax-playing, talking bear—an outsider's outsider, in other words—who experiences love and transcendent bliss through music. (Imagine the John Coltrane of *A Love Supreme*.) The descriptions of music-making, of the improvisational process, of life on the road, and of the grim financial reality of the professional jazz musician's life—all of these are richly, lovingly detailed, frequently technical, and thoroughly convincing. Let's hope that when this bear came home, he brought jazz fiction with him, pointing it in the direction of a rosy future.

NOTE

1. I would like to express my thanks to Lycoming College for the grant support and released time that allowed me to complete this study; and to the staff (especially Janet Hurlbert and Marlene Neece) of the Snowden Library at Lycoming College for their unfailing efficiency and good nature in providing me with answers and materials.

BIBLIOGRAPHY

An Annotated Bibliography of Jazz Fiction and Jazz Fiction Criticism. Compiled by Richard N. Albert. Westport, Connecticut: Greenwood, 1996.

Bell, Bernard W. *The Afro-American Novel and Its Tradition.* Amherst: University of Massachusetts Press, 1987.

B Flat, Bebop, Scat: Jazz Short Stories and Poems. Edited by Chris Parker. London: Quartet, 1986.

Breton, Marcella. "An Annotated Bibliography of Selected Jazz Short Stories." *African American Review* 26 (1992): 299–306.

Cataliotti, Robert H. *The Music in African American Fiction.* New York and London: Garland, 1995.

Cowley, Julian. "The Art of the Improvisers: Jazz and Fiction in Post-Bebop America." *New Comparison* 6 (1988): 194–204.

From Blues to Bop: A Collection of Jazz Fiction. Edited by Richard N. Albert. Baton Rouge: Louisiana State University Press, 1990.

Hot and Cool: Jazz Short Stories. Edited by Marcella Breton. New York: Plume, 1990.

Jazz Parody (Anthology of Jazz Fiction). Edited by Charles Harvey. London: Spearman, 1948.

Kennington, Donald, and Danny L. Read. *The Literature of Jazz.* 2d ed. Chicago: American Library Association, 1980.

Moment's Notice: Jazz in Poetry and Prose. Edited by Art Lange and Nathaniel Mackey. Minneapolis: Coffee House Press, 1993.

Sudhalter, Richard M. "Composing the Words that Might Capture Jazz." *New York Times,* Sec. 2, 29 August 1999: 1, 24.

Szwed, John F. "Joseph Škvorecký and the Tradition of Jazz Literature." *World Literature Today* 54 (1980): 586–590.

THE QUARTAL AND PENTATONIC HARMONY OF MCCOY TYNER

Paul Rinzler

I. INTRODUCTION

The purpose of this study is to document and analyze a special aspect of McCoy Tyner's music: his system of harmony based on quartal and suspended chords, and modal and pentatonic scales. This harmony is an essential aspect of what can be called Tyner's "sound," if not *the* crucial aspect of his sound.

OVERVIEW OF THIS STUDY

Music Examples

The musical examples I have used to illustrate Tyner's music come from a wide range of Tyner's recordings. Most of the pieces were written by Tyner. Some pieces are referenced once, and briefly; some are referenced several times. Much of this study relies upon transcriptions of Tyner's recordings, both published ones (the accuracy of which I have independently checked) and ones that I have transcribed. The musical examples in this study are generally short and no longer than necessary. Table 1 is a list of the tunes, albums, and transcriptions (when available) for tunes referenced in this study.

Date	Album	Tune	Transcription(s)
1962	*Inception*	Inception	*McCoy Tyner* (Toshiba)
1967	*The Real McCoy*	Passion Dance	*Inception to Now*
			McCoy Tyner (Toshiba)
1967	*Tender Moments*	Utopia	*World's Greatest Fake Book*
1968	*Expansions*	Peresina	*World's Greatest Fake Book*
1968	*Time for Tyner*	May Street	*Annual Review of Jazz Studies*
1972	*Echoes of a Friend*	Folks	*McCoy Tyner* (Hal Leonard)
1972	*Song for My Lady*	The Night Has a Thousand Eyes	*Annual Review of Jazz Studies*
1973	*Song of the New World*	Song of the New World	personal
1976	*Focal Point*	Theme for Nana	*McCoy Tyner* (Hal Leonard)
1976	*Fly with the Wind*	Salvadore de Samba	personal
		You Stepped Out of a Dream	*McCoy Tyner* (Hal Leonard)
		Fly With the Wind	*McCoy Tyner* (Hal Leonard)
1977	*Inner Voices*	For Tomorrow	*McCoy Tyner* (Hal Leonard)
			Inception to Now
1977	*Supertrios*	The Greeting	*McCoy Tyner* (Toshiba)
		Hymn Song	*McCoy Tyner* (Toshiba)
1981	*La Leyunda de la Hora*	La Vida Feliz	*New Real Book*
		La Habana Sol	*McCoy Tyner* (Hal Leonard)
1981	*Lookin' Out*	Señor Carlos	*McCoy Tyner* (Hal Leonard)
1984	*Dimensions*	Just in Time	*McCoy Tyner* (Hal Leonard)
1986	*Double Trios*	Latino Suite	personal
1987	*Live at the Musician's Exchange Cafe*	Port Au Blues	personal
1991	*Blue Bossa*	Traces	personal

Table 1: List of Tyner materials cited in this study

I have not included very many references to traditional or mainstream tunes in which Tyner takes a largely traditional or mainstream approach. Examples of such tunes are Tyner's own "Port Au Blues" and "Hip Toe" from *Live at the Musicians' Cafe* (RTV CD21301). While these mainstream pieces have occupied a larger and larger proportion of Tyner's recordings recently, and while a mainstream approach is certainly one aspect of Tyner's total musicianship, it is not such an important part of his unique, special sound, and so I have largely ignored it in this study.

A. GENERAL ASPECTS OF TYNER'S HARMONY

Harmony is one of the most characteristic parts of Tyner's style and is a major factor upon which his place in jazz is founded. The roots of Tyner's style of harmony lay in the music of John Coltrane and how Tyner played while with Coltrane. While Tyner certainly used many aspects of his style while with Coltrane (for instance, quartal chords), he did not develop his own unique style fully until around the time he left Coltrane and began to record as leader. Even so, his first recordings for Impulse were focused on more traditional material, including many standards, and it was not until he recorded for Blue Note that he recorded more and more of his own compositions in his own style. The complete establishment of this style might be somewhat arbitrarily set at his critically acclaimed recording *Sahara* (1972).

Tyner does use traditional II-V-I harmony, especially when he plays jazz standards, but for his own compositions and for his own unique musical style, he has used another type of harmony which will be the primary subject of this study.

The best and simplest single label for Tyner's harmony is "quartal." It is founded upon several features:

- the perfect 4th
- quartal chords
- the pentatonic scale
- modes
- minor harmony

Each succeeding one of these aspects of Tyner's harmony is founded the previous one. For instance:

- quartal chords are comprised of perfect 4ths (P4ths),
- the pentatonic scale can be derived from a 5-note quartal chord,

- some modes contain a pentatonic scale within them, and
- some modes imply minor harmony.

Each of these aspects above will be briefly explored and defined.

1. The Perfect 4th. The most essential part of Tyner's harmony, the simplest musical structure upon which nearly all other aspects of his harmony is based, is the P4th. It is ubiquitous as an interval in Tyner's harmony, and is the interval to which the term "quartal" refers.

The sound of the P4th in Tyner's harmony is most closely related to the suspended 4th (sus4) in common practice harmony. A suspended 4th is so called because the P4th is suspended into another chord in which it is a dissonance, and is then resolved. Example 1 by J. S. Bach shows a suspended 4th (in the alto voice) and its resolution.

Example 1: Suspended 4th

The suspended 4th for Tyner, however, is not a dissonance that requires resolution, and so does not usually resolve (although Tyner does sometimes treat a suspended 4th in the traditional manner, resolving it: see Examples 47, 48 and 49). Rather, the suspended 4 is treated more like a consonance by Tyner, and is used in several different types of chords, and even in tonic chords, as will be shown.

2. Quartal Harmony. Quartal harmony is based upon the interval of a 4th, and in Tyner's case, specifically the P4th. A quartal chord is defined here as a chord entirely built of P4ths. There are no standard terms in jazz usage today to label different forms of quartal chords. Furthermore, the term "sus chord" is sometimes used in jazz for what I have defined as a quartal chord. I am suggesting the term "quartal" (and the symbol "Q") be used in order to distinguish a chord built in P4ths from other chords, especially what I define as a sus chord. Example 2 shows three types of quartal chords that

Tyner uses, with the labels for them that I will use in this study. (See Example 7 for a summary of other chords and their labels.)

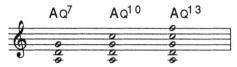

Example 2: Quartal chords

The special quality of quartal chords is a result of the fact that what would be an unresolved suspended 4th in traditional jazz or common practice harmony does not take on the quality of something needing or implying resolution when used in the context of Tyner's music but becomes a consonance in and of itself, as stable as any major or minor triad in common practice music.

Quartal chords are an essential part of Tyner's style: they are used as

- parts of voicings or textures that are not only used often by Tyner but also have a very distinctive sound (Tyner uses many different types of chord voicings and textures, including tertian chords, quartal chords, seconds, single pitches in the left hand, bass lines, etc.);
- left-hand comping chords in his improvisations, just as a mainstream jazz pianist will use tertian voicings for comping;
- two-handed chords in his improvisations in which a two-handed chordal texture provides variety to the normal right-hand melody and left-hand comping chords;
- the harmonic basis for chords in his compositions.

a. Tritones with P4ths. Levine suggests that using chords voiced in 4ths and that also contain a tritone is a way to create tension in what might otherwise be an unchanging (all P4ths) harmonic framework in modal tunes.[1] He includes examples of parallel 5-note chords voiced in P4ths that include some tritones as examples of chords that suggest the styles of Tyner as well as Chick Corea (Example 3).

Example 3: P4th and tritone voicings

Tyner's tendency, however, is to use voicings with tritones in II-V-I contexts, such as his composition "Inception," introducing some quartal chords, rather than with modal or suspended harmony as Levine suggests. The more characteristic part of Tyner's style is a modal, not II-V-I context, in which case he does not use voicings with tritones very often.

3. The Pentatonic Scale. There are two pentatonic scales in jazz: the major pentatonic and the minor pentatonic. Relative major and minor pentatonic scales, shown in Example 14, contain the same pitches.

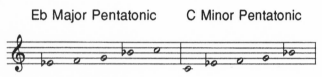

Example 4: Pentatonic scales

The pentatonic scale is crucial to Tyner's harmony, as the primary parts of his harmonic vocabulary can be generated through the pentatonic scale (see Example 14).

The pentatonic scales are closely related to the P4th and to quartal chords. Quartal chords are easily derived from a pentatonic scale: the entire pentatonic scale can be rearranged into a 5-note quartal chord (Q13), which also contains within it three Q7 chords and two Q10 chords (Example 5).

Example 5: Pentatonic scale and quartal chords

4. Modes. A minor pentatonic scale may be expanded by adding scale degrees $\hat{2}$ and $\hat{6}$) to produce a 7-note mode. Of the 7 traditional modes, only the dorian, phrygian, and aeolian modes contain within them a minor pentatonic scale (shown with open noteheads below) on the same tonic (Example 6).

The dorian, aeolian, and phrygian are the modes that Tyner uses the most frequently, and of these, the dorian is the most important. It generates more of the chords that Tyner uses, and he uses the dorian mode most frequently. He also uses the aeolian not uncommonly but less frequently than dorian, and the phrygian less often. The phrygian scale contains a $\flat\hat{2}$ (D$\flat$ in C phrygian), and Tyner's harmony depends more upon the natural $\hat{2}$ of the dorian

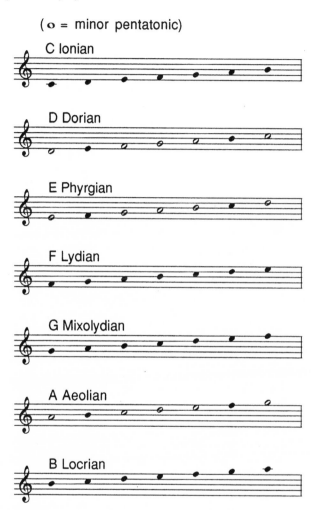

Example 6: Modes

and aeolian modes, as will be shown later. Tyner also uses the mixolydian mode commonly.

Both the dorian and aeolian modes contain the three Q7 chords that the minor pentatonic scale with the same tonic also contains. The mixolydian mode, however, does not contain a minor pentatonic scale beginning on $\hat{1}$ of the mixolydian mode. Tyner uses quartal chords on other scale degrees in the mixolydian mode.

Because the relative major pentatonic and minor pentatonic scales are comprised of the same notes, one must look to a related mode to determine which pentatonic scale (major or minor) is operative. For instance, in D dorian, one should assume that Tyner uses a D minor pentatonic scale instead of a F major pentatonic. Because the large majority of Tyner's music uses the minor modes (that is, those modes with a minor I chord: dorian, aeolian, and phrygian), Tyner favors the minor pentatonic scale.

5. Minor Harmony. Tyner's music is strongly oriented toward minor harmony, but in a particular way. Mainstream jazz harmony is founded on the II-V-I progression. Tyner's music establishes harmonic practices that are different from II-V-I jazz harmony. Tyner creates a different "flavor" of minor harmony. In contrast to tonality, which is based upon the minor as well as the major scale, Tyner's harmony might be called "minor modality," being based on suspended 4ths, the minor pentatonic scale, and the minor modes (dorian, aeolian, and sometimes phrygian). It is Tyner's great achievement to have been the jazz musician that has most thoroughly explored and developed this special type of minor harmony.

II. HARMONIC VOCABULARY

We all have a musical vocabulary, just like we have vocabularies to speak. When you converse with a person long enough, you can familiarize yourself with their vocabulary. But that doesn't mean they can't deviate from it, or inject new words.[2]

Tyner's insight about vocabularies and deviations is a useful one. The following is my attempt to outline the basics of Tyner's harmonic vocabulary, and while this vocabulary catches the essence of Tyner's harmony, he does certainly deviate from it.

Example 7 illustrates the essential chords that Tyner uses in his system of modal, pentatonic, quartal, and suspended harmony (some labels used in Example 7 are explained below). All the chords in Example 7 are all diatonic to C minor pentatonic with an added $\hat{2}$ (see "h. adding $\hat{2}$ to minor pentatonic" after Example 14), except for the Q13 chord, diatonic to C aeolian, and the sus2(6), diatonic to C dorian.

The chords in Example 7 form the basis for many different and important aspects of Tyner's music: it is a catalog of

- chords that Tyner uses in his compositions
- chords that Tyner improvises in his solos

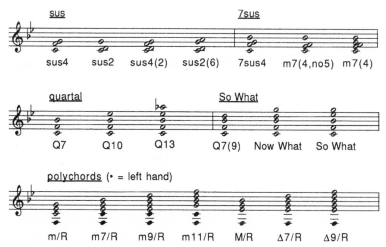

Example 7: Tyner's harmonic vocabulary

- parts of voicings for left hand and right hand that Tyner uses to build other chords
- harmonies used as the basis for melodic improvisation

Tyner also uses other elements in his quartal harmony, as well as traditional tertian harmonies over II-V-I progressions, which will be discussed later.

A. LABELS FOR CHORDS

There is some flexibility apparent in jazz with definitions of various quartal and sus chords and the labels applied to those chords. Levine identifies several labels that are used for a single such chord (Example 8).[3]

Gsus
F/G
Gsus4
G7sus4
Dm7/G

Example 8: Levine's labels for a sus chord

In order to catalogue Tyner's harmony and to identify many different varieties of quartal and suspended chords, I have created names and symbols for some chords that Tyner uses frequently but that are not commonly recognized in jazz theory. I have tried to base the names and labels that I have created upon existing principles of naming jazz chords.

1. Quartal Chords (Example 9). The labels for this group of chords follow the jazz practice of including all chord tones or extensions beneath and including a given number. For tertian chords, 3rds are stacked, producing the following sequence of chord tones and extensions: 1 3 5 7 9 11 13. For quartal chords, P4ths are stacked to produce the following sequence: 1 4 7 10 13. For instance, C11 (tertian) includes the 9th as well as the 11th, and CQ13 (quartal) includes the 4th, 7th, and 10th, as well as the 13th.

Example 9: Quartal chords

2. Suspended Chords. Jazz practice is not consistent about how suspended chords are defined, and Tyner uses many different variations of suspended chords, some of which are not commonly recognized in jazz theory. I therefore have created a new set of names and symbols, illustrated in Example 10:

Example 10: Sus chords

sus4—This defines the most simple chord (a triad) with a suspended 4th. A suspended note implies that the note to which the suspension resolves (in traditional theory, at least) is absent from the chord, so a sus4 chord does not have a 3rd. This symbol is widely recognized in jazz.

sus2—In this case, the principle that a suspended chord not include the note to which the suspension resolves is sacrificed for the convenience of a short chord name and one similar to the sus4 chord.

sus4(2)—Although an alternate label for this chord could have been sus2(4), I chose sus4(2) because sus4 is in general use, so sus4(2) merely adds an added tone (2) to an already existing label.

sus2 (6)—In this case a 6 is added to a sus2 chord.

7sus4—This chord name is consistent with the other chord names for suspended chords. This symbol and the sus4 symbol are the only sus chord symbols above that are widely recognized in jazz.

m7 (4, no 5)—While a little unwieldy, this name is the best option to accurately and exactly define this chord, consistent with other principles of naming chords.

3. *So What Family of Chords.*

AQ7(9)   A Now What   A So What   BQ7/AQ7

Example 11: So What family of chords

Q7(9)—This chord's label is borrowed from the label for quartal chords, but this chord is not comprised of all P4ths: its uppermost interval is a M3rd. This M3rd is the common element in the So What family of chords, which contain all P4ths except for one M3rd. This chord can also be labeled as a polychord (G/A for the first chord in Example 11).

Now What—I developed the name of this chord as a variation of the name for the So What chord. Like the So What chord, it has five notes and is composed of all P4ths except for one M3rd. The Now What chord has all the same notes as the Q7(9), with the addition of another P4th on top.

So What—This name for this chord is in general use in jazz practice. It comes from the voicing used by Bill Evans on Miles Davis's classic recording of the piece "So What." The So What chord is the same as the Q13 chord except that the top note is lowered a half-step. The So What chord can also be viewed as a Q7 chord with a major triad on top (C/AQ7 in Example 11). The M3rd of the So What chord is between two different notes than the Now What chord's M3rd.

Q7 polychord—This label is borrowed from the method of notating a polychord. It identifies two stacked Q7 chords whose roots are a whole step apart. This can be considered a different voicing of the Now What chord, as the Q7 polychord is merely the Now What chord with a doubled root two octaves above.

4. *Polychords.*
Jazz theory has no general labels for different kinds of polychords without also specifying the bass note and root of the chord. For instance, the symbol "F/G" is in widespread use and means an F major triad

over a G bass note, but there is no label in common use for the general type of that polychord, that is, a major triad with a bass note a M2nd up from the root of the triad.

Rather than developing a complete system of labeling such general kinds of polychords, I have only developed some labels for the polychords Tyner uses that are part of his system of quartal and pentatonic harmony. Furthermore, these labels do not contain symbols or numbers that specify the interval between the bass note and the upper chord, but merely indicate the quality of the upper chord, using standard jazz chords symbols, as well as the presence of a lower bass note, indicated by "R" for "root."

a. Left-hand Root-5th. Tyner sometimes voices these polychords so that the upper chord appears in the right hand and the root or a root-5th appears in the left hand (solid noteheads in Example 7), but sometimes not. In Example 12, a m7/R polychord is voiced in such a manner as to emphasize its polychordal nature: the right hand plays an inversion of a m7 chord over the bass note in the left hand.

Example 12: m7 / R, "You Stepped Out of a Dream," intro

In Example 13, the same basic polychord is voiced with a root-5th in the left hand (the 11th in the right hand, C, merely doubles the bass note).

Example 13: m7 / R, "Fly with the Wind," head

B. RELATIONS AMONG CHORDS

The chords in Example 7 are closely related to each other. All these chords can be derived from each other as well as from the minor modes and the minor pentatonic scale (although not with the same roots, as shown in Example 7). Example 14 shows these derivations and interrelationships.

1. Explanation of Example 14

a. Noteheads. In Example 14, different noteheads are used to indicate several important aspects:

Notehead	Indicates
o	found to have been used by Tyner
•	not found to have been used by Tyner
x	not part of the chord, but part of other chords from which the chord in question is derived (see "*g.* Chords derived . . .")
o	left-hand root or root-5th (R-5)

b. Based on A Minor Pentatonic. I have arbitrarily chosen A minor pentatonic as the fundamental minor pentatonic scale for illustrating these harmonies. Of course, all harmonies may be transposed to the other pitches of the chromatic scale. The horizontal lines underlining "A minor pentatonic," "A Phrygian," "A Aeolian," and "A Dorian" at the top of Example 14 extend over those notes in the first staff that comprise those scales. The heavy barlines on each staff indicate that the notes and harmonies lying between them are contained within A minor pentatonic. (The last system, with three staves, has only a single heavy barline and so contains no harmonies completely contained within A minor pentatonic.)

c. Chord Symbols. Chord symbols (with no pitch letter name indicated) are placed to the left of each staff in Example 14.

d. Roman Numerals Indicate the Root. The roman numerals below some chords in Example 14 do not necessarily indicate function as they normally do in traditional jazz theory or common practice harmony; at minimum, roman numerals in Example 14 only indicate on what scale degree of an A minor scale the chord is built, thereby indicating the root of the

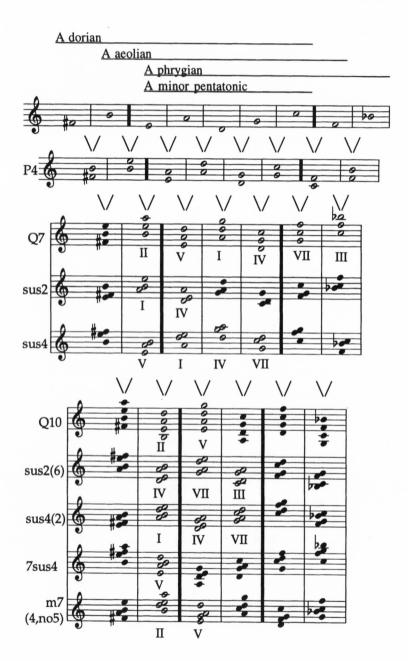

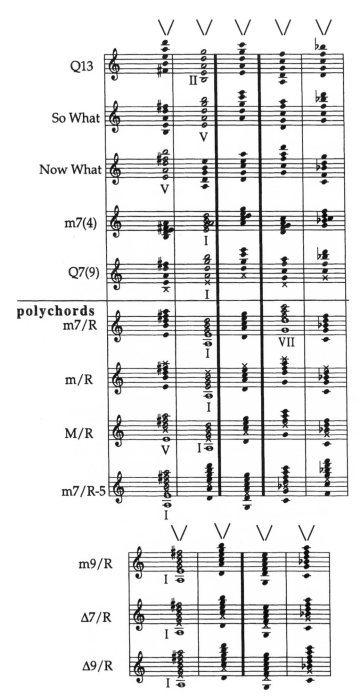

Example 14: Summary of Tyner's harmony

chord. Only chords found to have been used by Tyner (with open note-heads) have a roman numeral below them.

e. Similar Chord Qualities on a Staff. Harmonies with the same quality (internal interval construction) are placed on the same staff in Example 14. (In addition to the P4ths on the second staff, P5ths could have been included on another staff, but they are easily inferred by inverting the P4ths.)

f. Measures Define Chords. All chords occurring within the same "measure" on a single system of staves (that is, chords directly over each other vertically) are comprised of the same pitches. Such chords therefore could be considered inversions of each other, but see "j. Inversions" below.

g. Chords Derived from Upper Measures Connected by "\/". The pitches for all chords in the same measure are derived by combining all the pitches from the two nearest adjacent measures on the immediately higher system. This derivation is indicated by the "\/" lines drawn from the upper two adjacent measures down to a lower, single measure. More complex harmonies are thus gradually built up from simpler and closely related components. For instance, the IIQ7 chord contains the same pitches (B-E-A) as the two pairs of P4ths above it, B-E and E-A. Those two P4ths combine to derive the IIQ7. All chords in the same measure, because they contain the same pitches, are all derived from the same two upper measures. For instance, the IIQ7, Isus2, and Vsus4 are all derived from the P4ths B-E and E-A.

Furthermore, all possible derivations of a chord are not limited to the one system immediately above the chord in question, but may continue upwards through the lines connecting measures. For instance, the VQ10 chord contains within it not only a VQ7 and a IQ7 (as well as a IVsus2 and a VIIsus2, etc.), but, following the connecting lines higher, may also be derived from three sets of pairs of P4ths: E-A, A-D, and D-G. Only adjacent measures, whose pitches in all cases are closely related (separated only by a P4th/P5th, the most harmonically close interval except the octave), are combined to generate more complex harmonies.

The significance of this system of deriving chords from simpler, related components is important: various components of textures (single notes, intervals, 3-note chords, 4-note chords, etc.) distributed between the left hand and right hand in a voicing can be considered to be the relatively simple components from which a more complex harmony may be derived. For instance, a Q10 contains within it the harmonies shown in Example 15, any of which might appear as part of a two-handed piano texture that expresses that Q10 harmony.

Example 15: Harmonies within Q10

h. Adding $\hat{2}$ to Minor Pentatonic. $\hat{2}$ is the most important expansion of the minor pentatonic scale in Tyner's harmony. Adding $\hat{2}$ to a minor pentatonic scale allows for other quartal chords built on $\hat{2}$ (Example 14), in addition to the I, IV, and V quartal chords from just the minor pentatonic.

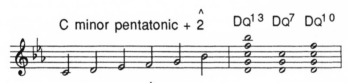

Example 16: Pentatonic scale with $\hat{2}$ and quartal chords

Chords derived from the minor pentatonic scale plus $\hat{2}$ can be considered an expansion of Tyner's quartal style generated by the pentatonic scale alone. In Example 14, the chords immediately to the left of the left-most dark barline are those derived with $\hat{2}$. The prevalence of these chords with open noteheads in Example 14 are evidence of the importance of the addition of $\hat{2}$ to the pentatonic scale in Tyner's harmony.

Another indication of Tyner's tendency to add the $\hat{2}$ to the pentatonic scale (as opposed to $\hat{6}$, the only other remaining scale degree to add) is indicated by the melody from the B section of "Fly With the Wind" (Example 17), which uses C minor pentatonic exclusively except for one pitch, and that pitch is $\hat{2}$ (D).

Example 17: Pentatonic with $\hat{2}$, "Fly with the Wind," head

i. Mixolydian Mode. Although the chord qualities in Example 14 are derived from the minor pentatonic and the minor scales, and therefore are contained with those modes that also contain a minor pentatonic scale on the same tonic (dorian, aeolian, and phrygian), these chords are also used by Tyner, sometimes on different scale degrees, in another mode that does not contain a minor pentatonic scale on its tonic: mixolydian. For instance, in the dorian mode, a Q7 chord appears diatonically on scale degrees $\hat{1}$, $\hat{2}$, $\hat{4}$, $\hat{5}$, $\hat{6}$. But in mixolydian, a Q7 chord appears diatonically on scale degrees $\hat{1}$, $\hat{2}$, $\hat{3}$, $\hat{5}$, $\hat{6}$. The mixolydian mode is not included in Example 14, but some examples of Tyner using the chord qualities derived from the minor modes but used in mixolydian are included in this study.

j. Inversions. The chords in Example 14 that occur in the same measure on a system have the same pitches as other chords in the same measure but are separately identified and labeled. This is different from common practice harmony in which chords with the same pitches, but which have different voicings or are in a different inversion, are merely different forms of the same fundamental chord with a single label.

Tyner's harmony approaches inversion and the uniqueness of chords in a certain way. The way in which chords in various inversions can act as tonics can sometimes seem contradictory. For instance:

- chords with different qualities (different pitches and internal interval construction), but built on the same root, can all be tonics;

- chords of the same quality but built on different roots can function as a tonic chord.

(i) Different Chord Qualities as Tonics. Examples 18, 19, and 20 show three excerpts from Tyner's music in which a Q7, a sus2, and a sus4 are all used as a tonic chord.

Example 18: Q7 as tonic, "Señor Carlos," intro

Example 19: Sus2 as tonic, "Señor Carlos," solo

Example 20: Sus4 as tonic, "Folks," solo

Rather than the I chord being established by a V chord and a leading tone, the Q7 chord in Example 18 is established through repetition (the short phrase in Example 18 is a vamp). The sus2 chord in Example 19 is made a tonic by harmonizing a modal ♭VII-I cadence at the end of a four-bar phrase. The sus4 chord in Example 20 is made a tonic as part of a ♭IIM6-Im7 cadence.

(ii) Different Roots as Tonics

Examples 21 and 22 shows two excerpts in which both a IQ7 and IIQ7 are used as tonics.

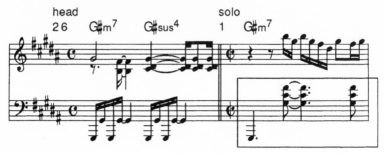

Example 21: IQ7 as tonic, "Theme for Nana," solo

Example 22: IIQ7 as tonic, "Passion Dance," solo

The Q7 in Example 21 is a tonic as the result of its root (G♯) having been established as the tonic in the head and because it is the first chord of Tyner's solo and of the head. The Q7 in Example 22 continues the tonic originally established by the root-5th that anticipates the downbeat of measure 33. This Q7 is made a tonic partially because the chord establishes the tonic melodically (the upper note in the voicing is F, the tonic), and because it is repeated over and over, immediately following the strong root-5th.

k. Limitations. Example 14 is not a perfect outline of Tyner's harmony. For instance, Tyner

- uses some, but not all the chords in Example 14,
- uses other chords not shown in Example 14, and
- favors some chords shown more than others.

Chords with filled-in noteheads, while not cited as being used by Tyner, are included to make a complete family of harmonies. Example 14 outlines a comprehensive set of chords based upon Tyner's harmonic system of the P4th and minor scales. So using chords from Example 14 not found to have been used by Tyner would still be true to Tyner's sound and general style.

C. POLYCHORDS

In traditional jazz harmony, polychords are chords comprised of a right-hand tertian chord and a left-hand bass note that is not a chord tone of the right-hand chord. The polychords that Tyner uses and that are part of his system of quartal and pentatonic harmony are also ones commonly used in jazz.

One way such polychords may be used is closely tied to a particular analysis of them that one might call the "functional" analysis of such polychords. This analysis considers that these polychords contain both subdominant and dominant functions. The subdominant function is carried by the upper chord, some type of II or IV chord. The dominant function is carried by the bass note, which is analyzed as $\hat{5}$. Examples of such polychords are F/G, Dm7/G, and the like.

These polychords actually function in the manner of this analysis when they move to a I chord (that is, the progression F/G-CΔ7). Tyner, however (as well as many other jazz musicians, influenced or not by Tyner), does not use these polychords in that functional manner. Rather, they are used in what may be called a "pan-modal" fashion and which is related to the rest of his system of quartal and pentatonic harmony: either as tonic chords themselves or in a parallel fashion.

1. Polychords as Tonics. When a polychord is used as a tonic chord, the tonic is the bass (lowest) note of the chord. In Example 23 this is mainly accomplished by the repetition of the chord (the change to FΔ7 can be considered a kind of change of mode, similar to a change to a parallel major or minor in common practice harmony). Example 24 shows a F/G polychord, or GQ7(9), functioning as a tonic.

2. Parallel Polychords. Example 25 shows three parallel Δ9/R polychords. The lowest notes in the treble clef are notated with their stems pointing downward to indicate that they were probably played in the left

Example 23: m7/R polychord as tonic, "Utopia," head

Example 24: Q7(9) as tonic, "Passion Dance," solo

Example 25: VIIΔ9/R, "The Greeting," head

Example 26: Δ7/R, "Traces," head

hand (along with the notes in the bass clef). Example 26 shows two alternating Δ7/R polychords a whole-step apart.

3. Polychords and quartal chords. The polychords in Example 7 are can be derived from quartal chords. The Q7 is the initial chord in this process. To this chord one can add a 9th, making a Q7(9), a chord already identified as part of Tyner's harmonic vocabulary. A Q7(9), however, is the same as the polychord comprised of a major triad with a bass note a major second above the root of the upper triad [GQ7(9) = F/G = G, C, F, A]. Because all the polychords in Example 7 can be considered to contain some type of subdominant chord over a dominant bass note, they can be viewed as substitutions or extensions of the basic Q7(9) polychord/quartal chord. Example 27 shows all the polychords in Example 7 (on a G bass note) along with the initial Q7 chord from which they may be derived. The jazz chord symbols above the staff also identify the root and quality of the upper chords (F or D chords) so that their function as a substitution or extension of the FM triad in the F/G chord can be easily understood.

Example 27: Polychords and quartal chord

4. Polychords and the Pentatonic Scale. D minor pentatonic is the minor pentatonic scale most closely related to these polychords in Example 27: Dm is one of upper subdominant chords, and one only needs to add to the D minor pentatonic scale Tyner's next most important scale degree, $\hat{2}$, to obtain all the notes in Example 27.

The tonic of the pentatonic scale to which the polychords are most closely related comes from one of the subdominant function chords in the upper chord (the II chord), whereas in the strict functional use of these polychords, the primary function of the polychord is as a dominant (the other part of the polychord), leading to I (even though it contains a part that functions as a subdominant—the upper chord). Functionally, the dominant aspect of the chord is emphasized, but, for Tyner, the related pentatonic scale comes from the subdominant part of the polychord, the upper chord.

D. LEFT HAND P5THS

The P4th as well as its inversion, the P5th, are the most important intervals in Tyner's harmony, forming the basis for quartal and suspended chords. As McCoy Tyner notes, however,

> There are other things [than fourths] involved. It's not just a pile of fourths. I play a lot of fifths in my left hand, you know, and they do the same things as fourths: They open the sound. . . . But there are thirds, seconds, octaves, and clusters there too.[4]

Still, P4ths and P5ths have given Tyner his special sound (along with other factors, such as his powerful left-hand pedal tones) and are a crucial part of his music.

One aspect of these related intervals is the use of the P5th in the left hand. Left hand bass lines occupy a significant part of Tyner's style. Tyner often plays bass lines and other bass figures with his left hand (including the common root, octave, or root-5th), even when playing with a bassist; his bass lines provide a strong counter-melody and sometimes have important harmonic considerations.

1. Melodic P5ths in Bass Lines. Tyner uses melodic P5ths extensively in his bass lines. The most common type of bass line that Tyner uses has the following characteristics:

- initial ascending contour
- shortness (no more than two bars in length)
- $\hat{1}$, $\hat{5}$, $\hat{8}$ (or $\hat{9}$ or $\hat{10}$ instead of $\hat{8}$)
- and-of-2 emphasized by contour and/or rhythm
- parallel motion when chords change
- repetition several times or indefinitely

The combination of these general tendencies produces bass lines that are distinctive and contain interesting variability. Example 28 illustrates several of Tyner's bass lines that follow most of or slightly vary the above general characteristics.

An important characteristic of these bass lines is the reliance upon the melodic interval of a P5th. This appears not only between the root and $\hat{5}$, which is perhaps the most common single characteristic of Tyner's bass lines, but also between $\hat{5}$ and $\hat{9}$ which appears in the bass lines to "Hymn Song," "You Stepped Out of a Dream," and "Peresina."

Example 28: Bass lines

2. Harmonic P5ths. The use of the harmonic P5th in Tyner's left hand is an important part of his style, occurring in Tyner's soloing as well as in the head. Tyner's P5ths, single pedal tones, and octaves in the bass register of his left hand have an important harmonic, rhythmic, and cadential function. These notes often strongly ground the tonic in a harmonic system that has a fair amount of ambiguity, and they often occur at major divisions in a tune. In addition to octaves or a single low bass note, harmonic P5ths are another way that Tyner produces the thundering pedal tones for which he is so well known.

Harmonic 5ths in the bass and left hand are featured perhaps most distinctively by Tyner in his arrangement of "The Night Has a Thousand Eyes" (Example 29).

Example 29: 5ths, "The Night Has a Thousand Eyes," head

In the intro and A section, the left hand breaks a Dsus4 chord into two P5ths, D-A and G-D. The bass doubles the lowest note of the left hand, except for the last note, which doubles the upper note D, emphasizing the tonic of the mode (D mixolydian) and helping the two-bar vamp phrase to cadence.

The B section introduces a variation of the left hand from the intro. Instead of successive 5ths, the left hand now outlines G7sus4 with a P5th and a P4th while using the same rhythm and contour.

Tyner uses P5ths to underlie three chords in the head of "The Greeting" (Example 30).

a. P5ths with Tertian Chords. In "Hymn Song," Tyner uses P5ths in the left hand to underlie triads, not quartal or sus chords (Example 31).

Some of the flavor of quartal harmony is carried by the P5ths in the left hand and imparted to the triads used in "Hymn Song," even though quartal chords are not being used.

In his composition "May Street," Tyner uses P5ths in the left hand as well as the right hand to voice major seventh chords in such a way as to approximate the flavor of a true quartal approach (Example 32).

Example 30: Harmonic 5ths in bass line, "The Greeting," head

Example 31: P5ths in bass line, "Hymn Song," head

Example 32: P5ths in bass line, "May Street," head

By using P5ths in both hands (while still producing a complete voicing for each major seventh chord) and moving in parallel motion, Tyner uses two important aspects of his quartal harmony that impart much of the flavor of quartal and pentatonic harmony to a chord from more tonal harmonic vocabulary.

Tyner also uses these strong left hand P5ths in tunes with tertian chords that use the II-V-I progression. Example 33 shows this in the tune "Just in Time."

Example 33: LH P5ths with II-V-I progression, "Just in Time," various excerpts

E. HARMONIC PROGRESSIONS

Four factors are responsible for the most common, recurring type of chord progression in Tyner's music:

- pentatonic harmony (quartal, sus, or polychords)
- parallel motion

- pairs of chords
- whole-steps between the roots of pairs of chords

The following examples illustrate these characteristics.

1. Pairs of Chords

a. Shorter Examples. "In Peresina," nearly the entire chord progression (the intro and the A section, but not the B section) consists of pairs of parallel, pentatonic-based chords. Example 34 shows several pairs of parallel chords:

- intro
    - GQ7—FQ7
- m. 1–2 in the A section
    - E♭/F—D♭/E♭
    - G♭/A♭—A♭/B♭
- m. 4–7 in the A section
    - E♭Q7—D♭Q7[5]

Example 34: Parallel chords, "Peresina," head

The B section of "The Greeting" begins with 2 chords for 8 measures, previously shown in Example 30. In this case, the left-hand P5ths and the basics of the pair of chords (Dm/G to Em/A) move in parallel motion, but the voice-leading is not exactly parallel. The highest note in each voicing, A, is sustained, and the Dm chord is a Dm9/G, while the Em chord is an Em11/A.

Two pairs of chords (F♯M—EM and DM—EM) share a common chord (EM) to total three chords that float over a pedal tone in the B section of "For Tomorrow" (Example 35). Tyner uses three pairs of parallel polychords to end his solo in "Passion Dance" (Example 36). Each pair contains two polychords a whole-step apart, and the pairs ascend chromatically.

Example 35: Pairs of parallel chords, "For Tomorrow," head

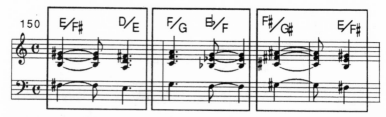

Example 36: Parallel polychords, "Passion Dance," solo

Example 37: Pairs of chords, "Salvadore de Samba," intro

Tyner composed two pairs of two chords separated by a shift of mode from phrygian to aeolian in the bass line to "Salvadore de Samba" (Example 37). The pairs are defined by

- a two-measure rhythm
- the direction of the root movement (up a step)
- the change of mode

The first pair, Am-B♭M, establishes A phrygian, but the second pair, FM-GM, moving to the tonic Am at the repeat sign, establishes A aeolian with the progression ♭VI-♭VII-I, thus shifting modes within the four-bar vamp. The phrygian portion of this bass line is the same (except for a slightly different rhythm) as the bass line for the intro to "Fly With the Wind" (Example 28).

b. Shorter Examples not Strictly Parallel. The B section to "Hymn Song" has two pair of chords (Dm-CM6 and CM-B♭M6) that are almost exactly parallel. The progression is shown in Example 38. Both pairs of chords have the same

- contour: in both cases the second chord descends by step under an upper pedal tone (notated as a whole note) in Example 38 to a M6 chord,
- length: two bars,
- left-hand P5th beginning: D-A and C-G, and
- harmonic rhythm.

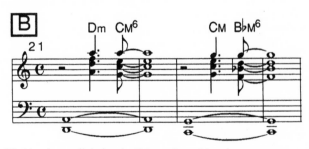

Example 38: Nearly parallel chords, "Hymn Song," head

The only way in which the two pairs of chords are not parallel concerns the quality of the first chord in the pairs; in the first pair, the quality of the chord is minor (Dm), and in the second pair, the quality of the chord is major. These chords are parallel diatonically (within D aeolian).

Tyner uses a polychord in two different forms, not voiced in parallel fashion, that obscure an underlying parallelism in the beginning of the A section of "La Habana Sol" (Example 39).

The two chords in question are G♭/A♭ and Cm7/B♭. At first glance and at first hearing, these two chords are not parallel. However, Cm7 in the upper part of the second polychord is a substitute for A♭Δ9 (Cm7 = A♭Δ9 without a root). G♭/A♭—A♭Δ9/B♭ is more easily understood as parallel. It is the voice-leading between the two chords that mostly obscures their parallelism. In Example 39, the open noteheads on the single staff show the fundamental parallelism (although the "x" notehead on A♭ in the second chord is absent).

Example 39: Parallel polychords, "La Habana Sol," head

c. Longer Examples: **abac.** Sections of several pieces by Tyner show a similar approach to chord progression throughout an entire 4- or 8-bar phrase. These sections share most of the following characteristics:

- one pair of chords per bar
- all chords sharing the same quality
- **a b a c** phrases (1, 2, or 4-bars each)
- chords on or near the downbeat and the and-of-2
- chords moving in parallel motion

- chords within each pair a whole-step apart
- phrases **b** and **c** a whole step apart

These characteristics produce progressions that are strongly similar.

The simplest example with single chords, not pairs, in an **abac** chord progression occurs in "For Tomorrow" in a vamp-like section after the A section (Example 40).

Example 40: Parallel chords, "For Tomorrow," head

The following examples from "The Greeting" and "Fly With the Wind" establish parallel motion among three chords, one of which is not adjacent to the other two in time. While this tendency does not occur in many of Tyner's compositions, it is specific enough to warrant special note.

In "The Greeting" (Example 41), each part of the **abac** phrase consists of a pair of chords, defined by their contour: that is, a new part begins with a skip in the melody.

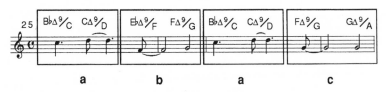

Example 41: Parallel chords, "The Greeting," head

Because the **c** phrase begins where the **b** phrase left off (the first chord of the **c** phrase, FΔ9/G, is the same as the last chord in the **b** phrase), and because it is in an analogous position to the **b** phrase (both the **c** and **b** phrases follow the same **a** phrase), the GΔ9/A can be heard as a continuation of the parallel motion from E♭Δ9/F—FΔ9/G in the **b** phrase, making a three-chord parallel progression E♭Δ9/F—FΔ9/G—GΔ9/A, albeit interrupted by the second **a** phrase.

A similar interrupted parallelism is heard in "Fly With the Wind," and although in this case the three chords do not appear in sequence in the same direction, they are still related and can be heard as connected (Example 42).

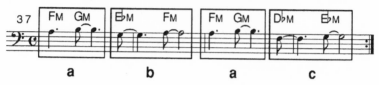

Example 42: Parallel chords, "Fly with the Wind," head

Similar to "The Greeting," the **c** phrase in "Fly With the Wind" is in an analogous position to the **b** phrase; both follow the **a** phrase. In the **b** phrase, the first chord, E♭M, chord ascends to the next chord, FM. But in the **c** phrase, the E♭M chord becomes the chord to which another chord (D♭M) will ascend. The **c** phrase does not pick up where the **b** phrase left off, as in Example 41 above from "The Greeting," but begins by preceding the common chord between the **b** and **c** phrases, E♭M, with another chord, D♭M. As opposed to the example from "The Greeting," the D♭M-E♭M-FM chords do not appear in sequence as they occur in pitch, that is, the lowest sounding of the three is not the first or last, the middle one in pitch is not the middle one in the sequence, etc. However, the implicit relationship between D♭M-E♭M-FM does occur when the entire **abac** phrase is repeated. The first chord in the next **abac** phrase is FM (not notated in Example 42), which completes the D♭M-E♭M-FM progression begun at the end of the first **abac** phrase.

"Hymn Song" establishes a similar type of phrase as that found in "The Greeting" and "Fly With the Wind," but elaborates it. "Hymn Song" contains two **abac** phrases (labeled **abac** and **ab'a'd** to distinguish them). The first one is very similar to the other **abac** phrase already discussed; the second one is a variation of the other **abac** phrases examined. Example 43 is the entire A section of "Hymn Song."

Bars 1–4 contain an **abac** phrase much the same as the others mentioned above. While the first two bars (**ab**) contain parallel triads of the same quality, that aspect of Tyner's **abac** phrases is not continued throughout the example, as Dm and B♭△7 precede GM later in m. 4 and m. 6. Other than that, bars 1–4 share all the other characteristics of Tyner's **abac** phrases noted above. This **abac** phrase in bars 1–4 also establishes a relationship between three parallel chords of the same quality (the initial FM—GM—AM triads) in a manner similar to "The Greeting" and "Fly With the Wind" above.

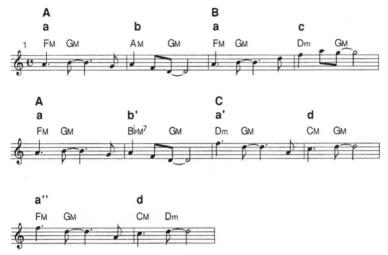

Example 43: Parallel chords, "Hymn Song," head

On a larger structural level, the entire excerpt in Example 43 is an **abac** phrase (labeled **ABAC**). It is primarily melody on this larger structural level that establishes the **ABAC** relationship. Whereas the **A** and **B** sections are two bars long, the **C** section is four bars long, containing an extension: the cadence CM-GM in m. 8 leads to the extension of the next two bars, which ends the progression on the minor tonic (Dm).

2. Tertian, Tonal Progressions

a. Tertian II-V-I. While Tyner's specialty is modal and pentatonic harmony, a significant portion of his repertoire includes tonal, mainstream II-V-I harmony. Some pieces by Tyner are largely or entirely based upon II-V-I harmony.

A good example of a II-V-I piece composed by Tyner is "Inception." This piece was written early in Tyner's career, 1962, and was recorded soon after he left Coltrane's group. At that time Tyner's recording was oriented more toward a traditional, mainstream repertoire, and he had not developed his special style of pentatonicism nearly as much as he would. In the head, "Inception" uses a cycle of dominant 7ths, a standard part of tonal jazz harmony. Overall, the piece is reminiscent of Duke Jordan's "Jordu," both in the contour of the melody, and the breaks. Other pieces composed by Tyner and largely based upon tonal II-V-I harmony are "Island Birdie," "Folks," "For Tomorrow," "Theme for Nana," and "Fly With the Wind."

Tyner's comping in this early work is strongly reminiscent of, and establishes the foundation for, his tendency to alternate pairs of chords, a tendency that recurs frequently throughout his career with quartal chords, suspended chords, and polychords. At the beginning of his solo to "Inception" (Example 44), he uses a pair of chords, F7(13) and G7(♭13) in much the same manner as he would comp with two quartal chords. In fact, the notes within each of these two chords are a 4th apart anyway, except that, because they occur within a piece based on tonal jazz harmony and are dominant chords, they include a tritone instead of all P4ths.

Example 44: Tonal chords, "Inception," solo

b. Sus4 resolves to $\hat{3}$. While a very large portion of Tyner's style relies upon the suspended 4th, Tyner also occasionally resolves the suspended 4th in a tonal fashion. This allows for a double aural interpretation of the suspended chord: at first hearing, it sounds like Tyner's typical use of suspended chords without resolution, but when resolved it sounds, in retrospect, like a tonal chord. Several examples are shown in Examples 45, 46, and 47.

Example 45: Suspension resolved, "Señor Carlos," head

Example 46: Suspension resolved, "Peresina," head

Example 47: Suspension resolved, "Fly with the Wind," head

3. Tonal and Quartal Harmony Juxtaposed. Tyner sometimes places tonal or II-V-I harmony directly next to quartal harmony. This is especially easy in a minor key, because Tyner favors the minor pentatonic, and can then use both a tonal minor I chord and quartal or suspended chord based on the corresponding minor pentatonic, dorian, or aeolian scales.

a. sus2 and m7. The vamp section to "Latino Suite" alternates a E♭sus2 chord (voiced as an FQ7 over an E♭ bass note) and a plain tertian voicing for a E♭m every bar (Example 48). Because the sus2 chord occurs in the first bar of the two-bar vamp, this section sounds as though it resolves to the sus2 rather than the minor chord.

Example 48: Sus2 and m7, "Latino Suite," head

b. Q7 and m7 ("Theme for Nana"). Another similar example occurs in "Theme for Nana," in which a bar with a G♯ pedal tone is repeated once (it could easily become a vamp if continually repeated). Within this bar G♯m or G♯m7, in minor tonality, alternates with G♯sus, from Tyner's pentatonic /quartal harmony. This measure and its repetition occurs at m. 8–9 and 25–26 in the head, and at m. 15–18 and 35–38 in the solo chorus (which is in half-time: each chord from the head is prolonged for twice its original length in the half-time solo chorus). Example 49 is a collection of all the voicings Tyner uses every time this G♯m—G♯sus section appears (the half-time solo and normal-time head excerpts are aligned vertically for easy comparison).

Example 49: Sus and minor chords, "Theme for Nana," various

Tyner primarily uses tertian voicings for G♯m, and sus voicings for G♯sus. These tertian voicings are defined by their inclusion of the 3rd and the 7th in the chord, which strongly establishes tertian harmony.[6] Tyner does use G♯7sus4 for G♯m (measure 25) , and once uses G♯m for G♯sus (m. 38): this demonstrates the compatibility of the two voicings.

c. m7/R and Δ7 as Tonics. In Example 23 previously considered, Tyner juxtaposes a tertian Δ7 chord and a m7/R polychord in a particularly striking way, as both chords can be heard as tonics.

d. II-V Progression. On a larger scale, the B section to Tyner's "La Habana Sol" uses tertian II-V progressions (Example 50) as well as chromatically descending Δ7 and dominant 7th chords as a contrast to the polychordal progressions in the A section.

A | A♭7sus B♭7 | C7| A♭7sus G♭7 | Fm7/B♭ | ∕∙ | A♭7sus B♭7 | C7 | A♭7sus G♭7 | E♭m7/A♭ |∕/∕/∕/∕|
                                 polychord   polychord

B | Gm7 C7 | Fm7 B♭7 | G∅7 C7 | F♯m7 B7 | E6 E♭| DΔ7 D♭Δ7 | Cm7 B7 | D♭m7 G♭7 |

Example 50: Chord progression, "La Habana Sol," head

4. Combining II-V-I and sus Harmony. Tyner's trademark of quartal and pentatonic harmony presents an interesting question in II-V-I pieces: whether to include aspects of his quartal harmony style in II-V-I pieces, and, if so, in what manner. Tyner has demonstrated the following techniques of incorporating aspects of quartal harmony in II-V-I pieces.

- quartal voicings
- left-hand P5ths and pedal tones
- right-hand pentatonic patterns
- right-hand P5ths & P4ths
- sus harmony vamps

a. Quartal Voicings. One of the foundations of Tyner's style is the use of quartal voicings in pentatonic harmony. Tyner, however, also uses quartal voicings within II-V-I harmony. He does this by extracting a quartal (all P4ths) 3-note voicing from standard II-V-I 4-note voicings. Example 51 shows the two standard 4-note voicings for II-V-I progressions (the voicings in the treble and the bass clef are inversions of each other).

Example 51: Standard II-V-I voicings

The only quartal voicings that can be extracted from the standard voicings for a II-V-I progression in Example 51 are for the I (CΔ7) chord, and are shown with open note-heads. These quartal voicings are conveniently labeled as Q7 voicings whose lowest note is the 3rd and the 7th of the Δ7 chord (IIIQ7 and VIIQ7).

Even though the 3rd and 7th of a chord must normally be present in mainstream jazz piano voicings, Dan Haerle gives the quartal chord EQ7 (in white noteheads on the lower staff in Example 51) as a voicing for CΔ7, omitting the 7th.[7] The other quartal chord for CΔ7 in Example 51 already contains the 3rd and 7th.

(i) IIIQ7 for Δ7. Tyner uses an FQ7 voicing for a D♭Δ7 tonic chord, as well as the standard 4-note voicings for E♭m7 (II) and A♭7 (V) in "Señor Carlos" (Example 52). Tyner's use of this quartal chord for I with tertian voicings for the II and V chords is within the tradition of mainstream jazz.

Example 52: IIIQ7 for Δ7, "Señor Carlos," solo

(ii) VIIQ7 for Δ7. Tyner uses a GQ7 chord to comp for A♭Δ7 in "Just in Time" (Example 53).

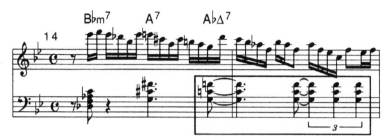

Example 53: VIIQ7 for Δ7, "Just in Time," solo

(iii) Quartal and Tertian Chords. Tyner also introduces quartal chords in a tertian context by alternating quartal and tertian chords, as shown in Example 54. The excerpt is from a blues in B♭. The standard blues chords are underlined above the chord symbols for the voicings that Tyner actually plays.

Example 54: Quartal and tertian chords, "Port au Blues," solo

Both of these quartal chords are very close harmonically to the standard blues (tertian) chords: they merely suspend the 3rd of the tertian chord:

$$
\begin{array}{lclclcl}
\text{FQ7} & = & \text{F B♭, E♭} & = & \text{5th, root, sus4} & \text{of B♭7} \\
\text{E♭Q7} & = & \text{E♭, A♭, D♭} & = & \text{root, sus4, 7th} & \text{of E♭7}
\end{array}
$$

b. II-V-I with sus Vamp. In "Folks," Tyner has composed the majority of the piece with tonal II-V-I progressions, but also includes a vamp-like section based on pentatonic harmony. Example 55 shows the II-V-I progressions in the A section of "Folks," ending with a repeated E♭7sus4 chord in which Tyner introduces the suspended 4th (A♭) through a variety of chord voicings (Example 56).

Gm7 C7 | Fm7 | Fm7 B♭7 | E♭m9 | D♭m7 G♭7 | D♭m7 G♭7 | C♭Δ7 | F♭6 | |: E♭sus4 :| |
Example 55: II-V-I & sus vamp "Folks," head

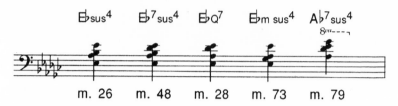

Example 56: E♭sus chords, "Folks," solo

c. Left-hand Pedal Tones. Examples of the use of pedal tones, including harmonic P5ths, with tertian chords were previously shown in Example 33.

F. FOCUS ON "YOU STEPPED OUT OF A DREAM"

"You Stepped Out of a Dream" as performed by Tyner offers a good opportunity to understand a wide range of Tyner's use of quartal chords, suspended chords, and pentatonic harmony within one small, recurring section of an entire performance. Example 57 illustrates the variety of chords used as components of voicings that Tyner is able to extract from relatively limited source material (the C mixolydian sections), as well as the consistent nature of the sound of much of this harmonic material.

Analyzing the chords in Example 57 above shows that Tyner derives them from two minor pentatonic scales contained with C mixolydian: G minor pentatonic and D minor pentatonic. Example 58 below shows the roots on which the voicings from Example 57 above occur, categorized by pentatonic scale. (Two voicings from Example 57 above, Am7 and CM, are tertian voicings available in C mixolydian, or which can be considered to have come from Am pentatonic.)

By emphasizing quartal and sus chords within pentatonic scales that are in turn contained with the prevailing C mixolydian scale, Tyner can be said to be imparting a strong quartal and minor pentatonic flavor to a mixolydian scale, a scale that does not contain a minor pentatonic scale that starts on its tonic. At times the pentatonic influence is complete: Fsus4 and Gsus4, alternated in both m. 32 of the head and m. 4 of the solo, contain all the pitches and no others of G minor pentatonic. Tyner alternates these two chords in his left hand for comping in several places

Example 57: Various related chords, "You Stepped Out of a Dream"

Gm & Dm pentatonics	Gm pentatonic	Dm pentatonic
Csus2		
Csus4, Gsus4	Fsus4	Dsus4
Csus4(2)		Dsus4(2)
G7sus4		
		G9sus4
GQ7		
		Dm
	Gm7	

Example 58: Mixolydian voicings, "You Stepped Out of a Dream"

in "You Stepped Out of a Dream." Tyner also briefly uses the complete D minor pentatonic scale: the notes in the G9sus4 chord in m. 51 of the solo, and in Dsus4 and Csus4 from m. 3 of the solo, are the same as those in D minor pentatonic.

G. AMBIGUITY IN TYNER'S HARMONY

The examples of chords presented so far are fairly unambiguous. For instance, in "Passion Dance," because the composed melody outlines F mixolydian, Tyner improvises in F mixolydian, and when the comping pitches are, in ascending order, F-B♭-E♭, one can reasonably state that the comping chord is an FQ7 chord and not an inversion of a B♭sus4 chord. What such a label actually implies is that the chord is a I chord, that is, the lowest pitch of the chord is the tonic of the harmony at that point, and so the chord is heard as a tonic chord. A similar situation holds for those cases in which Tyner alternates between the I & II quartal chords.

Suspended chords and quartal chords may be harmonically ambiguous, however, because they are inversions of each other and those inversions may have different harmonic implications. This is especially interesting considering that throughout most of jazz harmony, inversions play little role in determining fundamental harmonic implications, and chords are thereby freely inverted.

This harmonic ambiguity is founded on the fact that such chords contain a different suspended 4th, as well as different roots. For instance, in Example 59, a C quartal chord implies a C root with F as the suspended 4th that would traditionally resolve to E. On the other hand, the same pitches may be inverted to produce an Fsus chord, in which case an F root is implied and B♭ becomes the suspended 4th, resolving to A.

Example 59: Sus chords

This means that the two voicings or inversions of the same three notes may suggest two different roots, two different suspended 4ths, and therefore two different harmonic implications. Even though Tyner rarely treats a suspended 4th as a true suspension requiring resolution, one can still explore such harmonic ambiguities of the suspended 4th in Tyner's music.

Because the pitches themselves may lead to two different sets of implications, the best way to tell which root and suspended 4th is preferred is to listen to the harmonic implications of the chord in the context of the surrounding music. Sometimes such examination and listening will produce a clear and uncontroversial analysis. The previous examples of quartal chords as tonic chords noted above (Examples 21 and 22) are fairly direct and clear: the surrounding musical context (for instance, the quartal chord at the strong cadence in Example 21) is primary and effective in determining the proper root and suspension. But sometimes the analysis may be ambiguous.

1. A Musical Experiment. One such interesting example occurs in "Theme for Nana." The A section of the ending head ends on a vamp-like two-bar section. The chords in question here are the second and the fourth chords in Example 60. A published transcription labels both of these chords as G♯sus, but the last chord contains no 5th (D♯) of G♯sus, so G♯Q7 is more accurate; further, considering the last chord as a C♯sus4 over a G♯ pedal leads to an alternate analysis, which follows.[8]

The full harmonic implications and ambiguities of these chords may be more easily heard if a sort of musical experiment is done by resolving both potential suspensions in the second and fourth chords above and by comparing the results. Treating either of these two chords as a sus4 chord implies resolving the middle note of the voicing, while treating either of them

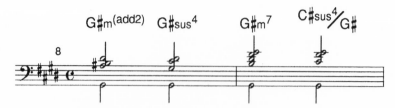

Example 60: Ambiguous chords, "Theme for Nana," head

as an inverted quartal chord implies resolving the lowest note in the voicing above the G♯ pedal. These resolutions are shown in Example 61.

Each staff in Example 61 (except the first) resolves the suspension in the second and last chords (notated as eighth-notes) differently based upon the following treatment of the chords in question:

staff 1–original progression
staff 2–both as sus4 chords

Example 61: Experiment, "Theme for Nana"

staff 3–both as Q7 chords
staff 4–2nd chord as Q7, 4th chord as sus4
staff 5–2nd chord as sus4, 4th chord as Q7

The richer and more convincing harmonic implications are present in staff 4 of Example 61, D♯Q7—D♯7 and C♯sus4—C♯M. (In staves 3 and 4 of Example 61, the clash between the pedal tone G♯ and the 3rd of the D♯7, F double-sharp, does not affect these implications.) Staff 4 allows for movement in the harmonic progression for both chords in question: in the other staves, one or both of the chords merely resolve to a chord on G♯, which provides no root movement for the progression.

So there is something inherent in the context and the progression that Tyner composed that allows for richer harmonic implications depending upon whether certain notes are considered to be a Q7 chord or sus4 chord. Furthermore, the beginning of the A section of the head repeats G♯m-C♯7. This progression is one of the most prominent in the piece, and interpreting the last chord in Example 61 as a C♯sus4 chord reinforces and recalls the earlier G♯-C♯ progression.

It is a measure of the harmonic ambiguity of these chords that no completely convincing analysis exists. If one's listening emphasizes the pedal tone, then all chords could be labeled with G♯ roots and the sus4s in each chord could be resolved to all G♯ chords (staff 5). On the other hand, the other option introduces a level of harmonic depth not present in the other. My favored approach is to label Example 60 with the chords that contain the greater harmonic depth from staff 4 in Example 61, but I also recognize that the other analysis is perfectly possible and justified. The important point is that this experiment illustrates the potential harmonic ambiguity inherent in Tyner's reliance on chords with a suspended 4th.

2. ♭VII-I or I-II? Another aspect of the ambiguity in Tyner's harmony is the following question: in what mode are two parallel, alternating chords (quartal, sus, and the like) that are a whole-step apart? Most often, with pairs of chords a whole step apart, the lower chord of the pair is the tonic. For instance, it was previously noted that in the intro to "Peresina" (Example 34) two chords alternate, FQ7 and GQ7, and the tonic of the prevailing mode is F.

However, in "La Vida Feliz," two parallel sus4(2) chords on G and A alternate in the intro, but it is the higher one, Asus4(2), whose root is the tonic of the prevailing A dorian mode (Example 62).

Example 62: Parallel sus4(2) chords, "La Vida Feliz," intro

These two chords are built on VII and I in A dorian, not I and II in G dorian, for three reasons:

First, the pitches of both chords, when collected into a single group, comprise A dorian with an added $\hat{2}$ which is the most important pitch to add to a pentatonic scale in Tyner's harmony. This supports hearing A as the tonic.

Second, a dorian is further supported in bar 15, in the A section of the head, by the presence of the F♯ in the melody, occurring with an Asus chord (Example 63).

Example 63: F♯ in A dorian, "La Vida Feliz," head

Third, in the solo section, Asus4(2) is embellished by B♭Δ9(♯11) chromatically from above and by Gsus4(2) diatonically from below (‖: B♭Δ9(♯11)—A9sus—G9sus—A9sus :‖), thereby establishing A, not G, as a tonic.

The fact that in one musical context the lower of two quartal or suspended chords is the tonic chord, creating a I-II progression, and in another context the higher chord is the tonic, creating a ♭VII-I progression, is a measure of the harmonic ambiguity inherent in Tyner's harmony.

III. SUMMARY

The essential aspects of McCoy Tyner's system of quartal, suspended, modal, and pentatonic harmony are summarized below:

Aspects	Comment
P4th & P5th	pervasive intervals
	P4th sometimes resolves to 3 in traditional manner
Quartal chords	stacked P4ths
Suspended chords	suspended 4ths, some with 2nds & 6ths
So What chords	stacked P4ths with a M3rd
Polychords	various kinds of II and IV chords over a V bass note
	V bass note considered to be the root
Chords in general	interrelated and often contain other simpler chords
	chords with different chord qualities but the same root can act as a tonic chords with different root but same quality can act as a tonic
Pentatonic scale	related to modes and all chords
	$\hat{2}$ is often added to pentatonic scale
Modes	minor modes favored
	mixolydian also used
Left Hand P5th	melodic P5th is common interval in bass lines
	harmonic P5th used as variation of pedal tone
Harmonic progressions	frequent use of quartal chords, suspended chords, and polychords
	parallel motion
	pairs of chords by step
Quartal and II-V-I harmony	sometimes juxtaposed
	quartal elements sometimes used in II-V-I context

Lastly, Tyner provides a good context in which to place study of his style:

> I mainly learned through trial and error. That's why when young pianists tell me, "Wow, I really love what you're doing," I tell them, "That's wonderful, but allow yourself to come out, too." Something I do may lead you to something, but it shouldn't distract you from finding your own sound.[9]

In the spirit of Tyner's comment, I encourage musicians to absorb as much as they can of Tyner's great music from the examples included here and the recordings referenced, as well as to let Tyner's music inspire them to new, creative work.

IV. A NOTE ON TRANSCRIBING

A written study on music published in a book or journal necessarily carries some limitations because it must rely upon transcribed versions of music, and transcriptions are incomplete versions of an actual aural experience. Even so, transcriptions can still be very valuable things. Tyner himself has said as much:

> A transcription can give people an idea of what you're trying to do, which is good. . . . [but] you can't really capture everything on paper. It's just a guideline.[10]

While many published transcriptions are accurate, and I have tried to ensure the accuracy of all musical examples in this study, transcribing is sometimes an imperfect enterprise. Steve Larson has noted these difficulties in relation to his own transcriptions in his dissertation on Schenkerian analysis and jazz:

> . . . in some cases I was unsure what was actually played. Modern jazz piano performances can be difficult to transcribe. Sometimes the harmonics generated by lower strings—particularly the first and second overtones (the second and third partials)—sound as loud as the notes actually played. In other cases, higher notes may "hide" in the harmonics of lower notes. These performers conceive their chords in many different ways. Their chords may be dissonant, dense, staccato, and soft. This sometimes makes it difficult to tell exactly which notes appear in these chords—and in which octave they appear.[11]

This type of honesty is rarely seen in print, but Larson accurately describes the situation.

Furthermore, discrepancies sometimes occur in different versions of published transcriptions of the same tune. I have found several performances by Tyner that have been transcribed and published by different transcribers, and some of them differ.

Tune	Transcription book title
"For Tomorrow"	*McCoy Tyner* (Hal Leonard); *Inception to Now*
"Passion Dance"	*McCoy Tyner* (Toshiba); *Inception to Now*
"Blues on the Corner"	*McCoy Tyner* (Toshiba); *Inception to Now*
"Peresina" (head only)	*The World's Greatest Fake Book*; *The Jazz Piano Book*

In such cases, it is sometimes easy to determine which transcription is accurate. For instance, at the very beginning of Tyner's solo to "Passion Dance," he plays left hand chords that are transcribed differently in the *McCoy Tyner* (Toshiba) version than in the "Inception to Now" version (Example 64). My hearing of the passage confirms the *McCoy Tyner* (Toshiba) version.

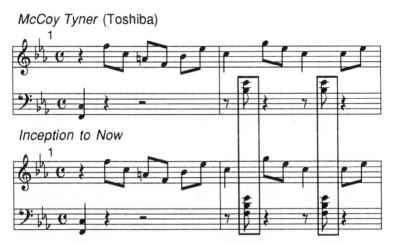

Example 64: Different transcriptions, "Passion Dance," solo

However, sometimes it is difficult to resolve discrepancies in transcriptions. For instance, there is a discrepancy between Mark Levine's transcription of the opening to "Peresina" and the published score that appears in "The World's Greatest Fake Book."[12] Levine transcribes the first several chords as So What chords. The first of these chords is the first chord shown in Example 65.

But the published score in *The World's Greatest Fake Book* notates the first several chords of "Peresina" as polychords: major triads over bass notes a M2nd above the root of the triad, an example of which is the second chord in Example 65. The only difference between these two versions is the presence of another note a P4th below the lowest note of the polychord. I believe that this chord in "Peresina" is not a So What chord, but is a polychord, because

- I do not hear the lower note (C for the first chord), and
- I hear the bass play F as the lowest note for the first chord, and move in parallel fashion after that.

Example 65: So What and polychord voicings

However, the sound and fidelity of the recording introduce some measure of doubt into this determination.

NOTES

1. Mark Levine, *The Jazz Piano Book*, Petaluma, CA: Sher Music Co (1989): 105–108.
2. Bob Doerschuk, "McCoy Tyner," *Keyboard* 7, no. 8 (August 1981): 38.
3. Levine, 23.
4. Doerschuk, 38.
5. The published score for *Peresina* [Chuck Sher, ed., *The World's Greatest Fake Book*, Petaluma, CA: Sher Music Co (1983): 307] labels the E♭Q7 chord in m. 4–7 as D♭(add 9, no 3) and the D♭Q7 chord as D♭7sus. However, it makes more sense to label them as quartal chords. These bars are the same harmonically as the intro, except they are transposed to D♭ from F, with a slight variation in rhythm. The essential parallel nature of the upper note on the and-of-two in the bass line as well as the horn harmonization is reflected by labeling these chords as parallel quartal chords. The first chord is labeled as a D♭ chord primarily because D♭ occurs in the bass on the downbeat, but in this case that D♭ should be heard as a pedal tone or as an embellishment of the higher E♭ in the bass line, which carries the more fundamental movement from E♭ to D♭.
6. The G♯m7(11) voicing in the coda also spells an F♯sus4 chord, but is also accompanied by a G♯ in the bass (left hand), which establishes G♯m7 as the basic chord.
7. Dan Haerle, *The Jazz Language* (Hialeah, FL: Studio 224, 1980), 24, and *Jazz/Rock Voicings for the Contemporary Keyboard Player* (Lebanon, IN: Studio P/R, 1974), 1.
8. *Jazz Giants: McCoy Tyner* (Milwaukee, WI: Hal Leonard, 1992), 85.

9. Doerschuk, 36.

10. Ibid., 36.

11. Steven Leroy Larson, "Schenkerian Analysis of Modern Jazz," Ph.D diss., University of Michigan (1987), 5–6.

12. Levine, 97; and Sher, ed., 307–308.

FROM POPULAR SONG TO JAZZ COMPOSITION: THELONIOUS MONK'S "RUBY, MY DEAR"

Michele Caniato

Traditionally, American popular song of the 1920s to 1940s did not feature a highly structured integration of melodic and harmonic materials.[1] To a great extent, melodies were composed to enhance a set of lyrics and fitted to an accompanying chord progression. Melodies and chords enjoyed a relation of basic interchangeability, with neither bound incontrovertibly to the other. This was made evident by the practice of writing new tunes to preexisting chord progressions and of reharmonizing existing tunes with new sets of chords.

While this relation can also be found in concert music, a characteristic of Western composition is the high level of integration of its materials that makes the relations within the work nearly inalterable without destroying the overall unity of the music. The procedures of chord progression borrowing and of chord substitution became widespread in the work of bebop musicians of the 1940s such as Charlie Parker and Dizzy Gillespie, who penned dozens of melodies to be fitted to chord progressions from existing popular songs and likewise made extensive use of substitute chords in standard tunes.

For the most part pianist Thelonious Monk showed a different approach: like his contemporaries he worked within the confines of the 32-measure popular songs and the 12-bar blues form, sometimes borrowing chord progressions or reworking existing tunes,[2] but his music exhibited a deeper preoccupation with compositional processes than that encountered in most jazz of the time. This applies to both his writing and improvising because, as Max Harrison has said, "the compositional mode of thinking is evident in everything he did." [3]

This study takes as a point of departure general characteristics of the popular songs of the 1930s and 1940s and their relation to the bop style. Following a brief overview of select concert music compositional techniques, I will examine a lead sheet of Monk's 32-bar AABA piece "Ruby, My Dear." [4] "Ruby" was copyrighted in 1945, first recorded in 1947, and composed probably a decade earlier.[5] The analysis focuses on the integration of melodic and harmonic elements, the alteration of structural events within the form, and the manipulation of minimal motivic material in the composition of this tune.[6]

Popular Song and the Bop Approach

The language of bebop infused the song of the previous decades with new melodic, rhythmic, and harmonic idiosyncrasies. While these advances were impressive (altered, symmetrical, and bebop scales; chord extensions, extended chromatic and diatonic approaches; sophisticated rhythmic concepts),[7] they did not alter the basic tonal structure of the lyric-inspired song of the Swing Era. Jazz musicians were more concerned with how they sounded (their individual and unequivocal voice), how they swung (their rhythmic interpretation of the beat and its subdivisions), and how they improvised on a tune and its chord progression, rather than with the alteration of the vehicle itself: the form.

After all, there were many improvisational techniques that could be used to "camouflage the harmonic and rhythmic regularity of the formal structure,"[8] such as utilizing "motivic events displaced from or straddling the hypermetric downbeats."[9] Any solo by a major jazz player underscores the centrality of these parameters in jazz.

At least three main features of the standard 32-bar AABA song form were, for the most part, adhered to: the closing of the second 8-measure A section in the tonic, the modulation of the B section to a different key, and the closing of the last A in the tonic (Example 1).

A 1
EbMa7 | Bb-9 Eb13 | AbMa7 | Ab-7 Db 13 | EbMa7 C-7 | F-7 Bb7 | G7 C7 | F9 Bb13 |

A 2   **closing in the tonic**
EbMa7 | Bb-9 Eb13 | AbMa7 | Ab-7 Db 13 | EbMa7 C-7 | F-7 Bb7 | Eb 6 | Eb 6 |

B   modulation to a new key
Bb-7 | Eb7 | AbMa7 | Ab6 | A-7 | D7 F7 | Bb7 Eo7 | F-7 Bb7 |

A3   **closing in the tonic**
EbMa7 | Bb-9 Eb13 | AbMa7 | Ab-7 Db 13 | EbMa7 C-7 | F-7 Bb7 | Eb 6 | Eb 6 |

Example 1: *Misty*, by Erroll Garner (1939)

Since many tunes started on chords other than the tonic,[10] the closing of the second A in the tonic provided a strong sense of home key and rounded off the main material before modulating to the bridge. The last two measures of the final A section fulfilled a similar function, where, after the close in the tonic, a turnaround or a dominant chord would lead to the repetition of the form with solos. In regard to the placement of the tonic gravity at the end of the last A section, Barry Kernfeld says:

> . . . the design allows it to repeat. This is achieved through the lack of coincidence between two points of arrival—the cadence on a tonic chord, which falls 2 (sometimes 4) bars before the end of a chorus, and the strongest metric downbeat, which falls on the first bar of the next chorus.[11]

The B or bridge section served as a contrast to the A material, with the lyrics frequently supplying a new message altogether. The music underscored the shift in psychological or emotional content with new melodic material and through modulation, either direct or prepared with a two-beat dominant chord or ii-V.

Clear key articulation at such points in the form was theoretically no longer indispensable given that bop was primarily instrumental music and the singer's need for a strong key reference no longer a practical necessity. Nonetheless this formula continued to govern much jazz of the time, and the emphasis on clear tonal articulation was retained by the new bop "heads."

Traditional Composition

If jazz adopted the simple periodic design of popular song, what are the elements that differentiate jazz composition from songwriting? Uncommon in much jazz of the mid-1940s are the following Western concert music techniques: integration of melodic and harmonic materials with the large-scale form, alteration of expected structural events within an accepted formal plan, progressive tonality, and interaction of octatonic-diatonic pitch cells. Beethoven worked in a way that brought "the details and the large structure together more intimately than with the work of any other composer" so that "not only the discursive melodic shape but the large harmonic forms as well have become thematic, and derive from a central and unifying idea."[12] Modifications of expected structural or articulative events occur in music where general norms governing formal designs are sufficiently established that they cry out to be altered. One can only marvel at the endless rearrangements of events in the deceptions and creative solutions found in sonata movements of the classical period by viewing them through the lens of sonata form concepts of the time. Ending a work in a different key from the initial one was not unusual for Mahler, whose symphonies progressed to new keys to underline the programmatic idea of the work.[13] New methods of pitch organization were devised in the early twentieth century to compensate for the dissolution of functional tonality. The interaction of diatonic, octatonic, and whole tone pitch cells provided organizational means for many composers, including Bartók and Stravinsky.[14] All of these techniques were rare in jazz until Monk came on the scene.

Whether Monk had knowledge of "serious" music or followed his ear and musical instinct in composing is a question beyond the scope of this paper. In a 1962 essay, critic Andre Hodeir questioned the depth of Monk's knowledge.[15] If his familiarity with "serious" music was not extensive, then his use of techniques generally associated with western concert music in "Ruby" is all the more remarkable.

"RUBY, MY DEAR"

Thematic Generation of the Harmony

The A sections, hereafter called A1, A2, and A3, are comprised of a series of ii-7/V 7/ I Ma7 chords, the most common cadential pattern in tonal jazz, connected by a scalewise accompanimental figure performed by the piano or piano and bass. After the third statement concluding on A♭ Ma7 (m. 6), the sequence is abandoned. The section closes on an AMa chord, placed on a weak part of the measure (beats 3–4), a tritone away from the initial key of E♭ (mm. 1–2).

Measure 8, the traditional place for a turnaround, offers two dominant or substitute dominant chords in the keys of A and E♭ respectively. Thus the function of the turnaround is both fulfilled and contradicted by pointing simultaneously backwards to A (A has not been tonicized, and we initially hear the E7 in m. 8 as its dominant) and forwards to E♭ (Example 2).

What determines the transpositional level of these sequential key centers? Generally, ii-7/V7/I patterns in jazz are governed by the overall key, which in the bop idiom encompasses secondary, extended, and substitute dominants (a tritone away from the original dominant chord) (Example 3).

Here the generating factor for the harmonic plan is the theme: the four-note motive at mm. 1–2, with the position of the first and last two notes re-ordered, generates the harmony (Example 4).

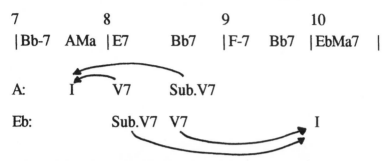

Example 2: Turnaround, mm. 7-10

Example 3: *Confirmation* (Charlie Parker), mm. 1-8

Melody mm.1-2	**Transposed a step down**	**Reordered=main chords of A1**
G F Cb Bb	**F Eb A Ab**	**EbMa7 FMa7 AbMa7 AMa**

Example 4: Melodic tetrachord generates the chord progression

A2 (mm. 15–16) extends the key center of AMa7 by proceeding to its supertonic B-7 and substitute dominant B♭7. The harmony lands squarely on AMa7 (m. 17) completing the four-note thematically generated sequence (E♭, F A♭, A) and supplying all the elements that had been withheld: rhythmic (AMa7 is now on beat one and occupies a full measure), harmonic (it is now tonicized like the other chords by its ii-7/ V7), and melodic (the melody note is scale degree 5 of the chord). The pitch E at mm. 8/16 had been displaced so as to not coincide with the AMa chord (mm. 7 and 15), creating an expectation fulfilled at B where this "double return" of the last thematically generated Ma7 chord joins the displaced pitch E, now rhythmically and harmonically aligned.

In other words, the traditional key relations of functional tonality have been replaced by a thematically generated chord progression that "derives from a central and unifying idea." [16]

Form

After AMa is tonicized (m. 18–19), the harmony cadences to c minor (m. 21). A ii-7/ V7 pattern in the key of D♭ follows. The D♭ never materializes, and the last A section follows and closes on F♯Ma (mm. 31–32).

What has happened to the standard structural events of the AABA song form? In place of a clear closing of A2 in the tonic we find an harmonically open section. Its resolution takes place only at B, shifting the expected harmonic repose to a place where contrast and continuation are traditionally found. The sectionalization of A and B is broken down and the two are linked by a common harmonic framework.

This unity is disguised by other parameters that make B sound like a new section: the melody is based on a fresh-sounding motive with a new rhythmic profile, the chord progression abandons the ii-7/ V7 pattern in favor of stepwise motion (mm. 20–22), and the ensemble adopts a double-time feel.

The F♯Ma chord that concludes the piece (m. 32) is only one beat in duration. Both the AMa at the end of the first two A sections (mm. 7 and 15) and this F♯Ma chord at the very end of the last A section lack any sense of resolution due to their weak rhythmic position and non-tonicization.

A glance at the coda indicates the final tonic as D♭Ma. The main chords can be summarized as in Example 5. The outline shows an AABA form where the customary harmonically closed sections are replaced by a continuous open form that progresses to a final tonic only at the very end of the piece, after the improvisations and the restatement of the tune or "head out."

The form is "perpetually energized"[17] by the lack of harmonic repose at the end of the A sections, and the strongest metric downbeat is displaced from the top of the form to the beginning of the B section. Also, the piece closes in a new key (D♭Ma), foreshadowed at mm. 23–4 by its ii-7/ V7 cadential pattern.

Motivic Material

The main motive x (mm. 1–2) is embedded in octatonic collection I Model B[18] (Example 6a). Considering the tetrachord that generates the pitch level of the harmony (F E♭ A A♭) as transposition 0, the three initial statements are x2, x4, and x7 respectively (Example 6b).The ensuing melodic material is derived from the manipulation of x; the "outer" intervals of a descending major and minor second are retained while the middle tritone is subjected to modification.

Motive y (mm. 31–32) uses augmentation: the final two pitches sink by a half step and a middle note C♯ is added. The descending melodic gesture remains unvaried. Y can beviewed as a diatonicization of x, where the octatonic-based interval structure is expanded to a configuration that fits the C-scale (or major scale model) on A (Examples 6 c–d).

Motive z (mm. 6–8) uses diminution: the melodic tritone is compressed to a major second. Z appears at two transposition levels, z and z1 (Example 6e). The rearrangement of z "in abstract form"yields a descending phrygian tetrachord where a whole step is flanked by the usual major and minor seconds (F E♭ D♭ C), transforming again the octatonically based x into a diatonic collection (Example 6f).

The first four bars of B (mm. 17–20) introduce a new motive w in combination with an elided statement of motive x (Example 7a). W is based on intervals 5/7 and 2/10 (perfect 4th and major 2nd) that duplicate the bass motion of the main ii/ V/ I cadential pattern found in mm. 1–2 ff. In the following measures (mm. 21–25), w disengages itself from x, and transpositions w8 (mm. 21–22) and w11 (mm. 23–24) emerge clearly (Example 7b). This goes in tandem with the harmonic movement where, after the resolution to AMa (m. 19), the harmony shakes off the previous ii-V-I pattern and moves stepwise to c and e♭.

Typically, such processes of motivic transformation are found in jazz improvisation[19] rather than in the actual composition of tunes. Also, displaying a technique encountered more often in concert music,[20] the first two bars of "Ruby, My Dear" introduce the elements crucial to the structure of the whole piece: tetrachord x generates melodic materials and harmonic relations, and the ii/ V/ I (057) cadential pattern spawns the material w found in the B section.

The A section chord progression and the harmonic roots of the B section partake in the same octatonic Collection II (Example 8). This collection not only links the A and B sections but reemerges in the coda where the final cadence reveals its large-scale implication as dominant of D♭ (mm. 33–34).[21]

Linear and Large-scale Considerations

The intense economy of means characteristic of Monk's work can be further observed in the background structural treatment of the melodic materials. The statements of x are, when consolidated linearly, connected by semitone or common tone. The voice leading continues with a whole

Form: A1-A2   B   A3   Coda

Measure: 2   4   6   7   17   23 24 26   28   30   32   33   34

EbMa7 FMa7 AbMa7 AMa <u>AMa7</u> Eb-7 <u>Ab7</u> EbMa7 FMa7 AbMa7 F#Ma <u>A7Ab7</u> DbMa7

Db: bVI*   ii-7 V7   IV*   V7   I

* enharmonically equivalent

Example 5: Chord outline

Example 6a: Main motive x embedded in octatonic collection I, mm. 1–2

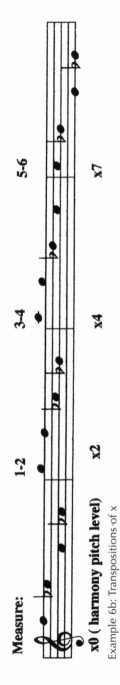

Measure: 1-2   3-4   5-6

x0 (harmony pitch level)   x2   x4   x7

Example 6b: Transpositions of x

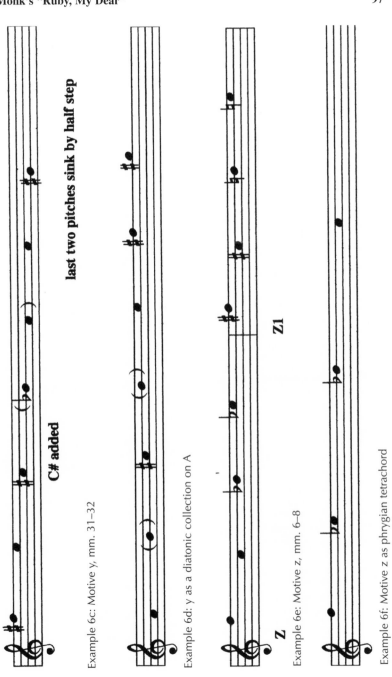

C# added

last two pitches sink by half step

Example 6c: Motive y, mm. 31–32

Example 6d: y as a diatonic collection on A

Z1

Z

Example 6e: Motive z, mm. 6–8

Example 6f: Motive z as phrygian tetrachord

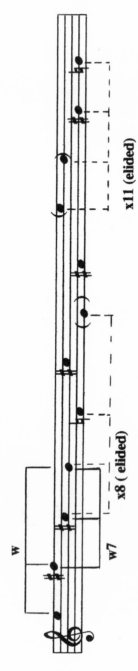

Example 7a: Motive w in conjunction with elided statements of x, mm. 17–19

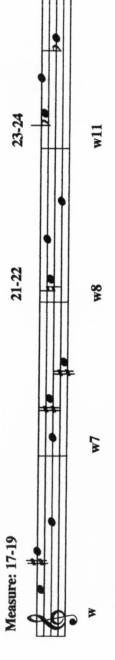

Example 7b: Motive w and its transpositions

Measure:		2	4	6	7				
		Eb	F	Ab	A				

Measure:			19	20	21	22	23		24
octatonic collection II:			A	B	C	D	Eb	(F) (F#)	Ab

                                      ↑ ↑
                            prominent in the melody

Example 8: Octatonic collection II-derived A and B section harmonic roots

step (m. 6) and expands to the first nonstepwise connection of a minor third in m. 7 to coincide with the delayed completion of the thematically gener-ated harmony (Example 9).

The first statement of w (mm. 16–17) begins on E, linking A2 and B by common tone before the stepwise thread switches from the melodic line to the bass for the duration of the B section. The ascending motion of the bass (mm. 19–20) yields a chromatically filled minor third A-C that is balanced by a descending "left-hand thumb-line" progression or "line cliché " (mm. 21–22) (Example 10a).[22] This symmetry recalls the arrangement of the melody notes that link A2 to B at mm. 15–17 (F♯ E E F♯) (Example 10b).

The intervallic boundary F♯-G♯ of motive y (mm. 31–32) carries a dou-ble semitonal approach converging on the G in m. 1 (Example 11). This gesture, at the end of the form, is foreshadowed by the F♯-G (mm. 8a-1) and

Example 9: Voice leading of motivic material in A1

Example 10a: Chromatically filled bass and "line cliché" in the chords, mm. 19–22

Example 10b: Symmetry in melodic link between A2 and B, mm. 15–17

Example 11: Double semitonal convergence, mm. 31-1

G♯-G (m. 20) motion. The coda also unfolds a stepwise melodic connection continuing the line from G♯ through G to G♭-F-E♭.

The descending semitone characteristic of x is echoed in the larger form: while x provides the pitch level for the chords in the first six measures of the A sections, the two final bars of A1 (mm. 7–8) and A3 (mm. 31–32) adopt transposition x1 a semitone higher as a chord generating structure. Here, the harmonies partake in the same tetrachordal transposition (Example 12).

x1= F# E Bb A   chords mm.7-8 reordered   mm.31-32 reordered

         Bb-7 AMa   E7 (F#)   Bb-7 (A) F#Ma E9
                          ↑   ↑
         elided but present in the melody   elided but prominent as a diatonic
                                              collection in the melody (m.31)

Example 12: Shared x1 tetrachordal structure of the harmony in mm. 7-8

This semitonal correspondence can be further observed in the final cadence in the coda (A7 A♭7) (m. 33), which summarizes and telescopes the AMa and A♭7 chord relation of the B section (mm. 17 and 24).

The three accompaniment figures (mm. 2 ff.) supply motion in otherwise static measures and an ascending counterharmony that balances the descending gesture of x. The progressive subtraction of chords (six, five, and four chords respectively), coupled with rhythmic variation (eighths, quarters, eighth-note triplet) generates the increased tension towards the third statement of x where the conclusive pitch of the counterline aligns with the statement of x, blending the two contrapuntal voices into a powerful rhythmic unison that underscores the highest point of the melodic curve (m. 5).

A comparison with similar figures in other jazz tunes highlights their augmented structural role in "Ruby, My Dear." In "Don't Get Around Much Anymore" by Duke Ellington, the figure (in the A sections) is static, apart from its adaptation to the changing harmony, in "Ruby" the counterharmony develops organically with the rest of the piece. Once again Monk transforms a traditional jazz cliché into an integral element of the work.

Beneath the surface of a lyrical ballad[23] Monk's characteristically essential and organized compositional thinking is in full effect. Like many of his other tunes ("Misterioso," "Skippy," "Straight No Chaser"), "Ruby, My Dear" is "an investigation of a perfectly specific musical idea" where "all elements of rhythm, melody, and harmony interact so closely that it is unrealistic to consider one without the other."[24]

While adopting the 32-measure song form inherited from the Swing Era, Monk infused it with processes of thematic transformation and structural integration uncommon to the style, facilitating the emergence of the genre of small form jazz composition. Thelonious Monk remains a unique and inimitable voice. In his work, jazz composition has found a pioneer for the setting of its own standards.

NOTES

1. I wish to thank John Daverio for his many insightful comments on an earlier version of this article.
2. See "Rhythm-A-Ning" and "Evidence" (Blue Note 1509) for chord progression borrowing, and "Smoke Gets in Your Eyes" (1954, Prestige 180) for the reworking of a tune.
3. Max Harrison, *A Jazz Retrospective* (Boston: Crescendo, 1976), 30.
4. *Thelonious Monk and John Coltrane* (1957, Jazzland 946). Lead sheet: *The Legal Real Book* , vol.1. Sher Music Co, Petaluma, California.
5. "Before the 1930s were over, in the family apartment Thelonious had written many songs, including 'Ruby, My Dear'" from Leslie Gourse's *Straight, No Chaser* (New York: Schirmer Books, 1997), 15.
6. Tom Simon's *"An Analytical Inquiry Into Thelonious Monk's Ruby, My Dear"* (Master of Music thesis: University of Michigan, 1978) surveys basic analytical concepts of jazz composition and improvisation, devises a model based on various settings of the piece, and focuses on a 1959 solo rendition of "Ruby" using functional harmony analysis and reductive analytical techniques.
7. For a primary source of transcribed solos, see *Charlie Parker's Omnibook* (Atlantic Music Corporation, 1978); for a pedagogical text that surveys bop in addition to earlier and later styles, see Scott Reeves, *Creative Jazz Improvisation* (Englewood Cliffs, NJ: Prentice Hall, 1995).
8. Keith Waters, "Blurring the Barline: Metric Displacement in the Piano Solos of Herbie Hancock," *Annual Review of Jazz Studies* 8 (1996): 19. Though the works analyzed are from the mid-1960s, the general techniques summarized are applicable to some of the earlier players too.
9. *Ibid.*, 31.

10. See, for example, songs such as "Body and Soul" (Johnny Green), "Sophisticated Lady" (Duke Ellington), and "Perdido" (Juan Tizol).

11. Barry Kernfeld, *What to Listen for in Jazz* (New Haven and London: Yale University Press, 1995), 41.

12. Charles Rosen, *The Classical Style : Haydn , Mozart, Beethoven* (New York: The Viking Press, 1971), 406–7.

13. Second Symphony: c minor-E♭major; Fourth: Gmajor-Emajor; Fifth: c♯ minor-Dmajor; Seventh: b minor-Emajor-Cmajor; Ninth: Dmajor-D♭major.

14. See Elliott Antokoletz, *The Music of Bela Bartók: A Study of Tonality and Progression in 20th-Century Music* (Berkeley: University of California Press, 1980).

15. Andre Hodeir, *Toward Jazz* (New York: Grove Press, 1962), 162.

16. Charles Rosen, *ibid*.

17. Barry Kernfeld, *ibid*.

18. See Pieter Van den Toorn's *The Music of Igor Stravinsky* (New Haven: Yale University Press, 1983), 50–51. Octatonic patterns are identified according to their pitch content as Collection I (E D C♯ B B♭, A♭, G F), Collection II (F Eb D C B A G♯ F♯), and Collection III (F♯ E E♭, D♭, C B♭, A G). A Models ascend; B models descend.

19. Gunther Schuller, "Sonny Rollins and the Challenge of Thematic Improvisation," *Jazz Review* 6, no. 1 (November 1958): 1.

20. For an analysis of the large-scale relations presented at the outset in Igor Stravinsky's *Symphony of Psalms*, see Elliott Antokoletz, *Twentieth-Century Music* (Englewood Cliffs, NJ: Prentice Hall, 1992), 279.

21. In jazz improvisation one of the chord scales used on an A♭7 would be octatonic Collection II because it outlines both the chord tones and the tensions (=chord extensions): 1 ♭9 ♯9 3 ♯11 5 13 ♭7
                A♭ A B C D E♭ F G♭

22. A minor key "line cliché" unfolds scale degrees 8-7-♭7-6 within the duration of the i chord. See "My Funny Valentine" (Richard Rodgers), "In A Sentimental Mood" (Duke Ellington), and other standard tunes.

23. I would like to acknowledge Barbara White for pointing out to me the relation between the four-note motive x and the syllables in the title (Ru-by-My-Dear). This hypothesis underscores the lyrical and programmatic nature of the impulse creating the main motive of the piece. Ruby Richardson was Monk's girlfriend in the 1930s, and the dedicatee of the song.

24. Max Harrison, *A Jazz Retrospective*, 30.

"CRISS CROSS": MOTIVIC CONSTRUCTION IN COMPOSITION AND IMPROVISATION

Clifford Korman

Scholars and performing musicians discussing the work of Thelonious Monk often remark on apparent motivic connections between the melody and the solos which follow. Pianist Fred Hersch observes that "[i]mprovising on a Monk theme is like an extension of the composition, because that's the way Monk plays, and that's the way he writes. So your improvisation grows out of the piece itself."[1] Whitney Balliett, in his obituary of Monk, states that "[h]is improvisations were molten Monk compositions, and his compositions were frozen Monk improvisations."[2] In his biographical and historical article on Monk in *The New Grove Jazz*, Ran Blake states that

> . . . Monk invented and developed ideas rather than merely embroidering chord changes . . . [h]is most important contribution as a pianist was his remarkable ability to improvise a coherent musical argument with a logic and structure comparable to the best of his notated compositions.[3]

In the preface to his publication of Monk compositions and arrangements for piano, Charley Gerard opines that

> . . . Monk's music is distinguished . . . by his extensive utilization of motivic building blocks. A melodic segment of a handful of notes is used as the subject of extensions, transpositions, ellisions [*sic*] and combinations of these techniques of transmuting the material at hand.[4]

Walter Bruyninckx observes this characteristic of Monk's style, yet considers it a detriment rather than an attribute: he states in his discography that

> . . . as a pianist Monk does not convince me of being a great solist [*sic*] . . . when studying [his] solos carefully it seems they are made up of several short fragments of notes, coherent in the context of that phrase, but incoherent in the entity of the entire solowork[5]

Motive is defined in *The New Harvard Dictionary of Music* as

> a short rhythmic and or melodic idea that is sufficiently well defined to retain
> its identity when elaborated or transformed and combined with other material
> and that thus lends itself to serving as the basic element from which a com-
> plex texture or even a whole composition is created. . . . A motive may con-
> sist of as few as two pitches, or it may be long enough to be seen to consist of
> smaller elements, themselves termed motives or perhaps cells. The potential
> for generating more extended material is most often regarded as essential . . .
> Music characterized by the pervasive use of a motive is said to be highly or
> very motivic. . . .

Monk's composition "Criss Cross" has often been used to exemplify the
use of motivic development in his compositions and improvisations.
Nowhere in the available literature, however, is a full transcription of the
composition with the subsequent solos and recapitulation of the melody
presented; nor is a thorough examination and discussion of the recorded
performances in support of these observations and conclusions to be found.
Unfortunately, in fact, the published transcriptions are often erroneous in
regard to rhythmical motives and form, and they do not specify the recording on which they are based.[6]

In this presentation I use as source material my own transcriptions of the
four recorded performances by Monk of "Criss Cross" currently known and
available (see the appended discography for specific information).[7] I intend to
use these as concrete evidence that Monk was a soloist who often related his
improvisations to the motives initially presented, and perhaps, in his capacity
as bandleader, was attempting to create in performance a work unified from
beginning to end by references to the thematic and formal structure of the
composition. For this he would need the help of the other performers (his
"sidemen"); if the attempt was successful, the performance could be considered a specific and unique entity comprised formally of an introduction (if
present), the initial statement of the melody, the subsequent improvisations,
the recapitulation of the melody, and coda. A significant distinguishing factor
of Monk's work is that such a performance would not necessarily include elements which belonged to the general pool of the jazz vocabulary of that time,
i.e., patterns and phrases accepted as part of a common language which could
be applied to melodically negotiate particular harmonic progressions.

An examination of these four performances raises ancillary issues which
I will discuss: the comparison of Monk's performances over a period of
twenty years, his use of nuance in the process of variation, and the extent
to which the other soloists use Monk's process of motivic development.

TRANSCRIPTION PROCESS

Before continuing, a few remarks about the transcriptions and my notational system will prove helpful.

(a) Where appropriate, I use stems to delineate the contrapuntal voices in Monk's part.

(b) The assumed subdivision of the quarter-note is the "jazz eighth-note," leaning to the triplet level of rhythm. However, Monk often varies the distance between the eighth-notes as a function of rhythmical nuance. Although difficult to represent precisely, I use the indications "swing" to denote the assumed subdivision, "hard swing" to denote a subdivision which leans to a deeper triplet feel, and "straight" to denote an even duple subdivision.

(c) In the transcriptions of the 1951 recordings, only the differences between the two takes are notated.

(d) Though they may occur at different times in each arrangement, the solos and final statements of the melody are aligned for the purpose of comparison. The measure numbers, consequently, do not coincide with the actual performance in the 1963 and 1971 recordings.

In order to confirm motivic development, we must first identify the basic elements of the work and follow them throughout the performance. The following two sections trace the introduction and subsequent appearance of these "building blocks" of "Criss Cross."

ELEMENTS OF THE COMPOSITION

See appendix for lead sheet of composition.

(1) The melody is constructed of two main motives, *a* and *b*, and the gesture motive *c* in mm. 23–24 of the 1951 recordings (Example 1). This gesture is omitted from the **B** section in the recordings of 1963 and 1971; it is used instead as the introduction in 1963 and alluded to in the final piano flourish in 1971 (Example 2). In the **A** section, motive *a* and its variants are stated four times followed by two statements of motive *b*. In the **B** section, the order is reversed; the unit *b-a* is heard twice.

(2) The reduction of motive *a* renders a descending major 3rd; the reduction of the final two-note fragment of variant *b1*, which ends the phrase of mm. 4–8, is a descending minor 6th. The reduction of motive *c* renders a compound motive composed of the descending minor 6th of motive *b*

Example 1: Motives

followed by the descending major 3rd of motive *a* (Example 3). The piano flourish which concludes the performances of 1951 and 1971 is a variant of *c*, whose descending major third reprises the exact notes of motive *a*.

(3) In the 1951 recordings, the rising chromatic line in the introduction (mm. x–z) form an inversion of motive *b*. This foreshadows mm. 2–3 in section **A** by "filling in" the interval f-a. (Example 4).

ARRANGEMENT AND PERFORMANCE

(1) The form of the song is **AABA**. In the 1951 presentation, each section is eight measures, creating a total of 32 measures. As stated above, in 1963

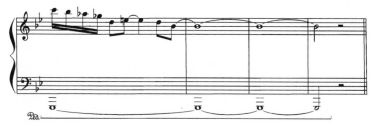

Example 2: Motive "C"

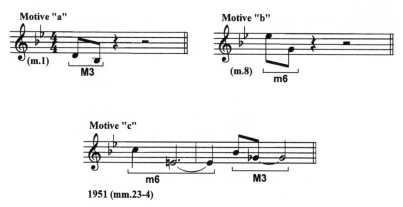

Example 3: Reductions

Example 4: 1951, mm. x-2

and 1971, Monk deletes mm. 7–8 of the **B** section. The result is a bridge[8] section of six bars, and the length of the form is consequently reduced to 30 measures.

(2) Each performance is presented at a different tempo. The fastest is the second take of 1951 at ♩=192; the slowest is the take of 1971 at ♩=163.

(3) The harmony of the 1963 and 1971 versions are slightly different than that of 1951. In the **A** section of the two earlier versions, m3 and the corresponding mm. 11 and 25 are harmonized as G♭7.[9] In the latter versions these measures remain Gm6.

(4) In terms of arrangement, the two performances of 1951 are identical. In a four-measure introduction, accompanied only by Art Blakey keeping time on the hi-hat, Monk presents motive *a* followed by three successive variants of *a,* each statement followed by a half-note, creating a three-beat hemiola. As noted above, the half-notes form a rising chromatic line, progressively widening the resulting interval from a perfect 5th to a minor 7th. The entire band enters and the melody is stated in unison by the saxophone, vibraphone, and piano through the thirty-two bar form. Milt Jackson improvises over one full cycle of the harmonic form. Sahib Shihab solos over the first half of the form (two **A** sections), and Monk completes the form (**B-A**). The melody is recapitulated once, and the performance ends with a piano flourish which evokes *c*. The full arrangement is consequently comprised of the four-bar introduction, four choruses, and the concluding flourish, which extends the piece by one bar.

The recording of 1963 begins with Monk alone, stating motive *c* in a three-bar introduction. The band enters as the piano and saxophone state the melody in unison. The form ends with the thirtieth measure. Charlie Rouse improvises through three cycles of the harmonic form, Monk follows with two cycles. The melody is recapitulated once; the final flourish is replaced by a high register cluster which represents the same harmonic content. The arrangement contains seven full choruses.

The 1971 recording also begins with Monk alone, this time stating motive *b*. The drums join him two measures later, and Monk follows with a statement of a full **A**. The bass enters with the second statement of *b*. This opening is ambiguous; only when the **B** section follows is it clear that the arrangement has begun in the fifth measure. The form concludes and, unlike the former recordings, is immediately restated in full. Monk begins his solo and takes two choruses; in the last **A** of the second chorus, he clearly states the melody (perhaps to balance the incomplete opening statement). He recapitulates the full melody, and concludes with five measures of extension; the first appears to resolve the harmony to g minor. Over this tonic bass, Monk plays the same flourish which concluded the recordings of 1951, and holds the concluding B♭ for two and one-half bars.

There is a clear logic and unity, then, in the motivic *construction* of "Criss Cross." The next issue is if and how these motives are reflected in the *improvisation* section.

THE SOLOS

Lawrence Koch in his article "Thelonious Monk: Compositional Techniques" states that "[p]erhaps the most ingenious aspect of Monk's writing is the total unity and balance of the composition . . . the piece expands from a single figure; it constantly adds elements together and intermittently returns to the original figure."[10] In considering the "Criss Cross" recordings, Koch's observation might be applied to Monk's improvisation process as well; it is rare for Monk to stray from the elements presented in the exposition of the melody. Each of his recorded improvisations is based almost exclusively on the primary motives; perhaps more significantly, though they may be varied by augmentation, diminution, rhythmic displacement or any of the procedures that I will describe later, *he tends to use the motives at the same location in which they originally appear.* Each solo contains examples of this tendency. For example, mm. 87–88 of the 1951 session, take 1, contain motive *c* in the place which corresponds to mm. 23–24 (Example 5). The subsequent eight measures, reflecting the last **A** of the form, continue with references to motives *a* and *b*. A comparison of these bars in all four performances is found in Example 6.

The improvisations of Monk are characterized by constant referral to the motives of the composition. Though he does introduce other phrases, the occurrences are infrequent, and may refer to the solos that have preceded his. In take 1 of the 1951 recording, mm. 81–86 begin with a fragment similar to one which appears in Shihab's m. 10; the bebop vocabulary Monk uses in this

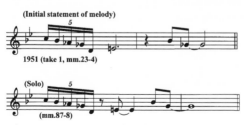

Example 5: Use of motives at corresponding formal location

Example 6: Mm. 89-96, all takes

passage may itself be a reference to the preceding solos (Example 7). Measures 105–112 in the 1963 version perhaps function as rhythmical accompaniment to the bass line (Example 8). Excluding these locations, Monk's improvised solos are comprised principally of variants of the motives.

As stated earlier, Monk in his role as bandleader may have intended to extend the procedure he used in his improvisations to encompass the work as a whole. To achieve this, the other bandmembers would have to relate their solos to the motives of the composition, with an awareness of their role in the performance. Let us look to the solos of the sidemen to see if this holds true.

Not every suggestion of a motive signifies the use of the motive. For example, in the first three measures of his solo in take 1 vibraphonist Milt Jackson uses a triplet three times, but does not resolve downward by a

93   94   95   96

Example 6: concluded

major 3rd (Example 9). A perusal of both his solos does not yield convincing evidence that he intended to use the motives as source material for his improvisation. Shihab solos in similar fashion, applying the bebop language (including common phrases, scales suggested by harmony, and quotation) to the chord changes rather than developing the motives of the piece. A case can be made that he opens his solo with a response to a fragment which appears in Jackson's solo of take 1 (Example 10). This is possibly a reference to the song "Louise," an example of quotation (a common element in jazz improvisation of the time period).[11]

It is interesting to note that Shihab opens both solos with the same three-bar phrase. He has clearly remembered a passage which worked on the first attempt and deliberately uses it to perform the same function.

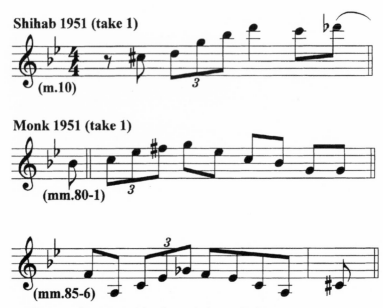

Example 7: Monk's non-motivic phrases in improvisation

Barry Kernfeld in *The New Grove Jazz* asserts that "In the 1960s (Charlie) Rouse adapted his style to Monk's work, improvising with greater deliberation than most bop tenor saxophonists, and restating melodies often. His distinctive solo playing with Monk . . . alternates reiterations of the principle thematic motif with formulaic bop runs."[12] In the 1963 recording of "Criss Cross," Rouse (who worked regularly with Monk from 1959 to 1970) confirms this observation as he refers frequently to motives *a* and *b*. He uses them literally, as in mm. 1–3 and m. 57 (Example 11a), but is more apt to embellish or vary them. If he introduces phrases unrelated to the motives; they become part of the developing solo, and generally appear again in some form. An example of this occurs in mm. 19–20 and 79–80. Though separated by two improvised choruses, a variant of the phrase played initially is stated in almost the same location in the harmonic form; it is displaced by just one beat (Example 11b).

It appears, then, that Charlie Rouse is the soloist who best serves Monk's purposes as a partner. This is reflected by the 13-year span in which Monk kept Rouse as his saxophonist.

Before drawing any conclusions I would like to touch upon an issue I consider important in a discussion of Monk's style. We have seen that

Example 8: Accompaniment to bass solo

Example 9: Milt Jackson solo, 1951 (take 1, mm. 1-3)

Jackson 1951 (take 1, mm.21-2)

Shihab 1951 (take 1, mm.1-3)

"Louise", mm.1-4

Example 10: Comparison on Milt Jackson fragment, Shihab opening statement, and the song "Louise"

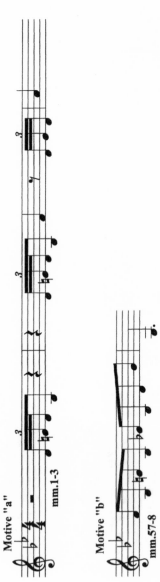

Example 11a: Charlie Rouse's use of motives in improvisation

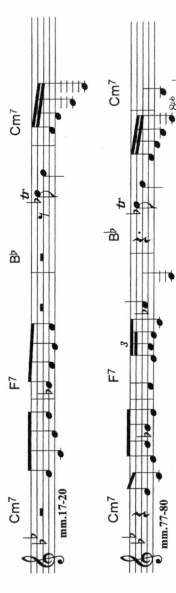

Example 11b: Rouse's integration of new motives into development of improvisation

during his improvisation, he deliberately refers to the motives of the composition. However, merely establishing a relationship between the principal motives and the development of the improvisation section does not completely expose Monk's procedure in creating a solo. A close examination and comparison of the "Criss Cross" recordings suggests that his is a process of nuance; we must look to a smaller level of detail than the fragments, motives, and phrases to investigate Monk's definition of "solo." It is not just the fact that he is playing the motives, but also *how* he plays them that more precisely defines the term.

NUANCE

To cite every occurrence of each element Monk uses would prove unwieldy given the space considerations of this paper, and probably redundant for its purposes. I identify and define, if necessary, the elements which I consider relevant, and provide a small number of representative examples.

Augmentation

Monk uses this device more frequently in the two latter recordings than in the 1951 set. This is perhaps due to the length of his solos; in 1951 he improvises only for sixteen measures.

(1) mm. 65–68 ,1971: motive *a* is stated in different rhythmic values and states of augmentation (Example 12a).

(2) mm. 77–78, 1963, 1971: motive *b* is transformed (Example 12b).

Example 12: Augmentation

Rhythmic displacement

(1) mm. 97–99 1971: motive *a* is augmented and displaced by a 1/4 triplet. Monk also creates a three-beat hemiola reminiscent of mm. 3–4 of the **A** section (Example 13a).

(2) A comparison of mm. 11–12 in all four performances demonstrates well Monk's use of this device. Each version contains a slightly different displacement (Example 13b).

Example 13: Rhythmic displacement

Distance in Time Between 1/8 Notes

As I have previously mentioned, Monk subtly varies the subdivision of the 1/4 note.

(1) m. 35, 1971: beats 1 and 2 are triplet 1/8 notes, beat 3 is straight, beat 4 returns to triplet feel (Example 14a).

(2) m. 48–49, 1971: Monk anticipates the downbeat of m. 49 by tying a triplet 1/8 over the barline. He changes the first beat of m. 49 to a straight 1/8 feel, and returns to the triplet feel on beat 3 of this same measure (Example 14b).

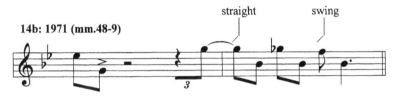

Example 14: Subdivision of quarter note

Left-Hand Voices

The left-hand voices of Monk are used to fulfill one of three functions: harmonic support, rhythmic punctuation, or counter-lines. Often one part fulfills all three:

(1) mm. 14–21, 1971: in mm. 14–15, harmonic support and rhythmic punctuation. The line begun in the tenor voice in m. 14 continues through m. 21 (Example 15a).

(2) It is probable that Monk considered the counter-voices as independent lines and was not concerned with avoiding resultant dissonance. Each line resolves with respect to the procedures of correct voice-leading. A perfect example of this occurs in the statement of the melody, **B**, mm. 18 and 21 of all four versions. Over an F7 chord, the soprano voice sounds a B♭, while the tenor sounds an A. The fourth and third degree consequently sound at the interval of a m9 and resolve by contrary motion in the following measures (Example 15b).

Length of Notes

A comparison of the four performances reveals differences in the length of certain tones, usually at the conclusion of fragments or motives. This is a

Example 15a: Mm. 13–22, 1971

significant element; whether or not a note is sustaining changes the articulation of a passage.

(1) mm. 31–32: the final note g of variant *b1* is played as a dotted quarter tied to quarter in both 1951 versions, an eighth note in 1963, and a dotted quarter in 1971 (Example 16a).

(2) mm. 131–132: the final note g of variant *a3* enters on beat 2 of measure 132 and is held as a dotted-half note in both versions of 1951, enters
on beat 1 as a quarter note in 1963, enters on beat one as a whole note in
1971 (Example 16b).

Simultaneous Tones

Vertical half- and whole-step intervals create dissonance and ambiguity as
to which note is intended for primary melody. The question must be raised

Example 15b: Independent lines, mm. 17–24, all takes (continued overleaf)

as to whether Monk intended the composite sound itself to function as "melody."[13]

(1) m. 32, 1971: the melody in the three previous versions is e♭-g. The addition of the a creates the possibility that it functions either as a whole-step "harmonization," a primary melody tone, or an element of the cluster g-a, to be considered as a single unit (Example 17a).

(2) mm. 92–93, 1971: these measures occur during the piano solo. Monk is using the shape of the motive *b,* but varying the rhythmic content. The vertical half-step intervals on beat 4 of mm. 92 and 93 might be harmonizing or simply "shading" the primary melodic tone, simulating a bend on a guitar or a slur into a tone that a horn is capable of creating (Example 17b).

Example 15b: concluded

Conclusions

With this information in hand, let us return to the main theme of this paper: the presence and ramifications of motivic construction and development in the presentations of "Criss Cross." I have discussed in detail Monk's approach, and I will briefly recapitulate my observations of the performances of the sidemen.

Charlie Rouse remains faithful to the motives, though he tends to embellish and/or use them in different locations more so than Monk. Though he is also apt to introduce phrases seemingly unrelated to the

Example 16a: Length of notes, mm. 31-32

Example 16b: Length of notes, mm. 131-132

primary material, he treats this new information as new raw material to
be varied or developed. His process is not identical to Monk's, but it is
quite similar. In contrast, Milt Jackson and Sahib Shihab retain the harmonic structure, but they present melodic ideas apparently unrelated to
the motives initially presented, using instead the vocabulary of bebop or

Ex. 17a: 1971, mm. 31-2

Ex. 17b: 1971, mm. 92-3

Example 17: Simultaneous tones

quotation. (Andre Hodeir defines this approach as *chorus phrase*.[14]) It might be argued, in fact, that Jackson does not completely succeed in negotiating the harmony: it is difficult, for example, to justify a major 3rd as a note of resolution on the final Gm7 (Example 18).

Example 18: Jackson resolution to maj. 3rd on G minor

The later recordings, consequently, more consistently hold together as complete and unified statements, from the perspective of both small- and large-scale structure. Perhaps this is due to the differences between the two ensembles; while Monk had recorded just once before with the 1951 ensemble, the personnel of the 1963 and 1971 recordings were more familiar and experienced with Monk's work. On the small scale, an initial reading and listening show that the melodic and rhythmic motives of the initial presentation are treated as the primary material available for variation and development in the creation of the improvisations. On the level of large-scale coherence, particularly in the case of Monk's solos, *careful listening shows that the discrete motivic fragments add up because of their temporal positioning, i.e., how they correlate with the original material.*

If we also consider nuance as a fundamental element of Monk's process, we can conclude that in his compositions based on motivic construction, exemplified by "Criss Cross," it is possible to view his approach to improvisation as operating on three distinct yet interrelated levels: the large-scale coherence of the performance, the small-scale level of motivic development, and the "micro" level of nuance. A remarkable quality of his work was his ability to remain true both to the content and the temporal position of the motives presented in the melody. His discipline and focus allowed him to compose and develop his ideas logically in the actual time of an ongoing performance, perhaps bypassing or accelerating the procedure of reflection and correction through which a composer putting his work to paper is able to pass. As a musician who spends much performance time trying to present a coherent improvisational statement, I can offer an appreciation; in the process of developing a solo, either information provided by the other band members or distractions caused by noise or loss of concentration come quickly and must be processed in the time that the presentation is unfolding. It is easy to rely on habit and preprocessed ideas to negotiate the harmonic sequences, and to lose one's awareness of the "big picture."

Martin Williams included Monk together with Jelly Roll Morton and Duke Ellington as a composer/performer whose ". . . sense of form extends beyond written structure and beyond individual improviser, to encompass a whole performance."[15] Williams continued by distinguishing Monk's process:

> Morton and Ellington hold together the jazz performance, give it form, by relating written and improvised parts. With Monk . . . the form is more improvisational—the "orchestration," one might say, is extemporaneous.[16]

The case can be made that Monk envisioned an improvised performance from beginning to end, and desired his bandmates to cooperate in realizing this vision by remaining focused on the primary material presented in the composition. Each performance can be considered an attempt to create a single, specific, and unique entity.

See lead sheet of "Criss-Cross," *notes, and discography on following pages.*

Criss Cross

NOTES

Acknowledgments: A number of people have offered encouragement, advice, and assistance during the development and completion of this article. Without them, it would not have taken shape. They are: Professors Dan Carillo, John Graziano, and Ronald Carter of the City College of New York, Professor Jeff Taylor of Brooklyn College, Professor Henry Martin of Rutgers University, and Kimson Plaut for providing computer-generated examples.

1. Paul Berliner, *Thinking in Jazz: The Infinite Art of Improvisation* (Chicago: The University of Chicago Press, 1994), 345.

2. Whitney Balliet. "Notes and Comments" in *The New Yorker*, March 1, 1982: 37.

3. Ran Blake "Thelonious Monk" in *The New Grove Dictionary of Jazz,* ed. Barry Kernfeld (London: Macmillan, 1988), vol . 2, 122.

4. Charley Gerard. *Thelonious Monk: Originals and Standards* (Brooklyn: Gerard and Sarzin, 1991), 11.

5. Walter Bruyninckx, *Sixty years of Recorded Jazz, 1917–1977* (Belgium: Mechelen, 1980), vol. 15, M590.

6. Bob Houston's "Jazz Masters" publication, for instance, cuts from the initial statement of the melody to the piano solo of the 1951 recording (take 1), both omitting and making no reference to the vibraphone and saxophone solos. (London: Wise Publications, 1977, 16–18.)

7. I omit from the discussion "Live at the Monterey Jazz Festival, 1963" (Storyville CD 8256 / Ultradisc gold CD 1755-686-2) since Monk does not solo on this recording.

8. Monk referred to this second section of the composition as the "inside."

9. I use the $G\flat7$ for ease of spelling in the melody. In fact, the harmony might be considered the enharmonic $F\sharp7$, perhaps as a dominant based on the leading tone of the key; probably as a substitution for a C7, the dominant built on the fourth degree of the scale.

10. Lawrence O. Koch. "Thelonious Monk: Compositional Techniques" in *Annual Review of Jazz Studies 2,* ed. Dan Morgenstern, Charles Nanry, David A. Cayer (New Brunswick, New Jersey: Transaction Books, 1983), 77.

11. Words by Leo Robin, music by Richard Whiting, *Louise* (New York: Famous Music Corporation, 1929).

12. Barry Kernfeld, "Charlie Rouse" in *The New Grove Dictionary of Jazz* (London: Macmillan, 1988), vol. 2, 397.

13. Jack Garner in his article "Monk: A Daringly Original Genius" offers Monk's explanation of this device: ". . . (he) once said he often played the adjoining keys on a piano specifically because he was trying to get to the impossible—the tone on the piano that hypothetically resides between the adjoining keys." *Courier-News* (Bridgewater, NJ), February 20, 1982, p. B-10.

14. Andre Hodeir, *Jazz: Its Evolution and Essence* (New York: Grove Press, 1956), 144.

15. Martin Williams "Thelonious Monk: Arrival without Departure," *Saturday Review*, April 13, 1963: 33.

16. *Ibid.*

DISCOGRAPHY

Three Thelonious Monk performances of "Criss Cross":

July 23, 1951, for Blue Note (78: BN 1590; LP: BLP 1509; CD: CDP 7 81511 2) with Sahib Shihab, alto saxophone; Milt Jackson, vibraphone; Al McKibbon, bass; Art Blakey, drums

February 26, 1963, for Columbia (LP: CL 2038, CD: CK 48823) with Charlie Rouse, tenor saxophone; John Ore, bass; Frankie Dunlop, drums

November 15, 1971, for Black Lion (LP: BLP 2460.152; CD: BLCD 760116) with Al McKibbon, bass; Art Blakey, drums

THE ARMSTRONG I KNEW

Dan Morgenstern

To be in the presence of Louis Armstrong was a gift. To get even closer than being in his audience was a blessing. I was among those who had that privilege. I first met him in 1949 and last saw him in 1971, and during the intervening years there were many encounters: at his home; in record, radio, film, and television studios; on the band bus; backstage in theaters, concert halls, clubs; and in tents. I saw that remarkable artist and human being at work, at play, at rest, among strangers and among friends. In every situation and circumstance there was something to learn, something to keep, something to cherish.

How did a 19-year-old nobody get admitted to the dressing room of a world-famous artist, backstage at New York City's second-largest theater, the Roxy in Times Square? A nobody who'd only arrived in the United States in the spring of 1947, after various adventures in Austria, Denmark, and Sweden (courtesy of that notorious tour guide A. Hitler), having first discovered jazz when taken to hear and see Fats Waller in Copenhagen as a nine-year old, then struggled to no avail with a violin, and had only a few years of collecting jazz records and reading about the music under his belt?

Well, when I first came to New York, I wanted to see 52nd Street, and once I found it, a girl I'd met introduced me to a little man she knew as "Face." He was carrying a trumpet, and his lips (he had a disproportionately large head, with the broad features of his Russian-Jewish peasant ancestors) had that instrument's signature. His real name was Nat Lorber; he made no records and is in no history books, but he knew more about jazz than most of those books will tell you. Nat became my friend and jazz Virgil—but that's another story. Among the many people I met through him was a remarkable woman, then about 25, who among other things was taking care of Louis Armstrong's fan mail. Letters would come from all over the world, some addressed as minimally as "Satchmo, USA," and she would sort them out. Those that merely asked for autographs or photos she would fill from a frequently replenished stock of Armstrong's recommended diet chart, but those that had more to offer were shown to the great man, who would an-

At the 1970 Newport Jazz Festival, the arriving star is greeted warmly by
Dan Morgenstern, with Bobby Hackett's approval. Photo by Harriet Choice.

swer most of them. (As I was to learn, he was dedicated to his friends and
fans; he was a hands-on man.)

Obviously, the lady had his confidence. Her name was Jeann Failows; she
was a publicist for jazz people, sometimes ran Sunday or Monday sessions in
night clubs, and generally devoted herself to the jazz cause. And she was a
Number One Louis Armstrong Fan. So was Nat, and they had long known
each other; he, of course, had already met his idol. After Jeann had approved
of me, my initiation came about during an engagement by the still fairly new
Armstrong All Stars (the edition with Jack Teagarden, Barney Bigard, Earl
Hines, Arvell Shaw, Cozy Cole, and Velma Middleton) at the Roxy—a movie
theater with stage shows and chief rival to Radio City Music Hall.

Our names had been left at the stage door, and we were escorted to
the star dressing room. Wrapped in a white terrycloth bathrobe, with that

famous handkerchief tied around his head, Louis greeted us all warmly. Jeann repeated my name, and Louis, having also been told that I'd recently arrived from Denmark (a country he never forgot for the marvelous reception Copenhageners had given him in 1933—the biggest up to then), weighed "Morgenstern" and "Scandinavia," and came up with "Smorgasbord," his nickname for me from then on. But when he autographed a photo for me, he inscribed it "To Dan"; it was the first of many, signed in green ink (at the time, he also used a green ribbon in his beloved typewriter). He had an amazing gift for making you feel at such ease that it soon seemed as if he were an old friend. (As, in a very real sense, he was, from those manifestations of his spirit I knew from records, films, and photographs.)

A real old friend soon dropped in—the pianist Joe Bushkin. He presented Louis with a long-stemmed red rose, announcing it as a gift from the actress Tallulah Bankhead (a great Armstrong fan), whom he'd just left. Louis smelled the rose, made a quizzical face, and extracted from the flower a large and well-rolled reefer. Laughter all around, not least from an even older friend. June Clark, who was Louis's age, had been a well-known trumpeter in the 1920s but had to give up playing due to a lung ailment (he always claimed that, in any case, there had been no reason for him to continue doing what Louis did so much better). For a time, he'd been Louis's road manager and later became the famous boxer Sugar Ray Robinson's right-hand man. Now, as Louis told us he needed a nap before the next show, June disappeared along with him behind a partition, and we fell quiet. Soon we heard the most beautiful whistling: It was Louis's 1930 "Sweethearts on Parade" solo, note for note, with perfect intonation and time. After the final note, June emerged, saying, "He's asleep." It was a very special lullaby, and my first experience with Louis's ability to fall asleep, quick and fast, and to wake up alert and fresh, no matter how long or short the nap, as he got himself ready to do the show. Jack Teagarden now stopped by to discuss a musical point; the rapport between these two was instantly evident. The stage manager arrived with the five-minute warning, and Louis firmly instructed him to find good places for the three of us from which to see the stage, leaving us with "Enjoy the show!"

That concern and hospitality would be repeated, in various ways, at future encounters. When Louis asked you how you were feeling, he expected an honest answer, and he was quick to detect if anything was bothering you. Throughout his long career, apparently from the time he was earning more than he felt the need to spend, this good and generous man helped hundreds—thousands—of individuals and many a worthy cause, but unlike so many others in the limelight, he never publicized such gestures. Many times I'd see him discretely pass some folded bills (and they were not small denominations) to someone with a handshake. Louis always carried a large roll of bills, and it was always replenished. He knew that some might take advantage of his good nature, but that was a risk he willingly took.

Louis had a marvelous talent for concentrating completely on whatever he was doing—enjoying a meal (he loved good food and drink—the latter always in moderation, and not until after work), writing a letter, watching an event, listening to music. This is what made him such a fabulously quick study when it came to new musical material. Twice I observed this aspect of his talent in the recording studio, first during the famous encounter with Duke Ellington, on the second of the two sessions. Midway through, Ellington unveiled a piece of music he had written long ago (words as well as music) but had never performed successfully (several studio attempts remained unissued). He claimed that he'd composed this piece, "Azalea," with Louis in mind. The trumpeter and singer put on his hornrimmed glasses—something that gave him a studious appearance—and looked intently at the music sheet, then nodded his head. Ellington moved to the piano, and Louis began to play the not-at-all-simple melody as if it truly had been written for him, and then negotiated the tricky Ellingtonian lyric, with some bizarre rhymes, as if it were a Shakespeare sonnet. Ellington beamed. Some six months later, Louis was in the studio with Dave Brubeck, who, with his wife Iola, had written a major work, *The Real Ambassadors*, that starred Louis and also featured his All Stars, Carmen McRae, and the vocal group Lambert, Hendricks & Ross. Here, however, it was just Louis and Brubeck, who, seated at the piano, handed his star the lead sheet to "Summer Song," one of the most beautiful pieces he'd ever composed, and, though less convoluted than "Azalea," also far from a simple song. Again, Louis donned his glasses, looked at the music with intense concentration (something a bystander felt rather than saw), nodded to the pianist, and then proceeded to sing the song as if he owned it. Tears came to Brubeck's eyes.

Louis Armstrong was the kindest of men—to watch him signing autographs for his fans after a performance was a special treat, for he would ask each person's name and make certain he had it right before writing (most celebrities just dash off their signatures, but Louis personalized each photo he signed) and also engage in a bit of conversation (not with everyone, but certainly with children, and whenever he felt a "vibration")—but it was most unwise to anger him. A marvelous demonstration of this came about at a Newport Festival in the early days of that annual event—in 1957. There was no "backstage" at the sports stadium, Freebody Park, where the festival was then held, but a couple of big tents had been pitched behind some stalls, and one of them was Armstrong's domain. It happened to be his birthday, and all sorts of things had been planned, none of them apparently discussed in advance with Louis, who had arrived in midafternoon on his band bus, hoping to get a little rest before going on. But he listened quite patiently to George Wein, who suggested that he make his first appearance with the Armstrong alumni on the program (Kid Ory, Red Allen, J.C. Higginbotham, Jack Teagarden), to which he reluctantly agreed. (Though a great improviser, Louis never relished impromptu public appearances, always preferring at least a runthrough.) Then, of course, there should be a visit during Ella Fitzgerald's set—these two had recently recorded together and soon would do so again, and producer Norman Granz was also present. And then, there was a good chance that Sidney Bechet might be there, and wouldn't that be something, those two together for the first time in almost twenty years! This was clearly less to Louis's liking—he and Bechet had never been close—but he didn't say no outright, although he was beginning to get annoyed. Then someone arrived with word that Bechet had just telegraphed his regrets—he was, he said, stuck somewhere. This did not seem funny to Louis—he no doubt recalled that Bechet had been set as a guest at his 1947 Town Hall Concert but cancelled in much the same manner—but now came the straw that broke the camel's back. It was suggested that, since Ella was on the program, it might be a good idea to cut Velma Middleton from the All Stars' set in the interest of time. Velma had been with Louis since 1942, when she first started to sing with his big band. Critics had no use for her (a very large black woman who, surprisingly, was very light on her feet—she'd been a dancer—and could do the splits, she made many white writers uncomfortable), but she was a surefire hit with audiences, a perfect foil for Louis's comedy routines, and a very loyal friend. Since the tent had no walls, Velma overheard what was suggested and burst into tears. Louis, who had in the meanwhile been changing from his traveling clothes and was now wearing almost nothing, rose from his folding chair, pointed to the exit flap, and roared: "Everybody out! We do our regular show, Velma sings, and *nobody* rides on my coat tails!" The tent emptied in record time, and exactly what Louis said took place on stage that night, though he consented to have Ella and Johnny Mercer wheel out a cake and sing "Happy Birthday." The next day, all the press reports painted Louis as an ungracious birthday celebrant who had been inexplicably rude to his well-intentioned hosts, even failing to show up for a dinner party, but many of us knew better, and as Jack Teagarden said, "It seemed like they wanted to crucify Pops!" Moral: Don't get Mr. Armstrong angry!

At home, Louis was a most gracious host. What he really enjoyed most was having his guest visit with him in his "den," the only part of the house that bore his imprint rather than that of his wife, Lucille (who promptly got rid of it after his death, turning the area into a proper sitting room; it is being restored for the 2003 opening of the Armstrong House in Corona, Queens, as a public attraction). Here was his collection of tapes, recorded by himself and entered into a log. He decorated each box with his own designs—clippings, photos, inscriptions—and he loved to play samples (these might as often be comedy routines and rather earthy jokes as well as music). He also enjoyed taping conversations with visitors. No visit to the Armstrong home was complete without using the bathroom, which had been lavishly decorated by Lucille with gold fixtures, lots of mirrors, and other accoutrements. If you were visiting for the first time, Louis would demand a reaction. "Something else, eh?," he might say, "at least for someone who grew up using an outhouse!" Digestive matters were in any case important to Louis, a firm believer in laxatives. His favorite, which he recommended to all and carried sample envelopes of, was Swiss Criss, an herbal mixture that is still quite au courant. It was very effective even in small doses, but Louis would sometimes play a trick on the unwary, especially when it was someone riding on the band bus for the first time. Waiting for the dose to take effect, Louis would eventually take pity on the poor victim and make the bus stop. The thus indoctrinated would feel like a member of a special club. On the bus, Louis might suddenly fall asleep in the middle of a conversation—something that stood him in good stead during a lifetime of almost constant travel.

When the bus was about to leave from Louis's house (he would always be the last one to board), his own 1956 recording of "When You're Smiling" would be playing in the background. Louis Armstrong was perhaps the only artist who enjoyed his own recordings, and that one was a special favorite. It put him in the right mood to deal with yet another journey on his chosen path, what he called "My living and my life," in the cause of spreading happiness. Making people feel good was his mission in life, and it was impossible not to feel good in his presence. On stage, where he was an absolute master, Louis Armstrong appeared larger than life, as any great artist will, but those who think that what he performed was an "act" are very wrong. The essence of Louis Armstrong, the man, was the same as the essence of Louis Armstrong, the artist. In the words of the pianist Jaki Byard, recalling his impressions when he first met Louis, "he was the most natural of men—so natural, the tears came to my eyes."

At a conference in Leeds, home of Britain's largest music school, in 2000 there were three of us—saxophonist, bandleader, and historian Loren Schoenberg; trumpeter, writer, and teacher Digby Fairweather; and I—who gave talks involving Louis Armstrong and his legacy, and each of us independently arrived at the conclusion that he might—just might—have come to us as a visitor from another sphere or dimension. Whatever the case, it is certain that there is only one Louis Armstrong, and that he will never be forgotten.

LOUIS ARMSTRONG:
A CENTENNIAL PHOTO GALLERY

Louis ARMSTRONG - Mrs. ARMSTRONG
& Castor Mac CORD. Tenor Sax.

Top: Armstrong and his com-
panion (and later, wife) Alpha
Smith, with tenor saxophonist
Castor McCord, on tour in
Belgium, November 1934.

Right: Armstrong and Lionel
Hampton in Culver City,
California, ca. 1930, when
young Hamp was the drummer
in the band backing the trumpeter at Frank Sebastian's
Cotton Club. Note Hamp's
hi-hat—quite a novelty then.

Top: Armstrong and Bob
Crosby in a CBS radio studio
in 1938. Did Crosby's shirt
serve as an inspiration for
Harry Truman?

Left: Timme Rosenkrantz,
the Danish "Jazz Baron,"
snapped a dapper Armstrong
on a Harlem street in 1938.
(Luis Russell is visible in the
background.)

A gorgeous Maurice Seymour publicity photo of Armstrong with his beloved Selmer trumpet, in the early days of his association with Joe Glaser (ca. 1935).

Top: Armstrong gives a pretty fan a trumpet lesson as pianist Joe Bushkin (r) and the lady's escort look on, backstage somewhere in New York City (possibly the Hurricane) ca. 1950.

Bottom: Two mid-1930s Armstrong portraits—pensive in front of his big band, and posing prettily in a photographer's studio.

An early edition of the All Stars surrounds champ Joe Louis and wife. Earl Hines, back to camera, has the attention of Ms. Louis, and Barney Bigard is at the Brown Bomber's side, flanked by a happy Velma Middleton. Big Sid Catlett looks amazed, and Pops, horn at side, Jack Teagarden, and a youthful Arvell Shaw round out the group.

Top, left and right: Armstrong during a publicity shoot for RCA Victor Records, ca.1945—did Pops drop the disc?—and, bottom, whatever he just did during a mid-1940s record date seems to have pleased a radiant Armstrong.

Book signing time at the Commodore Music Shop in 1946 for Robert Goffin's Armstrong biography *Horn of Plenty*. Proprietor Milt Gabler is on the far left, behind a pile of books, and his brother-in-law Jack Crystal (Billy's dad) is behind Armstrong, while brother Barney Gabler is between the two ladies.

Top: The triumvirate that
couldn't last—not least due
to the ever-present and
odiferous Hines cigar.
Must be Earl's tune that
Pops and Big T are reading.

Left: A loving Louis
and Lucille, his fourth
(and lasting) wife,
in the mid-1940s.

Armstrong and Wild Bill Davison, captured by Skippy Adelman during a 1946 "This Is Jazz" radio broadcast produced by Rudi Blesh.

Pops doesn't seem at all jet-lagged at the onset of a two-week Hawaiian tour. Dig that wrap-around top coat—a fashion touch introduced by Billy Eckstine.

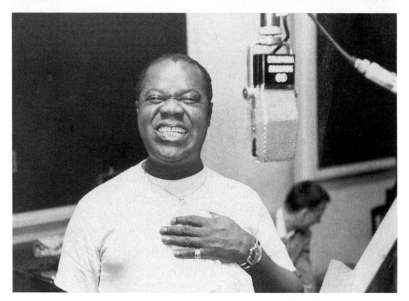

In the Columbia 30th Street New York studio, probably during the W.C. Handy sessions. Barrett Deems is in the background, and the good, uncredited photographer was probably Don Hunstein.

A high-contrast shot, by Teri Gili, of an elegant Armstrong in the 1960s, at the Paper Mill Playhouse in New Jersey.

Top: Listening to a playback in RCA Victor's 24th Street Studio A, during the session with Duke Ellington (in booth, as is Helen Dance). Evie Ellis (Ellington) is sitting in the corner. Photo by Arnold Myers.

Right: Jeann (Roni) Failows, one of Armstrong's closest friends, poses with Pops in Framingham, MA, ca. 1967. Photo by Jack Bradley.

In one of his early ventures as a photographer, Ed Berger struck gold, capturing a rare joint appearance by two kings of jazz (quite possibly the only such encounter on camera) at the Music Circus in Lambertville, New Jersey, July 1966. Top: Paul Whiteman is delivering a birthday serenade to Pops. Bottom: Louis and the All Stars, Tyree Glenn, Danny Barcelona, Buster Bailey.

During the 1970 Bob Thiele-produced recording session with many of his friends, Armstrong is seen here with one of the closest—personally and musically—Bobby Hackett.

A slim Louis and his Lucille arriving on June 17, 1968, in England for a two-week stand at the Variety Club in Batley, and Louis leaving Batley's town hall in a Rolls-Royce two days later, during a sightseeing tour of the Yorkshire town.

THE "STARDUST" FILE

Brian Priestley

One of the most enduring exhibits in the annals of American songwriting, "Stardust" is also an instructive example of the early influence of jazz on more popular music. For nearly three-quarters of a century, the song has also fed back into the repertoire of those jazz performers who are content to base their work on material that was well known to the general public. Another way of saying this, of course, is that it was created in an era when the divide between jazz and pop was less extreme than today, although there is no doubt that, already in the 1920s, there was in musicians' minds a tangible tension between "hot" and "sweet" styles. It was possible, how-ever, for a piece to start out as the first and migrate to the second camp, which didn't stop it being reclaimed by the hot fraternity from time to time.

The circumstances surrounding its composition are described by Carmichael in his two autobiographies, the second a dismemberment and reassembly of the first with much "as-told-to" in-filling by his co-writer.[1] The first book, published in 1946 after Hoagy had achieved on-screen fame in Hollywood movies (as opposed to merely providing classic songs for them), was actually conceived and probably completed in 1933. The im-mediacy, and indeed quirkiness, of its contents easily convince the reader of the essential truth of the details. In the summer of 1927, following a brief attempt to do "a proper job" as a lawyer, the 27-year-old Carmichael was back in Bloomington, Indiana, where he was born and raised and where he had previously been a student and active pianist-bandleader. Strolling across the former sports-ground Jordan Field at night, he was struck by a melody that came from out of nowhere, and immediately resorted to the pi-ano of the student cafe, The Book Nook, to try and hammer it into shape. In 1985, the present writer went on a pilgrimage to Jordan Field and the contemporary descendant of The Book Nook and—although no composi-tional urge resulted—the following reflections on the song itself did.

As to its origins, there seems no truth in the suggestion that "Stardust" was, however distantly, derived from Carmichael's 1925 composition "Boneyard Shuffle" (or, as given in one of the "reference books" on popular music, "Barnyard Shuffle"). There is more plausibility in the widespread notion about the influence of his friend and sometime colleague, cornetist Bix Beiderbecke, as has been claimed by many commentators, including such musicians as Bud Freeman and Nick LaRocca. The latter, quoted in the Sudhalter-Evans biography of Beiderbecke, claimed that the germ of "Stardust" was already present when Beiderbecke first sat in with LaRocca's Original Dixieland Jazz Band on the ODJB standard "Singin' the Blues." There is no hint of a direct "Stardust" connection in Bix's later contribution to the famous Frank Trumbauer record of "Singin' the Blues" done in February 1927 but, if Carmichael had already heard this disc (which seems quite likely), it may have brought to mind other Beiderbecke performances, including one he had witnessed as recently as April 1927.[2]

The Bixian inspiration was certainly acknowledged by Carmichael in a generalized way, especially in connection with the verse of "Stardust," although it is also worth noting that the verse's main melodic idea is similar to the second phrase of the 1919 standard "Dardanella." The composer's admiration of Louis Armstrong too, dating from at least 1923, may have influenced the melodic architecture of the song's 32-bar chorus. Specifically, there is the remarkable coincidence that bars 3–4 of the chorus are also heard in bars 25–26 of Armstrong's stop-time chorus on "Potato Head Blues"—it must indeed be coincidence, since this May 1927 recording was seemingly not yet released when "Stardust" was created, but again there may have been other similar Armstrong performances lingering in Charmichael's memory.

The other aspect of the chorus that deserves special mention and was significant in its appeal is the three-note pick-up subsequently associated with the words "Sometimes I..." This too can be related to other earlier songs, such as the 1917 "Poor Butterfly" (whose opening three notes have a similar half-step movement) and the 1919 "Rose Room" (whose first two notes are on the same pitch, subsequently moving to the third and fourth notes by half-steps). But, in both those cases, the pick-up phrases are in the lower part of the register covered by the song, whereas "Stardust"'s opening four notes are near the top of its range, only to be exceeded by the tune's highest pitch (in bar 3) preceding the words "dreaming of a song."

This was, however, not yet a song, even though the lyrics have been referred to in identifying particular notes. It was a jazzy instrumental, far removed from the slow ballad we know today, and intended to be played at the same tempo, or even a little faster, than Trumbauer's "Singin' the Blues." Certainly, this was the case when Carmichael got the chance to record the number at the Gennett studios in Richmond, Indiana, on October

31, 1927. Working with the members of Emil Seidel's Indianapolis-based band,[3] Carmichael apparently created the arrangement which, after a brief guitar intro, has trumpeter Byron Smart outlining the verse, playing it straight but with a style of articulation distantly recalling Beiderbecke. Altoist Gene Wood then plays the chorus, adding a couple of Trumbauer-like flourishes, to be followed by a solo for Carmichael's unaccompanied piano (oddly enough, this lasts 33 bars since one of the first 5 bars is an "extra"!). Though clearly worked out beforehand, this has a jazz feel to it and a couple of phrases which seem quite flamboyant, so much so that the prearranged clarinet lead of the last half-chorus is anticlimactic, possibly indicating it was conceived by the pianist rather than the clarinetist.

Apparently, the record didn't sell at all well, but it was the start of something big. The further adventures of "Stardust" began with two recordings in the fall of 1928 which define two different approaches to the number. This was significant for the composer, given that the 1920s was the decade in which records first began to play an important role in securing publication, since the main medium by which songwriting success was still measured was sheet-music sales. Carmichael wrote fondly of his association with the great black arranger Don Redman during his brief stay in Detroit the previous winter. Redman, who had done so much to establish Fletcher Henderson's New York group as the top jazz big band of the day, was then leading the Jean Goldkette-managed McKinney's Cotton Pickers. Because this session involved ignoring their contract with Victor Records, they adopted the name "The Chocolate Dandies" (previously the title of a 1924 Noble Sissle-Eubie Blake musical on Broadway). Redman was much taken with the melody of "Stardust" and his Chocolate Dandies recording keeps intact Carmichael's own arrangement, even down to the written clarinet solo of the last chorus, but with superior individual performances from Redman himself and guest guitarist Lonnie Johnson, and with a more sprightly tempo.

Only about four weeks later, however, "Stardust" was also recorded by Irving Mills, who had already published a couple of Carmichael songs and was about to publish "Stardust." (These first recordings and the composer's copyright registration in 1928 were done under the two-word title "Star Dust," whereas in Irving Mills's publication it became a single word.) Mills's recording was cut at one of the many dates for which he booked pick-up groups of New York's finest session men. These recordings were often known to collectors by one of Mills's many aliases, The Whoopee Makers, though on this particular occasion the billing was Mills's Merry Makers or, on the alternate take, Goody's Good Timers.

The Merry Makers recording was, in some respects, similar to the previous recordings; it uses the written clarinet solo for the opening chorus. However, what is most remarkable is that the tempo is much slower—around 29.5 bars to the minute or 118 beats per minute (bpm), compared with 40 bars (160 bpm) in the Chocolate Dandies version (Carmichael's 1927 recording is somewhat more variable in tempo, but eventually settles down to 36 bars or144 bpm). Thus, the 32 bars of the main melody chorus take only 48 seconds to be played by the Chocolate Dandies, 53.33 seconds by the composer's premier, and a total of 67 seconds by the Merry Makers. One consequence of this drastic change is that the arrangement no longer fits on a 78 rpm record and, after a full chorus (with no introduction) and a verse, the Merry Makers only have time for the first 8 bars of what should be a final chorus, followed by a most ungainly cut to the closing 4 bars.

Issued by the Cameo group of labels during a boom period for small record companies, the Mills's Merry Makers version actually set a precedent for subsequent hit recordings of "Stardust." But, before this became universally recognized as the most suitable approach, there were further versions put on disc, including one by another Irving Mills group with Carmichael himself at the piano. Surrounding him with such eminent players as Miff Mole, Pee Wee Russell, and Jimmy Dorsey—all as members of "Irving Mills's Hotsy Totsy Gang"—this September 1929 date elaborates the previous recorded arrangement by having the original piano solo chorus scored (by Carmichael?) for three saxophones, but the tempo is merely a steadier rendition of the very first recorded treatment. This may indicate that the composer still wished to retain some of the jazzy feel of his initial conception, and indeed black bandleaders such as Cab Calloway and Fletcher Henderson, who both recorded the number in 1931, tended to prefer the faster tempos. The arrangement commissioned by Henderson, incidentally, was by Bill Challis, who appears never to have scored the number during his Paul Whiteman days.

Carmichael always maintained in later life that it was bandleader Isham Jones's record which set "Stardust" on its road to success. More specifically, he claimed that this was the first version to slow down the tempo; he had clearly forgotten the relatively obscure Mills's Merry Makers version. The speed adopted by Jones in fact was a fraction less slow than the MMM, but what was important was that this recording had, in the composer's own words, "an immediate success." Cut in May 1930 and issued shortly after, it sold despite the start of the Depression—perhaps indeed because of it, for this was a superior example of the sweeter sounds with which the public was to console itself after the financial failure of the Jazz Age. In this respect, "Stardust" was truly ahead of its time (as were Beiderbecke and the other improvising soloists who had inspired Carmichael) and the earlier uncertainty over a suitable tempo might be said to symbolize the fact.[4]

Even more than the tempo, though, the arrangement on the Isham Jones recording was what made it so appealing. This was the work of Victor Young, later to become a successful conductor on radio and writer of such immortal songs as "Ghost of a Chance" and "A Hundred Years from Today" and film music like "Stella by Starlight" and "My Foolish Heart." In 1930 he was merely the featured violinist of the Jones band, and he saw clearly how to bring out the latent qualities of "Stardust" by playing the intro and the closing chorus himself, perfectly straight and in an upper register, the lead being taken in-between as an equally sweet-toned muted trumpet solo from Johnny Carlson.

There are two tiny but beneficial changes from earlier recordings, which are already enshrined in the 1929 song copy and the published stock orchestration by Jimmy Dale.[5] Firstly, the verse now begins with a tonic major chord, instead of the relative minor used in the 1927–9 records (and which Carmichael himself still retained, along with his arranged piano chorus, on the solo version done as late as December 1933). And, instead of the minor 9th chord in bar 9 of the main chorus, a simple dominant chord helps the sequence to flow more easily—incidentally making the eventual appearance of the minor 9th in bar 25 much more meaningful. The effect of these amendments was clearly subliminal except to musicians, but they made the relationship of melody and harmony more palatable and easy to grasp for the general populace.

Carmichael's own ambivalence about the potential of his tune is thrown into sharp focus by the knowledge that, as early as 1928, his last Gennett recording session includes an unissued "Stardust" (now doubtless lost forever), apparently performed as a duet between the pianist and violinist Eddie Wolfe. Was this perhaps quite close in conception to that of Isham Jones and Victor Young? Why indeed would he rerecord the number just a few months after its initial waxing, and for the same record company, unless the approach was markedly different from that first attempt? There is also the interesting fact that it was Carmichael himself who first conceived of the melody being fitted out with lyrics or, at the very least, originally considered that the addition of lyrics would increase its chances of being published. (Charles "Bud" Dant, the trumpeter on the 1928 Gennett session who was interviewed by Duncan Scheidt, claimed that this unissued "Stardust" in fact featured Carmichael singing his own early lyrics, a statement unlikely to be confirmed or disproved at this late stage.) The composer once

said that he had already written his words to the tune even before recording
it for the first time, thus countering the oft-repeated statement that it was
arranger Jimmy Dale who was responsible for the suggestion that the piece
be turned into a song.[6] Carmichael's original lyric was made public in the
1970s, and it contains the words "In my heart you will remain" and "Stardust melody" which, as we all know, were retained (with a slight change of
the first phrase to "In my heart it will remain"). The new official version
came about when Mills, according to Carmichael, "threw out my lyrics, put
Mitchell Parish to work on it, and one afternoon he knocked out the now
familiar words."

Parish, a staff writer for the Mills office, not only went on to write "Stars
Fell on Alabama" but was particularly adept at tackling strong melodies
originally created as instrumentals. "Moonlight Serenade" (composed by
Glenn Miller), "Stairway to the Stars" (Matty Malneck and Frank Sig-
norelli), "The Lamp Is Low" (Ravel, adapted by Larry Clinton) and "Don't
Be That Way" (Edgar Sampson) all have his lyrics, as well as "Sophisticated Lady"—perhaps Parish's masterpiece. It is run very close, however,
by his contribution to "Stardust," a contribution crucial to the song's long-
term success. One thing that the new vogue for sentimental sounds allowed
was an increased emphasis on the words used by a vocalist, with the result
that the standard of literacy in popular music has perhaps never been higher
than in the 1930s. The choice of vocabulary such as "reverie" and "paradise" has seldom seemed less precious than in the chorus of "Stardust,"
while the rhyming of "inspiration" and "consolation" is unflamboyant
enough to put most other writers to shame. It's true that the opening couplet of the verse

And now the purple dusk of twilight time
Steals across the meadows of my heart

is so riveting that the next two lines are almost bound to be an anticlimax,
and Parish seems to have deliberately ensured that they are. So, although it
is tempting to describe his work as a poem in its own right, it reads rather
unevenly on the printed page. What it is, however, is a brilliant example of
a lyric designed to fit a particular melody so that each is enhanced by the
other.

It is also an early instance of a lyric *about* a melody, attempts at which
are usually doomed to failure unless of a lighthearted nature such as "Sam's
Song" or "Opus One." But, as far as Parish's definition of the "song that
will not die" is concerned, performers seem to find each word an inspira-

tion. The first vocalist on record to accept this inspiration, in compensation for the challenge of a very demanding melodic line, was, of course, Bing Crosby. His classic recording of July 1931 does not entirely triumph over the tune for, though there is naturally no suggestion of inaccuracy, a certain strain is evident from time to time. However, the sincerity of Crosby's whole approach is emphasized by beautifully relaxed phrasing and breath control and the subtle inflection of individual syllables. The equally relaxed tempo, identical to the Isham Jones version, is occasionally slowed further to accommodate the vocal phrasing, and whoever conducted the accompaniment did a marvelous job of following Crosby *colla voce* without making it too obvious. (No one is credited as arranger or conductor for this session, and one would presume that Victor Young was involved—his introduction from the Jones record is used again—except for the fact that Young is credited on both earlier and later Crosby sessions.) Though not quite the first hit under his own name, this was a significant record in Crosby's career and, in an early example of media extravagance, copies were distributed free to promote his first solo radio appearances a mere two weeks later.

This recording draws attention to the final modification of Carmichael's original conception, as recommended by the published version. In the first notes of the verse, all the early recordings begin with the symmetrical phrase re-mi-do-re, which Crosby manages to sing fairly convincingly, clearly following his ear rather than the song-copy (he may have done this in recollection of a performance or a demonstration by Carmichael, as it seems reasonable to assume that the composer himself, now based in New York, would have made it his business to attend the tune's first vocal waxing). In subsequent versions, however, the starting note is changed to do (i.e., do-mi-do-re), doubtless on the assumption that this would be easier for untrained singers to emulate.

Later in 1931 one of Crosby's chief influences, Louis Armstrong, did a classic recording which, in order to leave room for vocal and instrumental improvisation, employs only the chorus (whether by coincidence or not, the verse is omitted from nearly all subsequent versions until it makes a big comeback in the 1950s). What is most notable about Armstrong's interpretation, though, is how he takes advantage of the public's growing familiarity with the song, displaying his ear for passing harmonies and often rendering the melody unrecognizable, especially when the famous opening phrase of the chorus is reduced to a single repeated note.

As with "Body and Soul," which Armstrong had recorded a year earlier, it was the inherent qualities of the song rather than his interpretation which ensured that it became a "standard." One of the features of the "Stardust" story is the speed with which it established itself or, to put it another way, the frequency with which it was "revived." In the spring of 1936, it was granted the honor of being recorded in two different versions on the same 78 r.p.m. single, almost certainly the only tune to receive this treatment until the 1970s fashion for coupling a vocal and an instrumental version of one number.[7] In this case, the two artists featured were the two top bandleaders spearheading the brand-new swing music boom, Benny Goodman (with a new instrumental score by Fletcher Henderson) and Tommy Dorsey, whose mellifluous trombone statement is followed by a pleasant, Mildred Bailey–inspired simplification of the melody by his vocalist Edythe Wright. Dorsey also adopted a slower tempo of 102 bpm, making a 32-bar chorus last 76 seconds.

It is remarkable that many of those who made a successful waxing of "Stardust" took a second or third bite of the cherry in the record studios. Apart from Carmichael himself, of course, Bing Crosby rerecorded the song as early as 1939, as did Louis Armstrong in 1950. A mere four-and-a-half years after his first version, Tommy Dorsey in November 1940 cut a new, considerably slower arrangement (70 bpm., requiring 110 seconds for one chorus) featuring Frank Sinatra and the Pied Pipers. This also enjoyed considerable sales, being coupled with Dorsey's performance of "Swanee River." And then, only seven months after it was first issued, this Dorsey/Sinatra recording was recoupled with his 1936 version.

Several instrumental interpretations earned impressive royalties in the intervening period. One specifically mentioned by Carmichael came in 1938, coupled with the first record to be titled "In the Mood," by the black bandleader Edgar Hayes. It consisted of a dreamy, bell-like solo by pianist Hayes with minimal accompaniment that sounds as if it could have influenced Erroll Garner, at a tempo nearly as slow as the subsequent Sinatra version (76 bpm). It may have served as a model for the following year's more band-oriented version led by pianist Eddy Duchin, while a similar piano solo is just one of the elements in a sumptuous, and commercially successful, 12-inch single by Andre Kostelanetz.

But the best-received instrumental by far was that of Artie Shaw in 1940, which is reported to have eventually sold more than two million copies. One of its highspots is the 8 bars by trombonist Jack Jenney, which are a deliberate reminiscence of his own band's recording of the previous year, in which he had created an entirely new improvised melody from the harmonic sequence of "Stardust." Widely admired by fellow musicians, this should perhaps be classed with the jazz versions of the tune, although Jenney's new melody (which seems to be the basis of the later pop-song

"Learnin' the Blues") remains within the wistful mood of the original piece.

Other notable jazz arrangements often depart further from the emotional climate of the song, such as Benny Goodman's second and very different version, recorded in 1939 with his sextet including Lionel Hampton and Charlie Christian. A famous public concert originally recorded for radio transmission on station KFWB, then issued on an early long-play album, also featured Hampton at a "Just Jazz" event in 1947. More than the prewar versions, this extended session comes closer to what is now thought of—at least in mainstream circles—as a normal tempo for a jazz ballad. Beginning at 64 bpm, the first chorus (featuring Willie Smith) lasts exactly 120 seconds, after which the piece slowly picks up speed, only to ease off slightly as Hampton's climactic solo goes into double-, then quadruple-tempo.

The English writer Charles Fox used to say that "Because 'Stardust's melodic identity is stronger than its melodic shape and because the harmonies and structure are unusual, few jazz musicians have improvised on it successfully."[8] The quotation referred to Coleman Hawkins's first reading (with Django Reinhardt in 1935), which adheres very closely to the song, but one of the present author's favorites is Hawkins's 1945 disc—his third account in ten years—which reintroduces Carmichael's verse as a trumpet solo by Howard McGhee. There are several other recorded performances which seem to disprove Fox's contention, and it is no coincidence that tenorman Chu Berry, in 1938 the leading contender for the expatriate Hawkins's crown, cut a fine "Stardust" at the same session as his pre-Hawkins version of "Body and Soul."

It is also striking that "Stardust" had quickly become a jam-session standard, as evidenced by the live recordings of Charlie Christian in Minneapolis (1939), Don Byas at Minton's and Dizzy Gillespie at Monroe's (both 1941). It remained a perennial in the repertoires of Ben Webster (from Ellington at Fargo onwards) and Sonny Stitt; it received notable recordings from Clifford Brown and Paul Desmond (with both Brubeck and Mulligan); and there are even versions by Parker and Coltrane. (Perhaps this is the place to mention the curiosity of a live recording from 1981 by trumpeter Freddie Hubbard, which uses the verse of "Stardust" played unaccompanied as his introduction to a performance of, and billed as, "Body And Soul.")

By the time in the mid-1950s that booming record sales were becoming accepted as a more appropriate indicator of a song's success, it was established that "Stardust" had sold more sheet-music units than any other popular song. But, if an observer had predicted its partial eclipse due to

changing tastes, he could not have been more wrong. According to one account, Carmichael told Nat King Cole, "The prettiest vocal version I ever
heard of my song 'Stardust' was by you"[9]—though it is not inconceivable
that he said the same thing to other performers at other times. Certainly
Cole's performance on the 1956 album *Love Is the Thing*, with its di-
aphanous string writing by Gordon Jenkins, is a placid and utterly straightforward reading. At 84 bpm, the album version consists simply of one verse
and one chorus although, for the single release, the verse was in fact edited
out. It played, however, an important role in the success of a 1957 single by
the rhythm-and-blues vocal group, Billy Ward and the Dominoes, where
the verse was taken out-of-tempo with the lead singer (apparently Ward
himself, at this stage of the group's career) using toned-down gospel in-
flections, before introducing the gentle rock-and-roll beat of the chorus.
The apotheosis of the song's verse was achieved in 1962 when Frank Sinatra returned to the subject in the album *Sinatra And Strings*. Almost out-of-
tempo but equating no more than 52 bpm, and with arranger Don Costa
providing a deceptively long introduction and coda to deter anticipation of
the chorus, Sinatra eclipses his earlier recording and pours all the song's
emotion into a single reading of the verse.

Strangely enough, this idea was not without a bizarre, instrumental-only
precedent set by one Eddie Dexter (very likely a pseudonym for either Paul
Weston or, possibly, Lou Busch). In 1955, he recorded a "novelty" arrangement—actually titled "The Verse Of 'Stardust'"—taken at a "businessman's bounce" and with instrumentation including mandolin, tack piano,
and both soprano and bass saxophones. The net result is rather like Spike
Jones without the sound effects, and the fact of playing four verses in quick
succession, each time in a different key, does banish any latent dependency
on the unheard chorus. There may well be other such oddities in the "Stardust" file, since it is surely impossible to hear all the recorded versions,
now comfortably into four figures—a recent catalog lists some 90 currently
available interpretations by jazz musicians alone, recorded between 1931
and 1998.

This volume of coverage is not a sign of quality, only of popularity,
which has been confirmed yet again by the BBC's 1999 poll finding that
"Stardust" was the second most beloved popular song of the century (just
behind Paul McCartney's "Yesterday," since you ask). But there can be few
other pieces which it is possible to listen to again and again in different versions—often consecutively, as this writer has done—and still find oneself
whistling in the street with redoubled appreciation.

NOTES

1. Hoagy Carmichael, *The "Stardust" Road* (New York and Toronto: Rinehart, 1946); Carmichael, with Stephen Longstreet, *Sometimes I Wonder* (New York: Farrar, Strauss and Giroux, [1965]).
2. Richand M. Sudhalter and Philip R. Evans, *Bix: Man and Legend* (New Rochelle, New York: Arlington House, 1974).
3. Scheidt, Duncan, *The Jazz State of Indiana* (Pittsboro, Indiana: Schiedt, c1977).
4. Bud Freeman more than once made the claim that Carmichael attempted to record "Stardust" for Victor in 1930, with one of his studio groups containing both Beiderbecke and Freeman: "I remember we recorded 'Stardust' at the wrong tempo—it was too fast—and everybody in the band said 'Oh, get rid of that stupid tune.' And six months later [sic] Isham Jones recorded it, as a ballad, and of course it became a world classic" (from an unpublished interview by Peter Vacher, July 1984).
5. Irving Mills first published the piece in early 1929 in a solo piano version, and there is reason to believe that the orchestral stock also dates from the period before the lyrics were added. Dale's arrangement has been recorded recently, possibly for the first time (certainly, the first time in its entirety), by a Canadian band, The Valentino Orchestra, whose musical director is the Ellington and Mingus specialist, Andrew Homzy.
6. See for instance David Ewen, *All the Years of American Popular Music* (Englewood Cliffs, New Jersey: Prentice-Hall, c1977). Of course, it might have required the word of Dale to convince Irving Mills of the need to publish "Stardust" as a song though, given Mills's aptitude for exploiting suitable Ellington works in this way, that seems doubtful too.
7. In the 1950s somebody had the bright idea of commissioning 12 arrangements of "Lullaby of Birdland" to appear on the same album.
8. Max Harrison, Charles Fox, and EricThacker, *The Essential Jazz Records, vol.1: Ragtime to Swing* (London: Mansell, 1984)
9. Dempsey Travis, *An Autobiography of Black Jazz* (Chicago: Urban Research Institute, 1983).

SELECTIVE DISCOGRAPHY

Hoagy Carmichael. 10/27. Gennett 6311

Chocolate Dandies. 10/28. Okeh 8668

Mills' Merry Makers. 11/28. Cameo 9012

Isham Jones. 5/30. Brunswick 4886

Bing Crosby. 8/31. Brunswick 6169

Louis Armstrong. 11/31. Okeh 41530

Coleman Hawkins. 3/35. La Voix de son Maitre K-7527

Chu Berry. 11/38. Commodore 1502

Benny Goodman. 10/39. Columbia DJ-26134

Jack Jenney. 10/39. Vocalion 5304

Tommy Dorsey (featuring Frank Sinatra). 11/40. Victor 27233

Duke Ellington (featuring Ben Webster). 11/40. Palm 30–11 (LP)

Coleman Hawkins. 2/45. Capitol 15854

Lionel Hampton. 8/47. Decca DL7013 (LP)

Sonny Stitt (as "Lord Nelson"). 6/48. Sensation 5

Eddie Dexter (titled "The Verse of 'Stardust'"), ?/55. Capitol 3121

Nat King Cole. 12/56. Capitol F80448 (single), W824 (LP)

Frank Sinatra. 11/61. Reprise 20059 (single), R1004 (LP)

Freddie Hubbard (titled "Body And Soul"). 11/81. Fantasy F-9615 (LP)

Valentino Orchestra (1929 stock arrangement). 7–8/97. Just A Memory JAM9137 (CD)

STRUCTURE IN JAZZ IMPROVISATION: A FORMULAIC ANALYSIS OF THE IMPROVISATIONS OF BILL EVANS

Barry Kenny

INTRODUCTION

The starting point in this investigation into the musical language of Bill Evans was the realization that, despite recent advances in music psychology and jazz analytic methodology, our present understanding of the processes involved in improvisation is still at best unclear. While a thorough understanding of these processes may appear naïve and perhaps ultimately elusive, if music analysis is to proceed beyond the complexities particular to individual improvisations, it must at least partially address the cognitive mechanisms which generate spontaneous composition over a wide variety of continuous forms. The identification of thematic characteristics applicable to a large bodies of improvised works may also greatly improve our present understanding of the representative improvising styles and key repertoire of historically important jazz musicians.

In this study, two analytic methodologies were employed to uncover recurring formulaic language in the improvisations of Bill Evans. The analyses involved an examination of nine improvised solos to identify the frequency of occurrence of melodic formulas, thereby establishing a hierarchy of Evans's most commonly used formulas. Individual formulas were additionally examined in relation to chord function and to one another to ascertain whether there exists an interconnected formulaic network of analogous themes within Evans's internal grammar. Results show a close relationship between the melodic contours of Evans's preferred formulas and chord function where, as a result of the analyses, it was possible to determine which chord functions were more likely to generate characteristic melodic responses over any given situation. Findings point to a high degree of analogous similarity between the formulas themselves and suggest a hierarchically organized formulaic network of themes. The associative application of this network to spontaneously created material demonstrates the extent to which Evans was successful in managing, adapting, and reworking material that had been assimilated into his technical and artistic resources as an improviser.

Improvisation and Cognition

Recent research in music psychology suggests that improvisers employ fragmentary and continuous cognitive structures, developed and added to in the course of an improvisation—a very different situation from the cohesive hierarchical structures employed by performers of notated music (Elliot 1995). In a computer program simulating the cognitive processes employed by jazz musicians, P. N. Johnson-Laird (1991) found that jazz structure (prearranged chord sequences, song form, and jazz harmony) required more computational processing power than the melodic responses generated by it. From this Johnson-Laird hypothesizes a hierarchy of cognitive processes, where higher level functions (i.e., harmony), which require greater processing power, are worked out prior to a performance. Lower level structures (melody) require less cognitive processing power and can therefore occur in the heat of the improvisational moment (Johnson-Laird 1991).

Jeff Pressing similarly concludes that skilled improvisers possess "a vast array of finely tuned and tunable motor responses which can be handled automatically (without conscious attention)" (Pressing 1991, 139). With considerable practice it becomes possible to "completely dispense with the conscious monitoring of motor programs, so that the hands appear to have a life of their own, driven by the musical constraints of the situation" (Pressing 1991, 139). The arrival at this heightened state of awareness, where one is able to unconsciously monitor the mechanics of improvisation is, Sudnow (1978) and Hargreaves (1991) would suggest, a distinguishing characteristic of experienced improvisers.

Eric Clarke's three-stage cognitive model of improvisation (Clarke 1991) further cultivates this notion of a preplanned and spontaneous duality. Clarke outlines a hierarchy of thought processes, employed proportionately in accordance with the level of structure demanded. These categories may be summarized loosely as follows:

a. repertoire selection—formulaic improvising characteristic of bebop
b. hierarchical—song form generated improvising structures characteristic of both bebop and hard bop
c. motivic—chain associative improvising characteristic of modal and free jazz.

Clarke argues that all three are generally present in most jazz improvisations but are employed in varying amounts according to the stylistic conventions of the situation and/or the taste or background of the improviser.

Studies by Owens (1974), Kernfeld (1981), and Smith (1983) have uncovered formulaic networks in the work of several seminal jazz musicians. These internalized cognitive resources, bearing many similarities to the syntax and grammar of spoken language, provide reference and impetus for the construction of spontaneously created melodies. When used across many improvisations, these internalized themes stylistically unify and characterize the thematic oeuvre of individual musicians. For a pianist as influential as Evans, who significantly spanned the breach between bop chord-generated improvising and modal/associative improvising (pioneering many of the techniques in this latter category), it is interesting that only one study to date (Smith 1983) has applied formulaic analysis to a study of Evans's improvisations.

Purpose of the Study

The purpose of this study, therefore, is to examine Evans's intrinsic musical language—defined as a grammar of motifs which are preconceived, internalized, and then applied with regard to both formal structure and to one another. Specifically, the task is to determine the extent to which this internalized formulaic language assists Evans in the creation of newly improvised melodies, thereby providing a unifying melodic thread to be found throughout his entire work.

In order to achieve this purpose, Evans's formulas will be examined in relation to formal structure—the song forms and harmonic progressions of tonal jazz that facilitate and generate the improvising process—by means of two distinct analytic methodologies. Using the duration of individual chord changes as the basic unit of melodic segmentation, *structural analysis* will examine the intervallic relationship between improvised melody and background harmony (i.e., chord changes), thereby establishing a structural relationship between note choice and chord function. *Intervallic analysis* will examine the same melodic segments but independently of chord function. From the data uncovered in both analyses, a list of Evans's most commonly used formulas will be identified and discussed. Of particular interest will be the relationship between the melodic contours of these formulas and the structural tones of the underlying harmony, and the way in which Evans is able to fashion and rework his formulas around these fixed structural markers to create fluid and interesting improvised melodies.

These purposes are reflected in the structure of this paper. Part one describes the procedure for each of the two analytic methodologies represented in this study. Part two discusses the results obtained from the two methodologies. Part three draws conclusions from the data, illustrating the way in which Evans was able to successfully synthesize and manage his internalized resources so as to satisfy the structural requirements of the situation and his own artistic requirements for individualized self-expression.

METHODOLOGY

Sample size and selection

To ensure sample comprehensiveness and stylistic consistency, sound recordings were chosen at regular intervals spanning Evans's recording career from 1959 to 1977. Further selection criteria were determined by the need to sample Evans's playing in a variety of settings (i.e., solo versus group, differing group members), of venues (i.e., recording studios, live concerts), and within a variety of compositional forms, tempi, and keys. This diversity of improvising stimuli and context precluded any bias that might have arisen out of a concentration of any of these parameters. Furthermore, the nine transcriptions were selected for their high proportion of improvised (i.e., nonhead or arranged) choruses (Table 1).

At this point, a necessary distinction must be made between Evans's *arranged* and *improvised* styles. The former bears many similarities to what Barry Kernfeld terms melodic "paraphrase" (Kernfeld 1981, 17), where most of the creative input is derived from textural and harmonic permutations of the original "head" melody, which largely remains intact. Evans's contributions to the harmonic and textural language of modern jazz piano playing are amply documented in other sources and an adequate treatment of these issues lies outside the scope of this study. Like many bebop and postbop pianists, Evans's *improvised* playing is generally characterized by a single-line right-hand texture accompanied by rootless left-hand cluster voicings. The right-hand improvised melody, bearing little similarity to the original "head" melody, is mostly generated by the harmonies or "changes" of the song. This improvisational method can be best understood by Kernfeld's definition of "chorus phrase" improvising (Kernfeld 1981, 17).

Analyses: Segmentation

For the purposes of formulaic analysis, the melodic lines for all nine transcriptions were initially segmented into short meaningful melodic

Recording Date	Album	Song Title	Composer	Key	Tempo	Setting	Excpt. (Bar nos.)
28/12/59	Portrait In Jazz	Autumn Leaves (outake-unreleased mono version)	Mercer	E Minor	4/4 Minim = 92	Recording Studio, 1st Trio: La Faro, Motian	105-200
29/5/62	Moonbeams	Very Early	Evans	C Maj.	¾ Crotchet = 116	Recording Studio, Trio: Israels, Motian	51-99
18/12/63	Trio 64	For Heaven's Sake	Meyer/ Betton/ Edward	F Maj.	4/4 Minim = 69	Recording Studio, Trio: Peacock, Motian	64-140
21/2/66	Bill Evans At Town Hall Vol. 1	I Should Care	Cahn/ Stordahl/ Weston	C Maj.	4/4 Crotchet = 168	Live Concert, Trio: Israels, Wise	33-127
10/68	Bill Evans: Alone	A Time For Love	Webster/ Mandel	D Maj.	4/4 Crotchet = 84	Recording Studio, Solo.	1-164
19/6/70	Montreux II	How My Heart Sings	Zindars	C Maj.	¾ Dotted Minim = 72	Live Concert, 2nd Trio: Gomez, Morrel	45-129
7-10 /11/74	Intuition	Invitation	Webster/ Kaper	C Minor	4/4 Crotchet = 152	Recording Studio, Duo: Gomez	95-202
5/12/76	Paris concert (posthumous release)	Turn Out The Stars	Evans	A Minor	4/4 Minim = 76	Live Concert, Trio: Gomez, Zigmund	37-116
13/5/77	I Will Say Goodbye	I Will Say Goodbye	Evans	Eb Major	4/4 Minim = 60	Recording Studio: Gomez, Zigmund	1-92

Table 1: The nine transcriptions

fragments—the starting and ending point for each fragment generally coinciding with the duration of a single chord change (Figure 1).

Exceptions to this segmentation rule included patterns which exceeded eight notes, which were divided into two (Figure 2), and syncopated patterns which semantically reached their logical harmonic resolution over the bar line, which were extended (Figure 3).

Structural Analysis

In accordance with this study's use of two distinct forms of melodic analysis, two different codification procedures were necessary to express a

Figure 1: Turn Out the Stars, mm. 12–15

Figure 2: Turn Out the Stars, mm. 55–56

Figure 3: How My Heart Sings, mm. 59–60

pattern's relationship to either harmonic structure (structural) or generalized contour (intervallic). In *structural analysis*, each note within the segmented fragments received a designated number from 0 to 11 *depending upon its intervallic distance from the root note of the chord it is associated with.*

If a melody note E, for example, was played over a C major 7th, it would be coded as 4—a major 3rd or 4 semitones from C. Structural patterns were ultimately expressed as strings of codified numbers, each separated by a decimal point (Figure 4).

Figure 4: A codified structural pattern (How My Heart Sings, m. 1)

All 878 structural patterns (from the nine transcriptions), now coded in numerical form, were entered into spreadsheets for the purposes of sorting and aggregation. Within this master list, like patterns (patterns with similar numeric codings) were brought together by virtue of the spreadsheet's numerical sorting capabilities (Table 2).

Table 2 further demonstrates the classification labeling scheme for the 878 patterns. In this scheme, all patterns that occurred more than once and shared the same first three numbers were given the same group classification. All sorted patterns from the total structural patterns were designated arbitrary classification groups according to the concordance of their first three notes. As shown in Table 2, patterns sharing the same first three digits 4.1.0 were assigned the grouping s4B— "s" is the structural pattern designator; "4" represents all the patterns commencing with 4 (i.e., a major 3rd from the root of the prevailing chord), and "B" arbitrarily distinguishes this pattern (4.*1.0*) from another sampled group such as, for example, 4C (4.*11.9*). The *Extension* column, simply the fourth note of each pattern, enabled a further subclassification of the three-note structural groups.

The *Direction* column, the upward (u) or downward (d) movement between adjacent tones (Figure 5), was included to preserve the original movement of a pattern across its original two-octave span, thereby avoiding the transposition limitations inherent in other single-octave analyses. It was additionally thought that this information could be analyzed in subsequent studies to ascertain Evans's generalized approach to melodic contour, thereby determining whether these generalized contours bear any significant correlation with chord function or with specific formulas themselves.

Sampled patterns consisting of fewer than three notes were deemed to be non-patterns (N/P), whereas those which only occurred once, and therefore couldn't be grouped together with any other like patterns, were labeled Non-Recurring Patterns (NRP).

Intervallic Analysis

Intervallic analysis—concerned with similarity of melodic movement irrespective of chord function—followed a different codification procedure. The intervallic codification principle identified the first note of each segmented pattern (the same fragments as used in *structural analysis*) as the

Song	Bar	Chord Type	Structural (Sorted by)	Direction	Group	Extension
HMHS	34	7th	**4.1.0.10.8**	dddd	4B	10
VE	47	7th	**4.1.0.10.9.7.5.4**	dddddd	4B	10
TOTS	67	7th	**4.1.0.11**	ddd	4B	11
AL	7	7th	**4.1.0.11**	ddd	4B	11
ISC	45	7th	**4.1.0.11**	ddd	4B	11
INV	86	7th	**4.1.0.11**	ddd	4B	11
TOTS	7	7th	**4.1.0.11.10**	dddd	4B	11
ATFL	72	7th	**4.1.0.11.10.8.7**	dddddd	4B	11
ATFL	86	7th	**4.1.0.7**	udd	4B	7
IWSG	57	7th	**4.1.0.8.5.4.7**	udddu	4B	8
ATFL	99	Maj7	**4.11.9.7**	ddd	4C	7
IWSG	46	Maj7	**4.11.9.7.5**	dddd	4C	7
INV	72	7th	**4.2.0**	dd	4D	
TOTS	44	Maj7	**4.2.0**	ud	4D	

Table 2: Structural analysis: sorting principles

Figure 5: Direction

fundamental (i.e., nonchordal, surrogate "root" note) for the rest of the notes or intervals that followed in the string. The first note of the pattern was always codified as 0, with the rest following as semitonal expressions of this fundamental note.

A string of four notes played over a C Major 7th chord—E, G, B, D— would be coded as 0.3.7.10. In contrast to *structural analysis*, the prevailing C Major 7th chord in *intervallic analysis* is deemed irrelevant—the fundamental note is E (by default—represented as 0), G is 3 semitones away (hence 3), B is 7 semitones away (hence 7).

The first four bars of Evans's improvisation on "Autumn Leaves" (Figure 6) illustrates the difference between structural (above stave) and intervallic (below stave) encoding principles.

Figure 6: Structural analysis versus intervallic analysis: codified procedure (Autumn Leaves, mm. 1–4)

Once decoded, all 878 intervallic patterns were similarly entered into a comprehensive spreadsheet for the purposes of aggregation and classification. Intervallic groups were labeled in accordance with their first *four* numerals, with a group number determined by the *second* number in each pattern (i.e., the first is always 0). Table 3 represents a section from the comprehensively sorted 878 groups. Here all patterns commencing with 0.1.4 were assigned the intervallic grouping of i1F—"i" is the intervallic pattern designator; "1" represents all the numbers beginning with 0.1 (i.e., a semitone) and "F" arbitrarily distinguishes this pattern (0.1.*4*) from another intervallic group F such as i1G (0.1.*5*).

Song	Bar	Chord Type	Intervallic (Sorted By)	Direction	Group	Extension
IWSG	51	7th	0.1.4.7.10.0.1.0.10	uuuuuudd	1F	7
VE	46	Maj7	0.1.4.7.5.4.2	uuuddd	1F	7
TOTS	4	Maj7	0.1.4.7.8.11.10.8	uuuuudd	1F	7
TOTS	13	Half Dim	0.1.4.8	uuu	1F	8
ATFL	68	7th	0.1.4.8.0.3	uuuuu	1F	8
TOTS	32	Min7	0.1.4.8.11.0	uuuud	1F	8
ISC	25	Maj7	0.1.4.8.11.10.9.5	uuuuddd	1F	8
TOTS	8	7th	0.1.4.8.11.9	uuuud	1F	8
TOTS	11	Min7	0.1.5.0	uuu	1G	0
INV	44	min7	0.1.5.8	udu	1G	8

Table 3: Intervallic analysis: grouping principles

RESULTS

Structural Analysis

The first feature apparent in the data was Evans's consistent preference for "functional" over "nonfunctional" tones (Figure 7). For the purposes of discussion, I will define "functional" as tones that function in a harmonic sense and which are either abstracted from the underlying triadic harmony (chord changes) or from the diatonic scales associated with the chord function.

Of the 878 patterns sampled, those which commenced on structural tones of the triadic major or minor chords (i.e., root (0) = 14%, maj/min 3^{rds} (3/4) = 11%/11%, 5th (7) = 16%) when combined, accounted for a staggering 451 of the total 878 patterns, or 52%. Other high scoring patterns were those which commenced on the major 2nd (2) = 11%, and the perfect 4th (5) = 9%.

Evans, in other words, demonstrates a clear preference for tones associated with the diatonic scale(s) over nondiatonic tones for commencing his formulas. This hierarchy of note choice emphasizes in the *Preferred First Group* the root (tonic) and the dominant (5th) (the pivotal notes of Western tonality); in the *Preferred Second Group* the 3rds and major 2nd; and in the *Preferred Third Group* the major 6th and the two 7ths. More interesting, however, is Evans's reluctance to use the more dissonant tones for commencing his patterns—the minor 2nd (20/878), the augmented 4th (58/878) and minor 6th all score poorly.

Individual Structural Patterns

Once all formulas were sorted and appropriately classified, it was possible to establish a hierarchy (based on rate of recurrence) of the individual patterns themselves. An examination of Table 4, the fourteen highest scoring structural patterns, reveals that all of pattern s4B's 23 appearances occur over dominant 7th chords (Table 4). This strong relationship between individual patterns and chord function is mirrored in the results for other patterns: 16/17 (94%) of pattern s3N's appearances occur over minor 7th chords; 10/12 (83%) of pattern s70's appearances occur over major 7th chords.

Chord Function and Melodic Contour

Notations of the top 14 structural patterns reveal a close relationship between melodic contour and the functional properties of the underlying chord

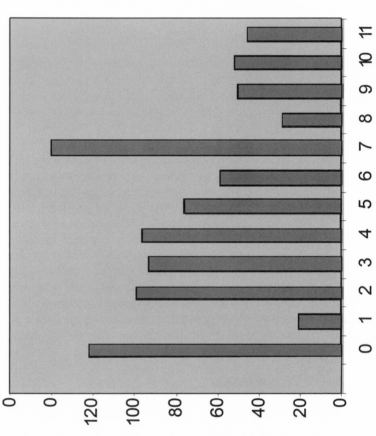

Category	No.	% Total
0	122	14%
1	20	2%
2	99	11%
3	93	11%
4	96	11%
5	76	9%
6	58	7%
7	140	16%
8	28	3%
9	50	6%
10	51	6%
11	45	5%
Total	878	

Figure 7: Distribution of total structural patterns by generic class

Pattern	N.	Maj. 7th	Min 7th	Dom 7th	Half Dim
s4B	23			23	
s4K	19	6		13	
s3N	17		16	1	
s5J	15	11		1	3
s0A	13		1	8	4
s0F	13		5	8	
s7U	13	9		4	
s0G	12	3	7	2	
s7O	12	10		2	
s11A	11	5	4	2	
s2E	10		9	1	
s2M	10		10		
s0B	9			7	2
s3H	9		4	3	2

Table 4: Top 14 Structural patterns: functional distribution

structures (i.e., of chord function). By virtue of its melodic contour, pattern s4B demonstrates its suitability for dominant 7th chords (23/23 occurrences), possessing a major 3rd (structural), minor 2nd (extension—♭9th), a root (structural), and a minor 7th (extension— ♭7th). See Music excerpt 1: s4B.

The third highest scoring pattern, s3N, on the other hand articulates the structural properties of minor 7th chords (16/17 occurrences). Reference is made to the minor 7th's ♭3rd, 5th and 7th and 9th extensions. See Music excerpt 2: s3N.

Pattern s0B's ♭2nd, ♭3rd and major 3rd—mirroring the semitone-tone-semitone proportions of the octatonic scale (a scale commonly used by improvisers over dominant 7ths)—renders it a suitable candidate for dominant 7th chords (7/9 occurrences). See Music excerpt 3: s0B.

Another pattern achieving a high proportional relationship with minor 7th chords (10/10 occurrences) was s2M. Here the structural tones associated with minor 7th chords (♭3, 5, ♭7) are embellished by a lower neighbor tone (2). See Music excerpt 4: s2M.

Generic Groups

As mentioned earlier, it appeared constructive to assess the impact of individual pattern repetition within a more defined framework. *Generic Group*

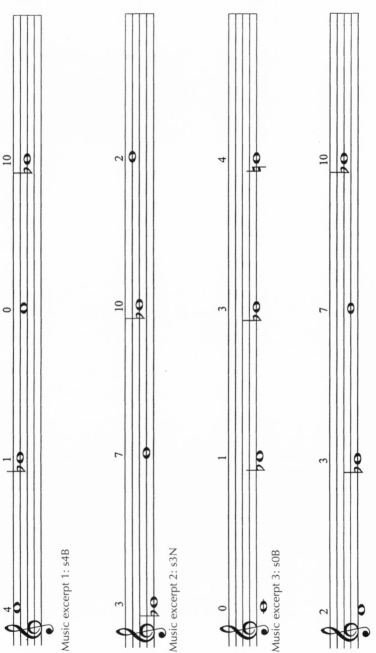

Music excerpt 1: s4B

Music excerpt 2: s3N

Music excerpt 3: s0B

Music excerpt 4: s2M

refers to the aggregation of individual patterns into groups defined by their commencing tones. Pattern s2A, for example, belongs to Generic Group 2—all patterns commencing with the number 2 (major 2nd). Table 5 places all the classified structural patterns within this broader generic context, a method of comparison that produced some interesting results.

Pattern s4B in this context accounts for 25% of all patterns commencing with 4 (major 3rd). Furthermore, patterns s4B and s4K when added together account for 46% (i.e., 25% + 21%) of the total Group 4 patterns. Even more significant is that each of these patterns, within Generic Group 4, individually outscore the nonrecurring patterns column (10%). This result is surprising in that one would expect such a broad based category as NRP, essentially amounting to a sundry or default column, to definitely score higher than any individual pattern.

Nonrecurring Patterns: Distribution

Another interesting trend is the inverse relationship between nonrecurring patterns and patterns commencing on diatonic structural tones. In the case of the triadic structural tones (i.e. root, 3rds, etc.), nonrecurring pattern incidence was low (see Table 6).

Patterns which commenced with nondiatonic tones, on the other hand, contained a much higher representation of nonrecurring patterns (see Table 7).

Intervallic Analysis

From the outset it was always expected that stepwise patterns would easily outscore patterns with wider or "gapped" intervals due to the astructural analytic methods employed by *intervallic analysis*. This prediction generally held true with results for smaller intervallic ranges (i.e., 0.1 to 0.3 or 0.9 to 0.11) scoring higher than wider intervals (i.e., 0.6). Aside from a few anomalies (data for categories 0 and 0.2) results overall collapsed inward, with the pattern representing the greatest distance (augmented 4th) between its first two notes, pattern 0.6, accounting for only 4 of the entire 878 patterns (Figure 8).

Individual Intervallic Patterns

Because intervallic groups reflect melodic contour independently of structure, it was also expected that there would not necessarily be a strong

Root

Root	No.	%
OA	13	12
OB	9	8
OC	2	2
OD	2	2
OE	4	4
OF	13	12
OG	12	11
OH	2	2
OI	2	2
OJ	2	2
OK	2	2
OL	2	2
OM	2	2
ON	3	3
OP	2	2
OQ	2	2
OR	2	2
NRP	28	26
Total	106	100

Min 2nd

Min 2nd	No.	%
1A	3	17
1B	2	11
1C	3	17
NRP	10	56
Total	18	100

Maj 2nd

Maj 2nd	No.	%
2A	2	2
2B	6	7
2C	2	2
2D	6	7
2E	10	11
2F	5	5
2G	6	7
2H	2	2
2I	3	3
2J	3	3
2K	2	2
2L	10	11
2M	2	2
2N	2	2
2O	4	4
2P	4	4
2Q	2	2
2R		
NRP	17	19
Total	91	100

Min 3rd

Min 3rd	No.	%
3A	4	5
3B	2	2
3C	2	2
3D	4	5
3E	3	3
3F	2	2
3G	7	8
3H	9	10
3I	5	6
3J	2	2
3K	4	5
3L	3	3
3M	2	2
3N	17	20
3O	2	2
NRP	18	21
Total	86	100

Maj 3rd

Maj 3rd	No.	%
4A	3	3
4B	23	25
4C	2	2
4D	4	4
4E	2	2
4F	2	2
4G	4	4
4H	2	2
4I	3	3
4J	3	3
4K	19	21
4L	6	7
4M	3	3
4N	6	7
NRP	9	10
Total	91	100

4th

4th	No.	%
5A	2	3
5B	8	12
5C	4	6
5D	4	6
5E	8	12
5F	4	6
5G	3	4
5H	2	3
5I	2	3
5J	15	22
5K	4	6
NRP	13	19
Total	69	100

Table 5: Generic Groups: proportional representaton of each pattern (continued below)

Maj 7th	No.	%
11A	9	20
11B	2	4
11C	5	11
11D	2	4
11E	2	4
11F	2	4
11G	3	7
11H	3	7
11I	8	18
NRP	9	20
Total	45	100

Min 7th	No.	%
10A	2	5
10B	2	5
10C	2	5
10D	6	14
10E	7	17
10F	2	5
10G	4	10
10H	3	7
NRP	14	33
Total	42	100

Maj 6th	No.	%
9A	2	4
9B	2	4
9C	2	4
9D	2	4
9E	2	4
9F	7	16
9G	2	4
9H	6	13
NRP	20	44
Total	45	100

Min 6th	No.	%
8A	2	9
8B	3	13
8C	2	9
8D	2	9
NRP	14	61
Total	23	100

5th	No.	%
7A	2	2
7B	2	2
7C	2	2
7D	2	2
7E	7	5
7F	2	2
7G	5	4
7H	2	2
7I	4	3
7J	2	2
7K	5	4
7L	8	6
7M	7	5
7N	12	9
7O	4	3
7P	3	2
7Q	2	2
7R	7	5
7S	13	10
7T	2	2
7U	5	4
7V	5	4
7W	5	4
7X	4	3
7Y	2	2
7Z		
7AA		
NRP	17	13
Total	133	100

Aug 4th	No.	%
6A	2	4
6B	2	4
6C	2	4
6D	3	6
6E	4	8
6F	3	6
6G	2	4
6H	3	6
6I	7	13
6J	3	6
6K	2	4
6L	3	6
6M	3	6
NRP	13	25
Total	52	100

Table 5: (concluded)

	Generic Group	Percentage
For patterns starting on the 5th	7	13%
For patterns starting on the Maj. 3rd	4	10%
For patterns starting on the Min 3rd	3	21%
For patterns starting on the Root	0	26%
For patterns starting on the Major 7th	11	20%

Table 6: Nonrecurring pattern incidence for triadic structural tones

	Generic Group	Percentage
For patterns starting on the Minor 2nd	1	56%
For patterns starting on the Minor 6th	9	61%

Table 7: Nonrecurring pattern incidence for nondiatonic tones

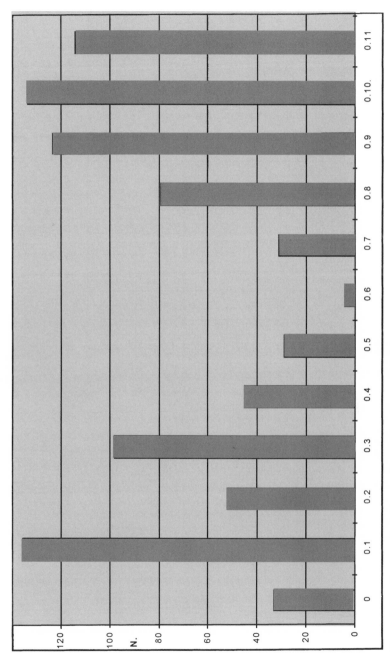

Figure 8: Distribution of total intervallic patterns by generic class

relationship between individual pattern groups and chord function. This prediction generally held true, with the three top scoring patterns (i11B, i10J and i1E) scoring evenly across all chord functions (Table 8). Notable exceptions to this trend were patterns i9F, i9I, i4F, i3F, and i10G. The greater distance between all of these patterns' first and second notes suggests that a gapped contour is more likely to implicate (and be used over) triadic patterns, hence achieve a high reciprocity with a particular chord function.

Pattern	N.	Maj 7th	Min 7th	Dom 7th	Half Dim
i11B	74	4	27	34	9
i10J	50	12	13	23	2
i1E	32	8	6	14	4
i8F	32	10	18	3	1
i2D	30	7	11	10	2
i1A	27	2	6	12	7
i9F	25	14	9	1	1
i9B	24	4	7	9	4
i9I	24		1	23	
i4F	23	5	17	1	
i10G	23	1	3	16	3
i1G	19	6	11	2	
i3G	18	5	9	3	1
i3F	17	1	1	15	

Table 8: The top 14 intervallic patterns: functional distribution

The choice of chord function among these "gapped" intervallic patterns is largely determined by the proportional relationship between the notes themselves within each pattern. i10J's stepwise motion, outlining a descending fourth, for example suggests the final four tones of the mixolydian mode (in reverse), a common approach to improvising over dominant 7th chords (23/50 occurrences). See Music excerpt 5: i10J.

Pattern i8F, associated with Minor 7th chords (18/32 occurrences), can be perhaps read as the 9th of a minor 7th chord proceeding to the 7th, to the 5th and on to the minor 3rd. See Music excerpt 6: i8F.

In a similar fashion pattern i9F suggests a gapped contour resembling the structural properties of major 7th chords (14/25 occurrences): 9th–maj 7th–5th–maj 3rd). See Music excerpt 7: i9F.

Pattern i3F, forming a strong association with dominant 7th chords (15/17 occurrences) is tantamount to a stacked series of minor 3rds outlining a

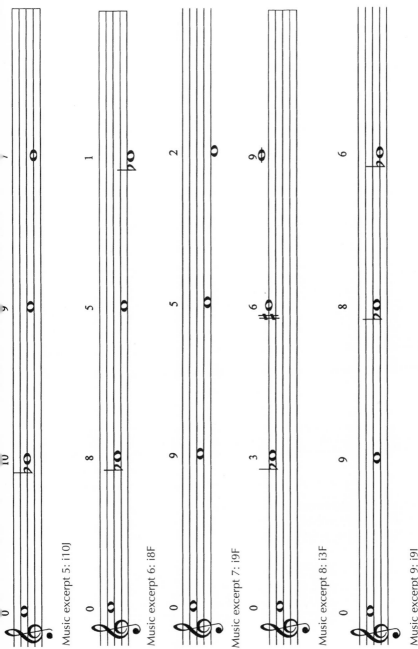

Music excerpt 5: i10J

Music excerpt 6: i8F

Music excerpt 7: i9F

Music excerpt 8: i3F

Music excerpt 9: i9I

diminished 7th arpeggio. It, like structural pattern s0B, maps perfectly onto an octatonic scale. See Music excerpt 8: i3F.

i9I's ambiguous pattern of intervals reveals itself on closer examination to be (23/24 appearances) identical to the contour of structural pattern s4B. See Music excerpt 9: i9I.

Intervallic patterns, therefore, in many cases represent an analogous extension of structural patterns. Evans demonstrates in these instances his ability to extend patterns—most likely originally internalized to cope with chord function situations (i.e., structural)—beyond the immediate limitations of tonality. Table 9 lists structural and Intervallic patterns which share identical melodic contours. The number each time the pattern appeared in each respective analysis is noted.

Structural Pattern	N.	Intervallic Pattern	N.
s4B	23	i9I	24
s0A	13	i1A	27
s2M	10	i1G	19
s0B	9	i1E	32

Table 9: Extension of structural patterns as intervallic patterns sharing the same melodic contour

DISCUSSION

Considering that most tonal jazz improvisers to a large extent superimpose their improvised melodies on to the prevailing network of "changes," it was not perhaps surprising to find that a large percentage of the patterns' commencing tones were in fact abstracted from the triadic structural tones of the underlying chord sequence. Evans's preference for diatonic tones in these instances suggests a hierarchy of note choice where, as suggested in the results, tones of high structural significance (*Group One*: tonic and dominant) are chosen in favor of lower structural significance (*Group Two*: thirds, major 2nd, major 6th and sevenths) which are in turn chosen in favor of those with little structural significance (*Group Three*: augmented 4th and minor 6th). Emphasizing a relationship between the patterns' commencing tones and triadic structure does not imply that Evans as a whole prefers structural tones to nonstructural tones. Rather, evidence suggests that many of Evans's internal patterns (prelearned or improvised) have been fashioned to reflect and embody significant moments in harmonic structure.

These findings, which underscore the importance of structural harmony in Evans's work, parallel Topi Jarvinen's theory of structural tones (itself modeled on Krumhansl and Shephard's [1979] research) which act as "cognitive reference points" in the unplanned course of an improvisation (Jarvinen 1995). In a tonal hierarchy similar to that found in the tonal repertory of Western music, Jarvinen similarly finds that tonal jazz improvisers abstract tones primarily from the tonic triad (in this study a suitable analogy can be drawn between chord function and key/tonal centers) "which is followed by the rest of the diatonic scale and finally by the nondiatonic tones" (Jarvinen 1995, 427). Figures 9 and 10 compare results from this study with Jarvinen's.

A further examination of some of Evans's favorite patterns—dubbed the "Top 14"—suggests a symbiotic relationship between chord function and melodic contour. The first four notes of many of these patterns articulate the structural tones suggested by each chord function.

Once individual patterns are examined in relation to their own generic class, Evans's preference for certain patterns, or pattern shapes, over others becomes even clearer. The uneven spread of the data even within each generic group, with the bulk of individual patterns scoring in the very low range (2%–4%) and some patterns scoring way and above others (i.e., pattern s4B as 25% of all Generic Class 4 patterns), suggests a hierarchy of choice among the patterns (within each generic group) themselves.

These large discrepancies in occurrence between Class One formulas (5 appearances and above) and Class Two formulas (2 to 3 appearances on average) proffer two essentially antithetical hypotheses. The first is that Evans's internal grammar is essentially limited to a few favorite formulas (i.e., Class One) within each Generic Group which are chosen according to the specific demands of the improvising situation. In this first hypothesis, Class One formulas are deterministically generated by the underlying chord sequences, with lesser used Class Two patterns remaining largely unrelated or incidental to a formulaic network. The second and more likely hypothesis is that these Class Two formulas constitute, in many cases, formulaic variants of those identified as Class One. While these Class Two variants may not exactly mirror the melodic contours of Class One patterns, they bear many similarities to them, in terms of melodic shape and gesture.

Figure 11 attempts to elucidate the hierarchical relationship between Class One and Class Two patterns within Generic Group 4. The left column represents Class Two patterns deriving in genus from Class One pattern s4B, the right column representing Class Two patterns deriving form Class

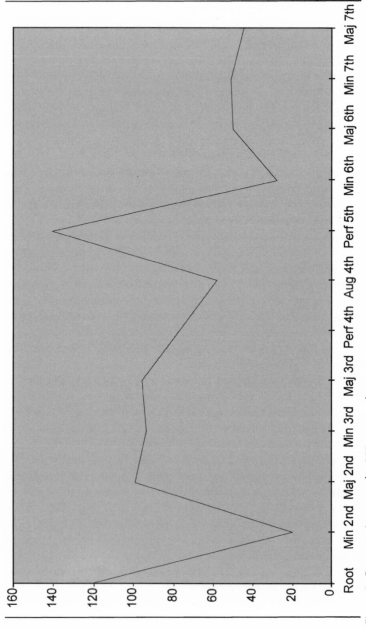

Figure 9: Commencing tones for 878 structural patterns

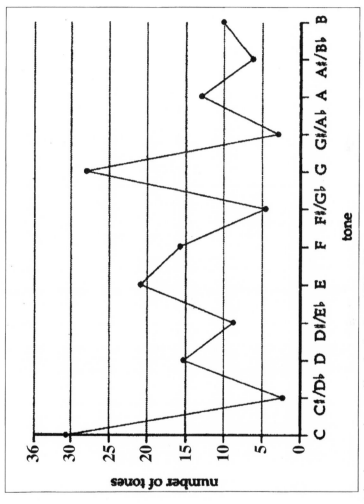

Figure 10: Weighted average key profile, after Jarvinen 1995, 428

Figure 11: Analogous pattern relationships within Generic Group 4

One pattern s4K. Bracketed numbers refer to the number of times each pattern group occurred in the total 878 patterns.

This Class One/Class Two variant hypothesis is further testified to in the unusually high incidents of nonrecurring patterns within generic groups commencing on nondiatonic tones (i.e., minor 2nd, minor 6th). To place this theory in a practical playing context, Evans as an improviser would be faced with his greatest challenges when confronted with the dilemma of having to resolve a nonstructural tone over the conventional structured "changes." Whether Evans chose on these occasions to deliberately subvert the structure (i.e., placing a clashing note on the strong beat of the chord change) or landed on these notes by accident, he would have been faced with a shortage of favorite analogous formulas and consequently may have needed to spontaneously create new material. Further evidence for this heightened spontaneity may be found in the lack of functional agreement (i.e., no strong attachment to any particular chord function) among nondiatonic patterns.

Figure 12, a gapped segmentation chart (transposed to C major to fit the ii–V7–I progression) demonstrates the manipulation and mutation of a single formula (s4B) across the course of a single song and attempts to show the way in which Evans is able to extend a simple three-note formula by analogy. It is worth noting how s4B is premiered three times by pattern s0A—a neighbor tone embellishment which connects the root of the D half-diminished chord to the third of the G7. The G7 itself connects with the E (3rd) of the C Major 7th chord five times (bars 3, 7, 19, 23 and 43) and with the G (5th) twice (bars 22 and 37). It is also interesting to note that aside from two instances (the E♭ over the C major 7th chord in bars 67 and 69), Evans consistently chooses structural tones to coincide with a change in chord.

Intervallic patterns represented, in many cases, analogous extensions of basic structural patterns beyond the dictates of structural harmony. Figure 13 illustrates Evans's ability to analogously apply structural pattern s2M in a more relative context (i.e., as pattern i1G). Although we can ascertain that Evans greatly favored pattern s2M as a way of approaching minor 7th chords (i.e., through structural analysis), intervallic analysis demonstrates that Evans was especially adept at extending principles in a more analogous or relative fashion (i.e., outside the dictates of chordal harmony). His associative "secondary" use of structural pattern s2M beyond its original "functional" purpose supports David Sudnow's theory of the steps improvisers take in developing their unique discourse (Sudnow 1978). Once a preset grammar of themes has been learned, often through repetition and imitation, they are (in Sudnow's first level) repeated note-for-note (i.e., unadorned) each time over a particular

Figure 12: Turn Out the Stars: segmentation analysis (transposed to fit ii–V–I in C major)

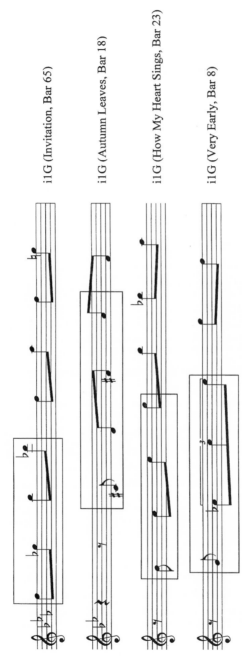

Figure 13: Analogous applications of structural pattern s2M (i.e., as intervallic pattern i1G)

chord function. In the second stage, they are employed more flexibly but still over a particular chord function. In the highest order of improvising, to which Evans evidently belongs, these prelearned themes are not only adapted to a range of limited situations, but also deconstructed and combined associatively according to the musician's wishes.

In this way, Evans's musical dialogue, which owes a great deal of its logic to his prearranged grammar of formulas, shares all the sophistication, syntax and meaning typical of fluent spoken dialogue.

CONCLUSION

Years after the advent of free improvisation (1960s) and more recent improvisational approaches advocated by Roger Dean and Derek Bailey, jazz improvisation in the 1990s remains largely taught through the internalization of a repertoire of formulas (McPherson, 69). While this application of note-for-note responses to recurrent structure may initially facilitate the efforts of beginning improvisers, it is the responsibility of jazz educators to demonstrate their application in more associative and flexible forms. This study, which identifies the formulaic grammar at the root of Evans's ability to spontaneously compose new melodies over a fixed structure and traces its associative application over a large representative number of works, analyzes the work of a skilled improviser.

Future research could develop the applicable scope of the analytic methods used in this study to include other domains such as "texture" or group interaction. These analyses could be additionally developed to include a intervallic study of formulas within formulas (i.e., secondary applications), a study of the way in which preceding formulas affect the choice and construction of those that follow and most effectively applied to a cross comparison study of several musicians.

In conclusion, this study supports recent findings in music psychology, namely that jazz musicians make use of continuous thought structures which are added to and embellished within the course of an improvisation. Consequently it is hoped that future jazz research will address the all-important mechanisms, used across a jazz musician's entire oeuvre, that facilitate and, in many cases, generate improvised response. Satisfactory analysis of these formulaic grammars may not only greatly enhance our present understanding of single improvisations but entire bodies of improvised music which, as a composite whole, may be said to be at least partially representative of an jazz improviser's style.

Acknowledgment

The author is indebted to Associate Professor Gary McPherson, University of New South Wales, for his assistance and enthusiasm throughout the study.

REFERENCES

Berliner, Paul F. 1994. *Thinking in jazz: the infinite art of improvisation*. Chicago: University of Chicago Press.

Blanq, Charles. 1977. Melodic improvisation in American jazz: the style of Theodore "Sonny" Rollins, 1951–1962. Ph.D. diss., Tulane University.

Clarke, Eric F. 1991. Generative processes in music, in J. A. Sloboda, ed. *Generative processes in music: the psychology of performance, improvisation and composition*. Oxford: Clarendon Press, 1–26.

Dean, Roger T. 1992. *New structures in jazz and improvised music since 1960*. Milton Keynes: Open University Press.

Elliot, David. 1995. *Music matters*. New York: Oxford University Press.

Hargreaves, David J., Conrad A. Cork, and Tina Setton. 1991. Cognitive strategies in jazz improvisation: an exploratory study. *Canadian Journal of Research in Music Education* 33, December: 47–54.

Jarvinen, Topi. 1995. Tonal hierarchies in jazz improvisation. *Music Perception* 12; no. 4 (summer): 415–437.

Johnson-Laird, P. N. 1991. Jazz improvisation: a theory at the computational level, in P. Howell, R. West, and I. Cross, eds. *Representing musical structure*. New York: Academic Press, 291–325.

Johnson-Laird, P. N. 1988. Freedom and constraint in creativity, in R. J. Sternberg, ed. *The nature of creativity*. Cambridge: Cambridge University Press.

Kernfeld, Barry Dean. 1981. Adderley, Coltrane and Davis at the twilight of bebop: the search for melodic coherence (1958–59). Ph.D. diss., Cornell University.

Krumhansl, C. L., and R.N. Shephard, 1979. Quantification of the hierarchy of tonal functions within a diatonic context. *Journal of Experimental Psychology: Human Perception and Performance*, 5, no. 4: 579–594.

McPherson, Gary E. 1993. Factors and abilities influencing the development of visual, aural and creative performance skills in music and their educational implications. Ph.D. diss, Sydney University.

Owens, Thomas. 1974. Charlie Parker: techniques of improvisation. Ph.D. diss., University of California.

Pressing, Jeff. 1991. Improvisation, methods and models, in *Generative processes in music: the psychology of performance, improvisation and composition*. Edited by John A. Sloboda. Oxford: Clarendon Press, 129–178.

Sarath, Ed. 1996. A new look at improvisation. *Journal of Music Theory* 40, no. 1 (Spring): 1–38.

Schuller, Gunther. 1958. Sonny Rollins and thematic improvisation. *The Jazz Review*, November 1958: 6–11.

Smith, Gregory E. 1983. Homer, Gregory and Bill Evans? The theory of formulaic composition in the context of jazz piano improvisation. Ph.D. diss., Harvard University.

Sudnow, David. 1978. *Ways of the hand: the organisation of improvised conduct.* London: Routledge and Keegan Paul.

TREADING THE BOARD—A PEDAL PLAY: THE ARTISTRY OF JIMMY SMITH IN PERFORMANCE

Tim Dean-Lewis

Jimmy Smith (b. 1925) is often described as the most influential jazz organist of all time. Smith became famous for the series of recordings that he made as leader of various "organ trios" for the Blue Note and Verve labels in the late 1950s and 1960s. His classic style is a kind of funky "soul jazz", often based upon bebop chord progressions and steeped in the blues. His characteristic, infectious vamps and astoundingly fast melodic improvisations have earned him enormous respect from around the jazz world, and have helped make the Hammond organ the legend of popular music that it is today.

Smith's parents were both pianists (his father played stride piano), and encouraged him from an early age. At the age of nine he won first prize in a radio competition (Major Bowes Amateur Hour) playing boogie-woogie. He went on to study harmony and theory (Halsey Music School), double bass (Hamilton School of Music), and piano (Ornstein School of Music), taking up the Hammond organ in 1951, and forming his first organ trio in 1955.[1]

THE ORGAN TRIO

The rise of the organ trio as a format was the result of a combination of factors. Since 1933, and the end of prohibition, small nightclubs had sprung up again all over the U.S.A. From the point of view of many club owners, the organ trio format showed one principal economic advantage over larger groups: in many states, a jazz venue was allowed a maximum of three musicians playing if it wanted to avoid paying for an expensive music license. The organ trio was a complete "made-to-measure" band for this situation.[2] The drums would supply the rhythm, while a guitar (or saxophone) played the melody. The Hammond organist, meanwhile, could double or harmonize this melody, as well as, crucially, supply the bass line (these techniques were initially developed by Wild Bill Davis and Milt Buckner).[3] When the guitarist was soloing, the organist would supply the bass line and chordal accompaniment. When the organist took a solo, the guitarist would play the chords. This opportunity to have a quartet sound produced by just three performers persuaded many club owners to buy a Hammond, and musicians toured these venues.[4]

This lack of a bass player was soon seen to have an advantage beyond financial considerations. From the perspective of the organist playing in the bop style, this trio format has an important musical difference (which could be described as either an advantage or a responsibility) when compared to the conventional jazz group: direct control of the bass line. Thus, the harmonic rhythm of bass and melody parts can be completely integrated or separated at will during both heads and solos without extensive group rehearsal. Similarly, chord substitution can be used in the bass part with the melody-playing musician always confident that it is about to take place.

It might be assumed from the above that the bass part would be played by the jazz organist using the Hammond's pedalboard. However, as we shall see, this is not precisely the case.

WATCHING BIG JOHN PATTON

A few years ago, I had the good fortune to play a Hammond B3 (with a pair of Leslie speaker cabinets) on a stage in Brighton (on the south coast of England). This rig had been hired for the main act: none other than Big John Patton, a fellow Blue Note organist of Jimmy Smith.[5] As the keyboardist in the support band, I had taken along my synthesizer (with organ presets), fully expecting to play it. However, not only was I allowed to perform on the B3 with my band, but Patton also encouraged me to watch him play close up during rehearsal and performance. What a difference! I was utterly amazed by the sheer physicality of the instrument; with the expression pedal down and the (200-watt) Leslies set to "tremolo," the bench shook so much that it felt as though I was driving a tractor!

Patton didn't have a bass player in his band, but he didn't use the Hammond's pedals either. Instead, he played all his "walking" bass lines on the lower manual of the B3 with his left hand, the relevant drawbars set to a simple 838000000 registration.[6] His right foot operated the swell pedal, and his left foot tapped away on the woodwork of the instrument, seemingly just keeping time.[7]

Since that (incredible) gig I have (a) looked for a Hammond that I could afford and (b) meanwhile, tried to improve my synthesized imitation by the use of various MIDI keyboards, volume pedals, and a Leslie simulator (much easier to carry!)[8] Realizing that part of a good emulation of the Hammond "sound" means playing within the tradition of this instrument, I have also studied the styles of the masters of the B3 such as Patton himself, Jimmy Smith, Jimmy McGriff, Charles Earland, and Brother Jack McDuff. From this aural evidence alone, I would have said that all of these organists played rapid, "walking" bass lines on the lower manual of the Hammond, imitating the technique of a double bass player, and did not use the pedals to produce notes (but see below). This technique is so much a part of the style that all of these organists will usually extend the trio format by adding more horns to the band in preference to a "real" bass player.[9] Indeed, to disrupt this method would be potentially damaging to the improvisational fluency of the organist concerned.

POPPING THE PEDALS

As suggested above, the pedalboard is not generally used by the jazz organist to produce notes. However, since watching Patton, I have learnt that many of these musicians use the pedals to add a percussive "pop" to each beat/note of the bass line generated with the left hand. Interviews of three organists by Robert L. Doerschuk (Jimmy McGriff, Tom Coster[10] and Joey DeFrancesco) describe a range of viewpoints with regard to this technique:[11]

(Jimmy McGriff) "You can get a string bass feel by using syncopation with the pedals. . . . It gives you the bass sound of pulling the string, like the aftereffect. If you don't play it like that on the organ, all you get is one solid sound. By using the bottom keyboard and the pedals, that's where your syncopation comes from. You don't play 'em together; then you only get that one sound, like hitting a bass drum. There's got to be a split second between when you play the pedals and the keyboard; that gives you the layover sound, and it sounds like a bass player playing with you."

(Tom Coster) ". . . if you hit the top B on the pedalboard, you don't get a note but you do get an attack sound. That, along with playing the moving bass with your left hand, is burning. As you're sitting in the correct position on the organ bench, the B pedal is almost right beneath your left foot, which makes it very comfortable. You play that very percussively, very staccato, and you get this amazing pop. When you play bass lines with your left hand, you play a lot of ghost notes with your thumb before the beat to get that real hip organ feel that Jimmy Smith and those cats were getting. The notes don't sound, but basically you feel them. And by attacking that B sharply on each beat, you get pop."[12]

(Joey DeFrancesco) "Do not keep time with the expression pedal! Some guys do that, and you get that *wuh-wuh-wuh* effect. It doesn't sound smooth. They may not do it consciously, but most people keep time with their right foot. If you start walking the bass with your left hand, pick one of the pedal notes and keep time with it. Use your left foot, and play real staccato; you'll get the plucked sound, and it'll also stop you keeping time with your right foot."

The author's attempts at this have led him to discover that this technique needs careful consideration to operate successfully. Firstly, the two sounds integrate most satisfactorily when the walking bass line is played with a strict legato feel; that is, with no gaps between the notes in the left hand. Similarly, the balance of note and "pop" has to be just right—too much "pop" and the pedal note begins to be heard, too little "pop" and the percussive effect is lost. Timing of the events is also important to integrate the two sounds successfully, as noted above by McGriff. However, something that makes this fairly easy is that the pedals respond well to the length of time taken by a comfortable tap of the foot. Because of this, there is no need to create uncomfortable tiny staccato pushes of the pedal, suggested by DeFrancesco's phrase "... real staccato". Similarly, simply playing both left hand and left foot directly on the beat seems to work very well; the author finds no need to interpolate a gap of a "split second," as McGriff suggests.

I believe that the choice of the note B by Coster is not merely influenced by comfort. Since most pieces in jazz and blues are in B♭, F, C, etc., this means that the note B is a relatively rarely sounded bass note, and thus the percussive "pop" of this pedal has a roughly equal effect upon all of the sounding bass notes. That is, the resulting timbre of the combined sound of lower manual and pedal is more consistent than if the pedal note chosen was, say, the tonic note of the piece being played. Thus, the B on the pedals always sounds like a "pop" (or a "bass drum," as mentioned above by McGriff) and never a confirmatory note an octave (or two) below the sounded bass line.[13]

In the light of this knowledge, I now wonder if Big John Patton was not just tapping his left foot to keep time, but whether that he too was adding this percussive effect to his bass lines.[14]

VIDEO EVIDENCE

Thus, while watching Jimmy Smith on a recent rebroadcast of the *Jazz 625* television series on BBC2,[15] I was a little surprised to see Smith moving his left foot *around* the pedalboard—and astonished by the thought that he might actually be using the pedals (as well as his left hand?) to supply the bass line. By video recording I have been able to watch the concert over and over.[16] This performance occurred on 30 May 1965, and Smith was joined by Billy Hart (drums) and Quentin Warren (guitar). Careful study of this video has persuaded me that Smith was using the pedals to add the percussive effect explained above, but was, simultaneously, *miming* the bass line with his left foot. Most of the time he played a "limited set" of just four notes on the pedals: B♭, B, C and D♭, which form a neat, bilaterally symmetrical "U" shape under Smith's foot, at the center of the pedalboard (Example 1). Meanwhile, of course, the actual bass part is heard to flow beautifully in various keys through all of the pieces; Smith is playing this with his left hand on the lower manual, as expected.

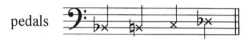

Example 1: The limited set of four pedals

Here is a little bit of notation of the "Jazz 625" broadcast which shows exactly what is going on (Example 2). It is a small excerpt (the last four bars) from the 5th chorus of Smith's solo on his 12-bar blues, "The Sermon." This piece was an established part of his repertoire by the time of this broadcast (it was first recorded in 1958). This notation shows what we hear as the bass line, and, underneath, what Smith's feet are actually playing.[17] I have chosen this particular example from "The Sermon" because it is (a) a well-known piece, (b) one of the longer shots of Smith's feet in the broadcast, and (c) generally representative of all such shots.

It can be seen from this notation that whenever Smith plays a white note on the lower manual, he presses either B or C on the pedals. Similarly, whenever he plays a black note in his left hand, he presses either a B♭ or a D♭ with his foot.[18] Also, he generally mimics the melodic contour of the bass line. Thus, to a static studio audience (even one with a knowledge of not only the keys of the pieces that Smith is playing, but also a not inconsiderable understanding of chromatic bass line structure) it appears that Smith is playing the bass line with his foot. From Smith's perspective, he is simply adding "punch" to the bass sound.

Smith tends to use fixed bass routines through his pieces, and does not attempt to improvise the bass line as a "real" bass player would. We should not be surprised, then, to find that bars 10 and 12 are identical, both with

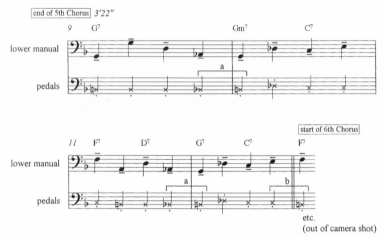

Example 2: The Sermon, 5th chorus, mm. 9-12

regard to the heard bass part and what we see at the pedals. Thus, the heard turnaround routine in the bass is matched with a mimed turnaround at the pedals.

At the 8th chorus of this piece the camera offers us an opportunity to study Smith's left hand in some detail playing these final four bars of the blues structure (Example 3). This notation shows Smith using a bass line that is essentially identical to that found in the 5th chorus (in terms of quarter-notes [crotchets]), but it gives further detail; here Smith can be seen to interpolate tiny, swung "ghost notes," as described by Tom Coster, above. These staccato notes are all played with the thumb, and, in this extract, are limited to Fs and As. By contrast, the on-beat notes are played, as before, with a strict legato feel. Fascinatingly, none of the rhythmic detail provided by the "ghost notes" is actually audible in either the 5th or 8th chorus. This is partly because of their extremely short duration, but also because they are lost in the mix. Billy Hart matches those in bars 11 and 12 with offbeat strokes of the snare drum, which suggests that these are rehearsed events. Thus, these four bars actually sound identical to those in the 5th chorus. The F marked with a "?" in bar 11 is played so lightly that I am not certain that it would be heard even if Smith was playing by himself, although Hart still matches this note. Seeing this use of "ghost notes" in the 8th chorus makes me suspect that Smith may incorporate them for the entire performance. However, they cannot be heard (or seen) in other places so clearly for me to make a clear judgment.

Example 3: The sermon, 8th chorus, mm. 9-12

I said above that Smith generally mimics the melodic contour of the bass line. However, if we look more carefully, in Example 2, at the individual movements taking place, we find the following exceptions:

1. If Smith is pedalling a B and the bass line moves *down* to another white note, then Smith's foot stays on B.
2. If Smith is pedalling a C and the bass line moves *up* to another white note, then Smith's foot stays on C—except at b, where he pedals a B where we might expect a C.
3. If Smith is pedalling a C and the bass line moves *down* to another white note, then his foot always matches this by a move *down* to B. However, by contrast, if Smith is pedalling a B and the bass line moves *up* to another white note, his foot always *stays* on B and does not move to C (e.g., bar 9, beats 1-2; bar 11, beats 2-3).

These exceptions suggest that the B pedal acts as a kind of "center of gravity" for his mimed bass parts (let's recall Tom Coster's choice of the B pedal, noted above—this has a charming resonance with the name of the instrument: Hammond "B3"). The particular movement back to the B natural pedal at b is best described as a kind of "return to base camp," which disallows more than 2 adjacent Cs in this section. This theory is supported by a simple frequency graph of the 17 pedal notes to be found from Example 2, which shows that B enjoys by far the highest frequency of use in this section (Example 4).

I suggest that B has become the center of gravity for the set due to the fact that Smith's heel is pivoting around a symmetrical point midway between the B and C pedals (at the center of the limited set), and naturally skews slightly to the left, as a left foot would naturally do if at rest.[19]

There are two further exceptions:

4. At those pairs of notes marked with an a, Smith is moving *downwards* with his hand and *upwards* with his foot.

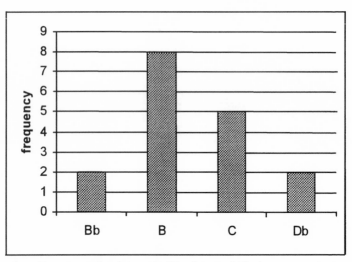

Example 4: Frequency of pedal use in "The Sermon," 5th chorus, mm. 9-12

   5. Similarly, at pair b, Smith is moving *upwards* with his hand and *downwards* with his foot.

Having tried to replicate them, I can attest to the extreme difficulty and un-intuitive nature of such maneuvers (even despite the fact that both occur-rences of a are identical). However, Smith obviously developed this tech-nique over time, presumably starting by using a single pedal to provide the percussive "pop." Further, the adjacency of the pedals used, combined with the regularity of a tapped foot, means that this strategy is fairly straightfor-ward when compared with the possibility of playing a complete bass line with the pedals alone. I suggest that these movements are conscious, but small, acts that are the consequence of the development of a series of rules that naturally evolved over a period of time, conditioned by the joint forces of (a) the use of a limited set, (b) the desire for realism, and (c) physical comfort. Thus, for some of the time at least, Smith's left foot seems to op-erate on a kind of autopilot, dislocated from the (similarly automatic) process of recalling the contours of the bass melody.

   As described above, Smith uses the limited set of B♭, B, C and D♭ most of the time. However, there is one shot of Smith's feet in "The Sermon" which shows him also to include a D. Similarly, during the head of "Who's Afraid of Virginia Woolf?," Smith is seen to play the A pedal a number of times. Incidentally, this last case is similar to exceptions 4 and 5 above, in that we can sees Smith's left foot casually moving in the opposite direction to his left hand (Example 5).

lower manual

pedals

Example 5: Opposite movements in "Who's Afraid of Virginia Woolf?"

The chosen pattern of quarter-note (crotchet) rests found here creates a specific problem, which is not found in the walking bass patterns of, say, "The Sermon". That is, if the organist chooses to use a single pedal, then he must endure holding his left foot up in the air for the crotchet rest, and thus risk the onset of cramp. However, by gently rocking from A to B in the pedals, Smith is providing comfort for his left foot and leg. This has the side effect of altering the timbre of the bass line (see above).

Let us note that these additional pedal notes, D and A, although rare, and occurring in distinct pieces, are immediately above and below the "core" set of B♭, B, C and D♭, and that the bilateral symmetry noted above is maintained (Example 6).

pedals

Example 6: The limited set of four notes extended by D and A

As noted above, for Smith's studio audience, the truth of the matter is very hard to see. Even with the relatively closeup view permitted by the cameras, the television audience of the original broadcast (assuming lack of video recorders) would also have had difficulty in seeing was really happening. As in many early TV jazz concerts, the musicians sit or stand just where they would on a conventional stage, and the television screen acts for most of the time as an undersize proscenium arch. Thus, although there is the occasional clear view of Smith's feet at the pedals, we should recall that the year is 1965, BBC2 is brand new, and these cameras are difficult to move around (they track and pan slowly, and even then the images shake quite a lot). Smith's Hammond is located stage right, at 90 degrees to the audience, so that he has a clear view (across the studio) of the other musicians.

Although the director of the program chooses only a few shots that show Smith's feet playing the pedals in each number, this discrepancy (between what we can hear and what we can see) is also, not surprisingly perhaps, to be found in most of the other tunes from the set: "Who's Afraid of Virginia Woolf?," "Wagon Wheels" and an untitled 12-bar blues (the playout). Although details of the notes played are affected by the key of the piece concerned, the same general rules (and exceptions) apply in these cases: the "core" set of Bb, B, C and Db is maintained, and the B pedal is noticeably the "center of gravity."[20]

"Wagon Wheels" is interesting, however, in that Smith shows the following frequency of pedal use: Bb: 1, B: 5, C: 8, Db: 4 (this is from the single close-up shot of his feet). The preference for C in this tune would seem to be influenced by the fact that this is the key of the piece. Thus, the timbre of combined note and "pop" is relatively simple. This directly parallels Smith's contrasting "straight" and (then, suddenly, aggressively) "outside" interpretation of the head of this cowboy tune.

Smith is extremely fluent at miming with his foot, and, upon reflection, I think that he seems to be hiding his left hand (the one really playing the bass line) from the studio audience's view. This left hand is absolutely as low as one could get it and still play the keys, with the palm against the key slip (the wooden part in front of the keys), and the tips of his fingers just reaching over the top of the manual. B3s have "waterfall" keys (i.e., slightly rounded at the front), which facilitate glissandi and further allow Smith to hide his hand. Of course, this rigid hand position is helping Smith maintain a strict legato feel in the left hand, and, as mentioned above, this facilitates realistic and consistent bass lines, at which he is absolutely superb. From the audience's perspective, his left hand is also partly concealed by his body and the sleeve of the right arm of his suit reaching out for the upper manual. By contrast, the TV audience is afforded extremely good views of both of Smith's hands, the Hammond's manuals and, occasionally, the drawbars.

Let's also note that Smith often floats his right hand quite high above the upper manual and flips his fingers downwards onto the keys. This is actually a standard expressive technique on the B3 due to the nature of the instrument: the "percussion" sound added to the second or third harmonic will only retrigger if all keys are released before playing a new note.[21] Holding the right hand low to the keys and playing in a legato manner will not allow the percussion to retrigger, but bouncing the hand high above the manual creates a distinctive percussive sound at the front of every note. So,

Smith's right and left hands are frequently in a rather contorted position, emphasized by the fact that the upper manual is above the lower by several inches on the B3.

A SECOND SPACE FOR THE BASS

However, having said all of this, there are in fact two places in this set in which Smith *is* using the pedals to generate the notes of the bass line:

1. At the climax of his solo (for a short period of time) in "Who's Afraid of Virginia Woolf?"
2. For the entire performance of the ballad "Theme from 'Mondo Cane'."

"Who's Afraid of Virginia Woolf?"

Here Smith builds his solo over 5 choruses, until, at the 6th chorus, he lifts his left hand off the lower manual and crosses his right hand on the upper manual to enlarge an already dense "chord melody." The bass line is heard to continue, however, which means that he must have started to use the pedals, not merely as a percussive addition but to generate genuine notes.[22] Careful study reveals that the Perfect 4th motif, upon which the bass line is constructed, has been substituted by a Major 2nd interval, which is easier to play reliably with the feet (Example 7).

Example 7: Pedal substitution in "Who's Afraid of Virginia Woolf?"

There is a small, but noticeable, change of sound in the bass part at this point, since Smith has the drawbars for the lower manual set slightly differently to those for the pedals (what appears to be 828000000 and 82, respectively).[23] This matches the author's impression that the combined sound of the note from lower manual and the "pop" of the pedal is best when the mix favors the note.

Repeated viewing of this section has suggested to me the manner in which Smith reliably makes this transfer of responsibility for the bass from his left hand to his foot. A few seconds before this climax, Smith lifts his left hand from the lower manual and reaches around his head to scratch his right ear. Here he is engaging in much the same distraction technique that magicians use when performing tricks incorporating sleight-of-hand. This maneuver allows him to examine the position of his left foot on the pedalboard in order to prepare for the changeover, without encouraging the audience to look down with him. Smith returns to his conventional, left-handed bass playing technique at the end of this solo section.

"Theme from 'Mondo Cane'"

The slow tempo of this ballad is clearly what allows Smith to perform what is a conventional bass line, consisting of a range of intervals. This leaves his left hand free for chordal accompaniment to the right-hand melody. He exhibits a general fluency with his left foot, although the bass line cannot be said to be as tight as those performed elsewhere in this concert with the left hand.[24]

Smith is clearly choosing sustained notes for this ballad and is not using the pedals for percussion. But I would suggest that Smith is also pedalling in this ballad not only because he finds it possible to create a satisfactory performance but also because the slower speed necessarily means that a mimed pedal part would be easier to spot by members of the audience. From this perspective, then, if we accept that Smith *requires* the pedals on the ballads, then, we could imagine, he must be seen to be pedalling on the other numbers in his set merely to be consistent. Thus, a set that includes a mix of fast and slow numbers encourages the miming.

Where Smith uses the pedals at the climax of his solo in "Who's Afraid of Virginia Woolf?," he does so without noticeably altering the pedal draw-bar settings. Similarly, before the start of "Theme from 'Mondo Cane'," there is no shot of him pulling out the stops in order to start generating notes from the pedalboard. Indeed, an examination of shots of these draw-bars throughout the broadcast reveals that they remain at a steady (82) setting.[25] The advantage of this method (of "popping" in the fast numbers, pedalling notes for the slow numbers) is that when Smith wants to operate the pedals, he does not have to alter the drawbars; all he has to do is to tread a little longer with his feet.

REVIEWS AND INTERVIEWS

It cannot be said that the subtleties of Smith's (et al.) pedal technique are well described. For example, in 1957, for the album notes for *Jimmy Smith's Houseparty*, Robert Levin wrote:

> The jazz organist needs not only to play chordal and (when in solo) melodic lines—the ordinary role of the piano—but, with a foot pedal, must simultaneously sustain the bass line as well. . . . Smith carries the bass line more firmly and clearly than any organist I have heard. . .[26]

Nearly forty years later, in 1995, Carl Woideck wrote the following album notes for *Jimmy Smith: Walk on the Wild Side*:

> With Smith playing the bass line with his feet, this tiny ensemble [organ trio] could produce sound that was not only musically complete but was also full enough to be heard in the loudest nightclub.[27]

Bill Dobbins produced a similar description for the *The New Grove Dictionary of Jazz*:

> Smith was the first player to make the organ effectively serve as a group (minus drums), providing walking bass lines with his feet, chordal accompaniment in his left hand, and a solo line in his right.[28]

Very occasionally during the television broadcast, Smith takes his right hand off the upper manual and plays a percussive interpolation on the lower manual, adding to the rhythmic drive of the piece. But this would not seem to qualify as the chordal method implied here by Dobbins. Elsewhere in *The New Grove Dictionary of Jazz*, Andrew Jaffe notes that Brother Jack McDuff's ". . . remarkably solid bass lines are equaled among organists only by those of Smith."[29]

In 1994, Allen Sears wrote (concerning Smith in his comprehensive history of the jazz organ) that

> If you played organ in the 1960s it was your aspiration to be able to fly across the keyboard with your right hand, play intricate rhythm chords with your left hand, play walking bass lines with your foot, and dynamically control the volume with your right foot on the swell pedal.[30]

While Gary Giddins accurately notes that Smith ". . . sustains bass walks and/or a drone in the left [hand] . . . ." he also mentions Smith's ". . . peerless ability to combine all the stops and pedals."[31] Whilst this is the best description I have yet seen of Smith's method (apart from Doerschuk's interviews in Vail's book), it cannot be said to represent "the whole truth."

These descriptions by Levin, Woideck, Dobbins, Sears, and Giddins have the advantage and attraction that they transmit a basic knowledge of the physical structure and layout of a Hammond organ to the lay reader. Unfortunately, they disregard how the instrument is actually played by most jazz organists of this period. However, if Smith (et al.) can, seemingly, trick such writers as these, then it is no wonder that the truth is not common knowledge.[32]

Tom Terrell's description of Smith's technique in the (more recent) album notes for the compilation *Jimmy Smith: Talkin' Verve: Roots of Acid Jazz* is similar, yet (cleverly?) avoids the direct association of pedalboard and bass. Terrell states that Smith's music

> . . . indeed had a new sound: phat [*sic*] bass lines; percussive left-hand work; and fluid, almost horn-like right-hand bursts of melody.[33]

It seems that Smith himself is at least partly responsible for the raising of this smoke screen, not just by miming at the organ but also by what he has said in interviews. For example, he described how he developed his skill at the pedals in an article for *Hammond Times* in 1964, published just months before the original broadcast of "Jazz 625":

> I never did take lessons, just taught myself. . . . When it came to the foot pedals, I made a chart of them and put it on the wall in front of me so that I wouldn't have to look down. My first method was just using the toe. In the earlier days I was a tap dancer so the transition to heel and toe playing was made without too much trouble. One thing I learned was that you had to have a relaxed ankle. I would write out different bass lines to try for different tempi in order to relax the ankle. One useful learning technique was to put my favorite records on and then play the bass line along with them to see if I could play the pedals without looking down and only occasionally using my chart on the wall. This worked out fine.
>
> When you are properly coordinated, you get an even flow in the bass. Most often, organists are uneven in their playing of the pedals, heavy here and light here.
>
> Soon I was putting hands and feet together and achieving co-ordination.[34]

Smith's statement that he was previously a tap dancer is intriguing—what an advantage this must have been in learning to "pop" and mime at the pedals.[35] Note also in the quotation above that Smith emphasizes use of the toe as his "first [= primary?] method", and also the emphasis upon "coordination" between hands and feet—compare this with McGriff's description of "popping" the pedals, above.

Similarly, in an interview in the mid-1980s with Brian Case, Smith said:

> . . . I put up a big chart of the pedals so I wouldn't hafta look down. I could look up and see where C was, D was, D-flat. That's how I taught myself to pedal. . . . See, I'd ask Wild Bill Davis how long it'd take me to learn organ. He told me it'd take 15 years alone to learn the pedals. 15 years! I'd have a fuckin' beard! I was playing in six months and playing opposite him in the same club a month after that! He felt bad, bad, bad—git this young muthafucker away from me!. . . . Most guys just play with two hands, but you got all those pedals down there. Why don't the rock players play those pedals? Because they're too fuckin' lazy to use them. When I teach, I'm there on the floor putting their feet on the pedals.[36]

As Smith says, many organists simply avoid learning the pedals; they have the reputation of being the hardest element of the Hammond organ to master.[37] Further, in an interview Smith gave to Pete Fallico in July 1994, he described a suggestion from Bill Doggett with regard to coping with the pedals:

> Bill Doggett gave me another way of playing the pedals to relax your leg. Bill plays straight up and down, with his heel, not his toe, 'cos he told me the toe gets tender faster than the heel on the pedals.[38]

On the "Jazz 625" recording, Smith appears to use his toe exclusively when miming, and toe and heel combined when pedalling (as far as I can see). The use of the toe alone gives a more consistent percussive effect and reduces the risk of accidentally playing a full bass note on the pedalboard. Actually, in most shots, his heel doesn't even look as if it would reach the pedalboard; the bench is close to the organ, and Smith seems comfortable sitting right back. This fairly rigid position in the body also helps to maintain good pedal percussion.

Fallico makes no comment upon Smith's claims, although in his liner notes for Jimmy McGriff's album *Straight Up*, he notes that this organist's "right-hand fingerings mesh smoothly with the foot [expression] pedal and left-hand finger bass that he builds his music on."[39]

Woideck reports the following in his 1995 album notes for Jimmy Smith: *Walk on the Wild Side*.

> [Wild Bill] Davis told Smith that mastering the organ was a big job, and just learning the foot pedals would take four years. Smith took Davis's statement

as a challenge. . . . After four months of hard work, Smith sought out Davis: . . . . "I'm playing like Bud [Powell] in my left hand and throwing some Bird [Charlie Parker] licks at him."[40]

This latter statement by Smith could be seen as misleading in that ". . . playing like Bud in [the] left hand . . ." would be understood by most pianists as referring to a particular set of left-hand chord voicings. Indeed, Powell is seen as the source of this material: many jazz piano teachers and texts specifically associate his name with these particular voicings.[41] Woideck seems to interpret Smith in just this way when he goes on to write that

> . . . Smith brought Powell-like technique to the organ. . . . Smith mastered the organ's bass foot-pedals, getting the elements of the bass line, chords, and melody all within his creative control.[42]

The interview with Fallico also shows that while learning piano at Ornstein's School of Music (from 1949–50),[43] Smith could not read music and tried to hide this:

> Jimmy didn't read music and remembers how cleverly he hid this from his teacher. "She would play a thing by Brahms, maybe a minuet or just a little waltz, and she would say, 'Now James, you think you can read this?' I'd say, 'Yes ma'am.' I hated for her to find out I was just doing it by ear. She'd say, 'James, are you sure you're reading music?'"[44]

While Fallico sees Smith as heroically partaking in the oral traditions of jazz ("how cleverly"), this quotation also suggests that the environment in which the young Smith developed as a musician was not a comfortable one for this approach to an instrument ("hated for her to find out"). While his experience with his piano teacher cannot be said to be rare, perhaps this did little to discourage deceit in the young Smith with regard to his music-making.

Let's admit that (especially for someone like Smith who initially trained as a pianist) it is much easier to play an emulation of a fast walking bass line on a Hammond B3 organ using the lower manual than with the pedals. Thus, given the evidence of the "Jazz 625" recording, it seems that, by miming, Smith spent a good part of his career concealing the fact that he didn't use the pedals.

JIMMY SMITH AT THE JAZZ CAFÉ

In March of 1999 I had an opportunity to investigate further this question at the Jazz Café club in London, where Smith had a week's residency. At this venue the (hired) B3 was placed at the front of the stage, and I was able to gain a space standing right at the front, which placed me three feet away from the pedals.[45] I was not surprised to see that Smith used the B♭, B, C and D♭ pedals at the center of the board for bass percussion for the majority of the gig, and that the B pedal was the "center of gravity". However, it was intriguing to see that there were one or two patterns that he performed correctly within uptempo numbers when the note durations were sufficiently long to be conducive to an accurate performance.[46] For example, a piece mostly composed of a quarter-note (crotchet) walking bass line included a cadential motif, which Smith performed verbatim (Example 8).

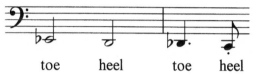

toe   heel   toe   heel

Example 8: Pedalled cadential motif

The chromatic structure and long note durations found in this motif allowed Smith to use easily both heel and toe in the conventional rocking action.[47] These held notes sounded, of course, although I was hard pressed to hear any difference; the balance between the bass lines performed on the lower manual and pedals was carefully maintained.

Similarly, for "Got My Mojo Workin'" (Muddy Waters), he initially played a G, D, G, D quarter-note (crotchet) vamp with both left hand and left foot (toe only); here the pedals function percussively (Example 9).

Example 9: Got My Mojo Workin', introductory vamp

As the head unfolded, Smith's foot movements gradually dissolved into the B♭, B, C and D♭ approach (continuing the same rhythm), and his left hand moved on to play the conventional bass line (Example 10).[48]

Example 10: Got My Mojo Workin', conventional bass line

At the very end of the concert, I noticed Smith glance for the first time at his left foot as he played the tonic C at the bottom of the board—the last of the few sounding pedal notes of the entire gig. Despite the high volume of this moment from the trio, I did not specifically notice Smith take the opportunity to alter the relevant pedal drawbar(s), and, again, I could not hear any specific difference in the Hammond's mix.

Friends at the gig took a little convincing that Smith was not playing the sounding bass line with his feet for the entire concert. I also spoke with a German Hammond player who had assumed that Smith played the bass line on the pedalboard but who then guessed that the pedals were used percussively. He then recalled that he had read that Smith had been challenged (possibly some time in the 1950s) as to whether he really played the pedals and that an experiment had been devised involving ultra-violet lights and painted shoes! Unfortunately I have been unable to source any material to examine further this intriguing image. Similarly, the sound engineer that I spoke to was certain that Smith was using the pedals for notes (he had placed his microphones at the two Leslie speaker cabinets, of course).

From the experience of (a) this concert, (b) the pieces on the "Jazz 625" broadcast where he does actually pedal, and (c) taking an open view of the interview quotations above, I would say that Smith does actually have a reasonable technique with the pedals which he has developed over the years.[49] However, the style (and speed) of walking bass line which he incorporates into the majority of his hits prohibit reliable performance with the pedals, and thus he chooses, in performance, to play the bass with his left hand, adding percussion with the pedals. At the Jazz Café, apart from those moments noted above, Smith's left toe gently bounced on the pedalboard for the entire evening (he played no ballads).

It has been rightly written that Smith plays "with all the refinement that one expects from a double-bass player"—this is unsurprising, given that he studied this instrument for two years.[50] Perhaps only an organist with this specific background—and the feet of a tap dancer—would realize the difficulties of transferring authentic walking bass lines (with their characteristic large intervals, nonadjacent grace notes, triplet details, etc.) to the pedalboard, and thus reject this as a possibility, yet then go on to develop such a good emulation with his left hand and left foot.[51] Further, any such bass line played on the pedals would have to be performed with the left foot alone if the right foot were to be free to operate the expression pedal (an element of the instrument that Smith uses continuously in his playing). Further, as noted above, Smith prefers the sound of three drawbars to shape the sound for the lower manual (a registration of 828000000); by contrast, the pedalboard is only provided with two drawbars (which he sets to 82).

Smith's experiences on the double bass and as a tap dancer were not the only factors that may have acted to his advantage. I suggest that Smith's hand was likely to have been strong when he first approached the Hammond. Let us recall that his father played stride piano, a style known for its challenging left-hand riffs, and that Smith won that radio competition playing boogie-woogie. Thus, given the influence of his father and that success, it seems likely that Smith would have had (or at least valued) an accurate left hand from an early age.

That Smith has never been comfortable to describe his true technique is understandable. This would be at odds with trying to satisfy the not necessarily compatible views of audiences and reviewers. Fierce competition saw to it that, from the beginning, Smith had a professional interest in separating himself in the eyes of his public from the competition of his numerous contemporaries, as well as his more than capable students such as Jimmy McGriff and Groove Holmes.[52] Indeed, this pressure would seem to be the motivation for pedalling in the first place. Smith has often derided his students as mere copycats. Similarly, a recent student, Joey DeFrancesco, has been described by Smith as

> . . . playing Jimmy Smith. He says he's not, but he lies. He's a nice kid, but he can't help but play me.[53]

Maintaining this competitive stance, Smith pronounced that he was "the greatest" on a number of occasions at the Jazz Café.[54] Further, at this gig, Smith was a musician who clearly saw his role as being that of an entertainer as well as an artist. He was a consummate performer who made certain that he was in tight control of both his fellow musicians (Jim Mullen on guitar and Martin Drew on drums)—as well as his audience. Between numbers he spoke and joked for long periods of time and would not be interrupted. He maintained strong eye contact with the audience for the entire concert, expressing the music with facial gestures directed at individuals in the crowd. Let us recall that Smith studied that chart on the wall so that he "wouldn't have to look down" at the pedals, which would damage this area of audience communication. There was also some audience participation (counting to eight and stopping on cue) on "Organ Grinder's Swing." Thus, it could be argued, for Smith not to mime the pedals in his uptempo numbers would simply have resulted in a distraction from the entertainment that is his performance.

In conclusion, I suggest a small philosophy: namely, that Smith is only miming for those in his audience that he perceives might be disappointed to see him pop on a single B or to ignore the pedals entirely. It is fascinating to think that this great musician has spent a good deal of mental and physical effort, both in concert and interview, concealing the fact that he prefers to play the bass line with his left hand and his left foot when, at the same time, he has produced so many performances of such stupendous musical virtuosity, complexity, and emotional depth. Indeed, when I saw him in London he was, at the age of 73, playing with just as much clarity and power as ever. And, I should add, the authenticity, accuracy and rhythmic drive of his bass parts was quite phenomenal. Whereas most musicians spend their careers either playing or miming, Jimmy Smith has, for many years, done both simultaneously. How long did it actually take, I wonder, for the young Jimmy Smith to learn how to pretend to pedal so well?

NOTES

The author wishes to extend his gratitude for assistance and encouragement with this article to Dr. Gerry Farrell (at City University, London, England), Jim Howard, Mike Watkinson, and my wife, Eme, as well as the others mentioned in the notes below.

1. Ouellette, Dan, "Jimmy Smith: The B3 Messiah," *Down Beat*, January 1995: 30–33; also Carr, Fairweather, and Priestley *Jazz: The Essential Companion* (London: Paladin, 1987), 462; Shipton, Alyn "Organ" in Kernfield, Barry (ed.) *The New Grove Dictionary of Jazz* (London: Macmillan, 1988, 941.
2. In fact, Smith's first gig on a Hammond was a mere duo with a drummer in a Philadelphia supper club. See Smith, Jimmy, "Incredible!", *Hammond Times*, 26, no. 2 (July–August 1964); found at <http://www.theatreorgans.com/hammond/jsmith.htm>.
3. Shipton, 941.
4. This was one of the major contributions to jazz by the Hammond organ; in a standard trio, quartet, etc., with an absent bassist, the bass line provided by a piano was, in the main, simply too quiet to compete with a drummer and soloist in a noisy club. Further, a Hammond B3 is able to create a strikingly good imitation of an acoustic bass, if played as described here.
5. I believe that this was the only concert given by Patton in the U.K. at this time.
6. These registration details refer to how far each of the nine drawbars are pulled out: 8 is maximum, 0 is minimum (i.e., no sound). On a B3, there are

two (switchable) sets of nine drawbars for each of the upper and lower manuals, and a further two drawbars for the pedals (16' and 8'). Patton's setting of 838000000 is often used by many of the jazz organists, including Smith.

7. For an excellent general description and history of the B3 and other Hammond organs, see Vail, Mark, *Keyboard Presents The Hammond Organ: Beauty in the B* (San Francisco: Miller Freeman, 1997)

8. The author now owns a Hammond T-202. Despite weighing approximately half as much as a B3, this 1969 organ could not be described as easily portable.

9. An exception to this rule is where the organ is supported by a larger jazz orchestra—for example, Jimmy Smith's recordings with the Johnny Pate and Oliver Nelson orchestras for Verve in the 1960s (listen to "Ode to Billy Joe" and "One Mint Julep," both available on *Jimmy Smith: Talkin' Verve: Roots of Acid Jazz* [Verve 531 563-2, 1996]). Here Smith does not double the (acoustic) bass part in the left hand, but mostly plays upper manual (melody/solo) with occasional chords on the lower manual (as accompaniment to other soloists). Relatedly, a photograph of Smith recording with a large group under Oliver Nelson at Webster Hall, New York City, in March 1963 shows Smith resting his left hand on his left thigh, while George Duvivier plays acoustic bass (printed in the album notes of *Jimmy Smith: Walk on the Wild Side: Best of the Verve Years* [Verve 527 950-2, 1995]). Incidentally, Smith plays a duet with bassist Christian McBride on "Angel Eyes" (Verve 314 527 632-2, 1996).

10. Tom Coster is best known for his work with Santana in the 1970s.

11. These three interviews are to be found in the chapter "Tips from the Stars," in Vail 1997, 160–169.

12. I suspect that Coster is actually referring to the B pedal in the middle of the pedal board, and not, in fact, the "top" B.

13. As an aside, the author notes the frequent use of deep-pitched sampled sounds/instruments to replace the kick drum in much contemporary (1990s) dance music. Although these sounds often have a more precise pitch than the conventional kick drum found in a drum kit, this characteristic is often offset by composers/programmers assigning the sound to a pitch outside of the key of the piece.

14. I find it hard to tell if Patton used this technique on his recordings; his bass sound has a simpler timbre than Smith's, and many of his recordings are mixed so that the kick drum of the drummer often obscures this part of the audio spectrum (for example "The Turnaround" from *The Organization* (Blue Note CDP 8307282).

15. A public broadcasting channel in the United Kingdom.

16. This video has also proved useful for my doctorate research at City University, London, which concerns strategies used by various musicians (including Smith) when playing "outside" the conventional tonality. Without focusing here on my doctorate work, I would like to add that careful listening and

notation of parts of this "Jazz 625" performance has led me to further appreciate the rhythmic complexity and certainty of Smith's music. For example, his left and right hands (and left foot) achieve a consistently high level of rhythmic (and durational) integration between bass and melody (as well as the harmonic integration noted above). Perhaps this is unsurprising, given that it is just one person playing these parts. Other bop (etc.), where the bass and melody parts are performed by two separate people (often proud of their individuality), achieves significantly lower levels of such integration. However, Smith maintains this integration even when playing flat out. No wonder, then, that his music is so satisfying to dance to!

17. Here, and in the later examples, sounded notes are notated as conventional quarter-notes (crochets), whilst "popped" pedal notes are written with crossed noteheads. In the interests of clarity, I have used the C which occurs at two spaces up on the bass clef to refer to the C at the center of the (25-note) pedalboard on the B3, and have then notated Smith's left hand bass line in the equivalent region. This is in the tradition of organ notation, which, being for an instrument built around stops, tends to be written conveniently around the middle of the relevant stave, regardless of the octave actually sounded in performance. The chords are representative of the core material, and do not necessarily relate to Smith's actual performance.

18. That Smith matches black notes with a black pedal and white notes with a white pedal must have an effect upon the resulting timbre of the combined sound; compare this with Tom Coster's use of the (solitary) B pedal, described above in the main text. A detailed analysis of the harmonic content of the combined bass sounds of various jazz organists would be an intriguing study, yet beyond the range of this one.

19. One of several still photographs of Smith (by Carl Settles), playing in November 1998 at "The Mercury Lounge" (Austin, Texas), shows his left foot in this central area of the pedal board. This image was found at <http://www.gullylove.com/jazzrevolt/jimmy.htm>.

20. There are five clear close-up shots of the pedalboard (a total of 36 seconds), and 6 less clear wide shots of the trio (83 seconds). These latter shots, although distant, provide some supporting evidence with regard to discovering, say, in which general area Smith's left foot is operating. There are no close-up shots in "Theme from 'Mondo Cane'." The entire broadcast lasts 32:25.

21. This was a feature added to the B3 that separated it from its predecessors; see Vail 1997, 50.

22. In the course of my studies, I have managed to find just one other example where I am confident that an organist is actually using the pedals to produce notes in the course of a piece. At the end of the head of "Our Miss Brooks," Brother Jack McDuff appears to hold a chord with his right hand, play a rising glissando on the lower manual with his left hand, and transfer the melody of the bass line to his left foot. Mind you, this is only for two chromatically

adjacent notes (B♭ and A), and these are whole notes (semi-breves) at that. For the interested, this event occurs a few times: at 2:57, 3:50, 6:52 and 8:56. "Our Miss Brooks" originally appeared on *Steppin' Out* (Prestige 7666), and is currently available on *Legends of Acid Jazz: Jack McDuff* (Prestige PRCD 24184-2, 1997).

23. The similar setting of 838000000 is often given for the lower manual when playing a walking bass line; for example, see Vail 1997, 181.

24. Of course, suddenly playing held notes with the left foot, after such an extensive period of "popping" the pedals, represents a significant change of task for brain and muscle; this might at least partly explain the lack of "tightness" of this section.

25. These settings are consistent with many photographs of Smith at the Hammond: for example, Vail 1997, 20; album notes for *Jimmy Smith: Walk on the Wild Side: Best of the Verve Years* (Verve 527 950-2, 1995), 8 and back cover.

26. Robert Levin's album notes for *Jimmy Smith's Houseparty* (Blue Note 84002, 1957).

27. Carl Woideck's album notes for *Jimmy Smith: Walk on the Wild Side: Best of the Verve Years* (Verve 527 950-2, 1995).

28. Dobbins, Bill "Smith, Jimmy," in Kernfield (ed.) 1988, 1139.

29. Jaffe, Andrew "McDuff, Brother Jack" in *ibid*, 729

30. Sears, Allen *A Walk on the Wild Side: The Story of the Jazz Organ* (1994); found at <http://www.theatreorgans.com/grounds/wildside.html>.

31. Giddins, Gary "Return of the Organ Grinder" in *Rhythm-a-ning* (Oxford University Press, 1985) p. 166.

32. I now wonder how many people (including journalists or writers of album notes) understood that Smith is miming, yet chose not to mention the fact. It has crossed my mind that, presumably, the manufacturers of this instrument would find it difficult to sell organs with pedalboards to a public wishing to emulate Smith (et al.) if the pedals (i.e., the entire pedalboard) were not considered strictly necessary. Despite their massive success, and great influence upon sales of the product, Smith and other jazz organists did not benefit from close relationships with the Hammond Organ Company (see Vail 1997, 28).

33. Tom Terrell's album notes for *Jimmy Smith: Talkin' Verve: Roots of Acid Jazz* (Verve 531 563-2, 1996). However, Terrell also writes here of "the double-time rumblings of a piano's bass pedals . . ." [*sic*].

34. Smith (1964) "Incredible!"; Ouellette (1995) reports Smith as saying that it was "an artist at the Ornstein school . . . [that made him] . . . a three-foot by three-foot chart of the pedals. . . ."

35. However, I have found no reference to this part of Smith's life in any of the biographies.

36. Case, Brian, "Organ Grinder," *Time Out*, March 17–24, 1999. This interview was originally held in the mid-1980s, but was rejected for publication at that time for its colorful language (a characteristic, incidentally, of Smith's live performance in London in 1999—see below in main text).

37. The story of jazz organ includes a charming anecdote that tells of how Count Basie used to sit on the floor and watch while Fats Waller played at the organ. Basie says that he learned to pedal by imitating the movement of Waller's feet with his hands. Art Hilgart recalls this in his album notes for a reissue of Smith's *Bashin': The Unpredictable Jimmy Smith* (Verve 314 539 061-2, originally released in 1962). Art has kindly provided me with two references for this: Morgan, Alun, *Count Basie* (Tunbridge Wells: Spellmount, 1984), 9; and Basie, and Murray, Albert, *Good Morning Blues* (New York: Random House, 1985), 69. See also Crow, Bill, *Jazz Anecdotes* (New York, Oxford University Press, 1990), 41–42.

38. Pete Fallico interviewed Smith in July 1994; found at <http://theatreorgans.com/grounds/doodlin/smithj.html>.

39. Pete Fallico's album notes for *Jimmy McGriff: Straight Up* (Milestone MCD-9285-2, 1998).

40. Woideck (1995).

41. See, for example "Shell Voicings in the Style of Bud Powell" in Gardner, Jeff, *Jazz Piano: Creative Concepts and Techniques* (Paris: HL Music/ Editions Henry Lemoine, 1996), 207–209.

42. Woideck (1995).

43. These dates are from Dobbins (1988), 1138.

44. Fallico (1994).

45. Most of the audience was on the dance floor (as I was), and could not see Smith's hands. Only those of us at the front could clearly see Smith's feet at the pedals. There is a balcony at the club which wraps all the way around the sides of the stage, but members of the audience who sat there (including an ex-student of mine), although they had a clear view of his hands, could not see the pedals. Thus, although the layout of the Hammond was perpendicular to its orientation in the "Jazz 625" recording 35 years earlier, and thus afforded me a good look at Smith's pedalling, nobody in the club was in a position directly to compare Smith's left hand and left foot.

46. Of course, this sort of event could have taken place during the "Jazz 625" broadcast, but I have been unable to find any hint of this. I suggest that they are more recent additions to Smith's performance.

47. Unfortunately, I am unable to name this (wonderful) piece, which involved rich, sweeping chords over this bass line. Indeed, my notation is based upon the presumption that Smith played with his left hand in the same key (of C).

48. On Jimmy Smith's celebrated 1965 version of this tune, the bass line is actually performed by bassist George Duvivier (currently available on *Jimmy Smith: Walk on the Wild Side: Best of the Verve Years* (Verve 527 950-2, 1995).

49. In the above quotations, the truth has been obscured, either by Smith, or journalistic editing. Everything Smith is quoted as saying may be strictly true, yet the impression given to the reader is that he must be continuously using

the pedals to play the bass line when performing live. These quotations only accurately describe Smith's "ballad" pedal technique.

50. "The Incredible" from *OKEY: Magazin für Orgel und Keyboard* (1997); found at <http://www.okey-online.com/storys/incredible.htm>; I am uncertain of the author of this article; the name Ralf Hoffmann appears, but I suspect that this is just the photograph credit ("Jimmy Smith in einem portrait von Ralf Hoffmann"). Many thanks to John Dean, my father, for translating this German article for me.

51. To the author's mind, Jimmy McGriff and "Brother" Jack McDuff at least match Smith in producing realistic bass parts Listen to McGriff's "Kiko" (Blue Note 7243 8 30724 2), originally released in 1964, and McDuff's "Misconstrued" (Prestige PRCD 24184-2, 1997), originally released on *The Midnight Sun* (Prestige 7529). The "ghost notes" found in these bass lines are much easier to hear than those of Smith found in Figure 2, for example — partly because the drummers concerned play in a more syncopated manner in relation to the bass line. However, it is Smith who seems to be able to achieve the greatest forward rhythmic drive in the bass. For example, listen to Smith's 1963 take of Dizzy Gillespie's bop blues "The Champ" and Smith's astounding 1968 performance of his own "The Boss," both to be found on *Jimmy Smith: Walk on the Wild Side: Best of the Verve Years* (Verve 527 950-2, 1995).

52. Sears (1994).

53. Ouellette (1995).

54. Issues of virtuosity have always been part of the pecking order of jazz, coming to a head in the cutting contests of the boppers, and Smith's style is all about such virtuosity. For example, listen to the flamboyance of the very fast melodic runs and the use of extremely rapid tremolo patterns in the slow "Blues in the Night" from *Jimmy Smith: Talkin' Verve: Roots of Acid Jazz* (Verve 531 563-2, 1996).

"PARKER'S MOOD" REVISITED

Kwatei Jones-Quartey

"Parker's Mood," the slow-tempo blues piece originally recorded for Savoy records on September 18, 1948,[1] seems to hold a special fascination for both jazz analysts and jazz musicians. This fascination has manifested itself in the form of both comments on and in more detailed analysis relating to the piece. Examples of this commentary are contained in analyses by the following five writers.

Thomas Owens, in a dissertation on techniques on Parker's improvisation techniques, commented: "Its wealth of melodic invention, its rhythmic subtlety, and its emotional intensity qualify it as one of the classics of jazz."[2] An example of improvisation-pedagogy that one finds in jazz magazines, and improvisation methods is provided in a short study by the jazz guitarist, Remo Palmieri, who on occasion actually performed with Charlie Parker. Working from his transcription of the piece, he ends his two-paragraph commentary with the following: "I believe this is one of the most prolific blues solos ever recorded."[3]

Analysis with a more specific focus appears in Henry Martin's broad-based work on Parker's improvisation. Using Schenkerian methodology, he analyses aspects of "Parker's Mood" as part of a chapter on the blues. Here he relates melodic aspects of Parker's improvisation during the body of the piece to the opening figure heard in the *rubato* introduction.[4]

Lewis Porter, in an article on blues connotation in Ornette Coleman's playing, makes a reference to "Parker's Mood" as part of general comments on the blues and its characteristics: "In vocal blues with instrumental accompaniments . . . the instrumentalists can fill in whenever the voice is resting. In instrumental jazz, this translates into the soloist filling in for himself or herself, creating a complex kind of rhythmic style such as in Parker's Mood."[5] Finally, in a section of his monograph on Parker's life and music, Carl Woideck conducts a comparative analysis of important surface motives found in the piece, using the nonissued recorded versions or takes as a basis for comparison.[6]

For each of the above writers, the pursuance of general or particular analytic goals within their respective articles or monographs precluded discussion of other issues that would have solely related to the analysis of "Parker's Mood." Reference to the piece was thus invoked in the service of their aims. Yet each of their references or brief discussions offers a tantalizing hint of issues that might be fruitfully explored through an analysis devoted specifically to "Parker's Mood." This paper therefore, seeks to engage just these issues through exploration of problems posed by the following five questions: (1) What general approach does Parker adopt towards improvising during the piece? (2) How does the improvisation within each twelve-measure chorus of the piece reflect such an approach? (3) In a comparative sense, what differences occur within each chorus? (4) Is there a background source that provides musical resources for the foreground musical surface? (5) What analytic methodology provides the most effective means of investigation and yields the most effective results in the examination of the piece?

QUESTIONS CONCERNING METHODOLOGY

On the question of an effective methodology, my approach is two-pronged. First, I discuss aspects of Parker's style as it appears on the surface of the music. Elements involved in this viewpoint include the following: his manipulation of the blues scale and his use of blues phrases; his use of idiosyncratic elements of the bebop style, not necessarily drawn from the blues genre; his approach to the harmonic progression within the twelve-bar blues cycle.

The second aspect of my analysis involves what lies below the surface of this blues. Examining the extant analyses, or passing comments about "Parker's Mood," there are, I feel, certain specific aspects that will respond to reexamination, hence my title—"Parker's Mood Revisited." The main stimulus for such a revisitation stems in part from Porter's statement, "this translates into the soloist filling in for himself or herself."

To an extent this statement describes my sonic impression of the piece as a multilayered improvisational process. In this view the process results from the combining of compositional resources collectively available on what I label a "background or compositional palette." On this palette Parker had various musical options available to him—blues phrases, the whole bebop harmonic and melodic language, rhythmic devices, idiosyncratic timbral qualities of his own instrument. All of these elements are fashioned into a coherent whole. However the finished product is best analyzed by viewing it as a construct of successive layers. As an aid to the discovery and display of each improvisational layer and its constituent elements, this analysis employs both descriptive and Schenkerian techniques as its two-pronged approach.

DESCRIPTIVE ANALYSIS

1. Approach to Form

At its core, the form of the blues is based on vocal precedents. Parker, in his interpretation of these precedents, observes some of the tradition, but since the context is improvised jazz, he adjusts his approach to fit his environment. Two main adjustments take place. First, he bypasses the sequential repetition that one normally hears in a vocal rendition of the blues, i.e., the AAB stanza format. In addition, or as a consequence, he omits any type of thematic melody, i.e., a "head," to the blues prior to the improvisation proper. Indeed, many of Parker's blues "heads" do not follow the AAB vocal format. "Au Privave," "Billie's Bounce," "Bloomdido," and "Cheryl" are examples of such typical Parker blues melodies. "Now's the Time" provides an example of a blues melody that does follow the AAB format.

With the setting aside of such formal conventions, a different means of synthesis is necessary to maintain the coherence of the twelve-bar form. Parker achieves this through a fairly uniform approach to each chorus. As a consequence, three elements from his palette of resources figure most prominently. His application of them is in a compositional fashion; they are the resources he employs to fashion his improvisation. Using the twelve-bar blues harmonic form as a template, the most prominently utilized of these resources, as compositional means, are the following: dramatic melodic devices associated with the blues (dramatic in a rhetorical sense, if we liken the improvisation to the telling of a story); rhythmic devices; bebop-style chord-scale passages.

Based on the use of these elements in each chorus, we may sketch out the following general form template, and consider the application of resources from his compositional palette (see Example 1—choruses 1, 2, and 3 appear in score form for comparison).

2. Form Template (Applicable to Each Chorus)

Measures 1–4. This first section of each chorus may be further subdivided into two units—mm. 1 through 3 as the first , and m. 4 as the second.

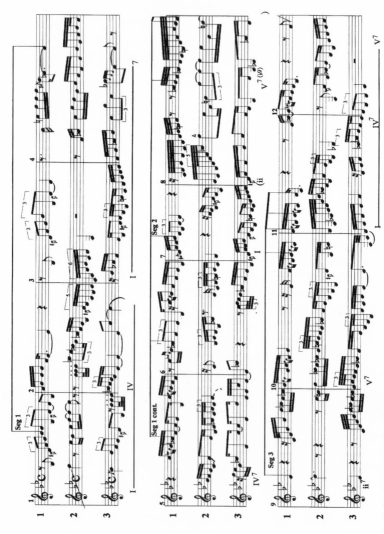

Example 1: Parker's Mood solo, choruses 1, 2, 3

Mm. 1–3. For the traditional tonic with IV interpolated at m. 2, Parker introduces each chorus with a dramatic blues melodic figure. Even though this is a blues piece, Parker's use, throughout it, of blues material is extremely judicious. At the outset of each chorus, his introductory phrase seems to characterize the particular affect that he will apply to the chorus and that we, the listeners, will experience. Thus, for instance, one difference between choruses 1 and 2 concerns intensity of attack—the deliberately held-back entry of the main figure in chorus one contrasted with the dramatic opening rip, in chorus 2, up to F5. In addition, differences in phrasing appear: mm. 1–4 of chorus 1 are laid out as a pair of subphrases in an antecedent-consequent relationship; in contrast, mm. 1–3 of chorus 2 contain a single blues gesture.

M. 4. In most blues this is a subdominant-preparation measure, and Parker treats it as such. Hoewever, in each chorus, a gradual expansion of resources is used for this preparation. In chorus 1, a relatively direct move to the pitch A♭ transforms the tonic into a secondary dominant of IV. In choruses 2 and 3 Parker brings into play common substitution or harmonic expansion formulas that were becoming standard elements of the bebop practice. For instance the passage found in m. 4 chorus 2, is built upon the common harmonic expansion of V7, ii7–V7, in this case four beats of B♭7 become two beats each of Fmin7 and B♭7. Over such a harmonic formula Parker applies another of his resources—bebop-style passagework which outlines the harmony. In "Parker's Mood," the placement of such passages confers a bridge function on the measure(s) in which they are placed. The measure(s) in question therefore provide continuous articulation between the natural formal boundaries of the blues, as in precisely this junction between mm. 1–4, and mm. 5–6.

Measures 5–8. This section also breaks down into two units—mm. 5 and 6, then mm. 7 and 8.

Mm. 5–6. These measures contain a compressed repeated rhythmic figure, varied on each repeat. To create the figure, Parker uses a segment of the blues scale D♭,B♭, A♭, F, E♭,) but adds C and juxtaposes it against D♭. In each chorus (see Example 1, m. 6), Parker highlights C and D♭, whether, for example, through the turn figure in chorus 1, or through the wide intervals of chorus 3. Further, except for a lone note in chorus 2, he avoids G, the third of E♭7. Note that the rhythm section adheres precisely to the conventional boundaries of the blues form, sounding the IV chord on the downbeat of m. 5. Parker's turn to the subdominant harmony occurs, in each chorus, on beat 2 of m. 5. Thus, in chorus 2 the first beat of m. 5 completes scalar material left over from the previous measure, whilst the slide up to F4 on beat 2 marks that note as the first in a new phrase.

Mm. 7–8. These two measures mark a return to tonic, and in a traditional blues these two measures would contain the tonic. For a bebop-style blues, the tonic of measure 8 is often replaced by a secondary dominant formula which prepares m. 9. In each chorus, the preparation for m. 9 takes on a different aspect, as Parker makes use of different resources from his palette. Contrast, for instance, the rapid double time scalar passages of chorus 1, m. 8, with the rhythmically complex registral play of chorus 2, m. 8. This flurry of activity in m. 8 (and to some extent in m. 7 of choruses 2 and 3) of each chorus, heads inexorably for an important goal tone occurring, in all three courses, on the first beat of m. 9 (although in chorus 2 the downbeat of m. 9 is anticipated).

Measures 9–12. Again the four-measure unit subdivides, here into two two-measure units.

Mm. 9 and 10. M. 9 establishes a breathing space in preparation for cadential activity. The cadential ii7–V7 pattern in mm. 9 and 10 substitutes for the pattern, V7–IV, that would normally occupy these two measures in a traditional-style blues. The actual melodic material used for the cadential approach is virtually identical in each of the choruses, and the technique is the same—an embellished octave, descending from B♭4.

Mm. 11–12. M. 11 is the goal of the cadential material found in mm. 9 and 10, and in each of the choruses the structural tonic arrives at some point within the measure. M. 12 contains melodic material that reinforces the tonic, basically a "tag."

This completes an illustration of Parker's general approach. Details of this improvisational approach, as found in each chorus, now follow.

LAYER ANALYSIS

I. Chorus 1

Of the three choruses, this is the simplest in terms of surface melodic approach, and, in effect, its nature is introductory. Below the surface activity, the structural melodic path involves a gradual octave descent from B♭4 (see chorus 1 in Example 1; extended stems mark off the structural pitches (these have been beamed together). This descent divides into three segments, of which the first best illustrates how Parker utilizes his compositional palette to give the first chorus its introductory character (see Example 2).

The first segment terminates at melodic pitch G4 (m. 7). During this segment, two events occur which provide an explanation for the music's fore-

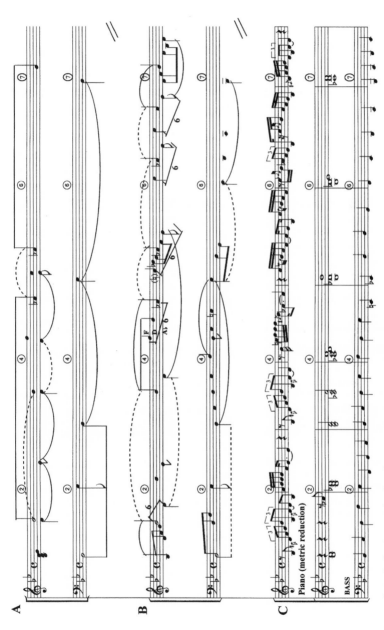

Example 2: Parker's Mood solo, chorus 1, mm. 1–7, segment 1

ground surface. The first involves the projection of several sixths, through the end of the first structural segment (as shown on level B); using this interval as his background, Parker fills it in, so to speak, in three different ways. The first sixth, D/B♭, yields the introductory blues gesture (mm. 1–3); the second, A♭/F (m. 4), is split by D5, registrally transferred from below and prefaced by the same C♯ inflection it receives in the lower register; the third sixth, E♭/C, surrounds the structural pitch A♭, and is filled in to create the repeated blues scale segment of mm. 5 and 6. This surrounding of A♭ arises as a result of the second event—the retention of A♭ as a structural pitch during mm. 5 and 6.

Parker's assertive move to A♭4 in m. 4 strongly establishes an expected resolution to G4, the third of the approaching subdominant. However this expectation is thwarted, and for the following reason—the primacy of the blues scale as a compositional resource. In effect A♭ represents this blues scale. For mm. 5 and 6, other choices were available to Parker. He could have resolved to the G4, and then outlined the subdominant harmony by scalar or arpeggiated means. However, for a blues in the key of B♭, the pitch, G, is not part of the blues scale. By eliminating this pitch therefore, Parker affirms that the idiomatic tradition of the blues is more important than harmonic correctness. He gives us the more sophisticated bebop harmonic spinning out, but at the opportune moments (for instance mm. 3 and 4 of chorus 3).

Juxtaposed against the subdominant seventh harmony, the structural A♭ (best seen in Example 2, level A, mm. 5 and 6) creates a chord tension tone.[7] In this piece A♭ is a structural pitch functioning as a tension tone. It replaces and is related by step to G4, which arrives in m. 7, quite distant from the harmonic region (mm. 5 and 6) where it could have been placed. Not coincidentally, m. 7 marks the return of the tonic, the end of the seven measure period begun in m. 1, and an area of relative stability.

II. Chorus 2

Chorus 2 (see Example 3), the climax of Parker's three-chorus essay, contains a variety of elements that contribute to make it the most complex, and the most emotionally expressive, of the three choruses. From his compositional palette, Parker shapes resources in three main ways in order to create the defining characteristics found in this chorus: (1) at the surface level, he intensifies the scope of the blues and chord-scale figures that outline the harmonic template (previously discussed); (2) at a deeper level he links two occurrences of melodic pitch F; (3) at an even deeper background level he replaces the structural F with D.

As previously illustrated in the general consideration of form, each chorus divides into three sections. In this chorus however, the background level of reduction seems to indicate a bipartite division. This reading is based upon the importance that Parker seems to attach to the pitch F at various registral levels, and the interdependence of F with the pitch D.

With the high point of the chorus established in dramatic fashion at m. 1, a subsequent descent is inevitable. In this descent, F5, as the structural tone, triggers every important musical figure found between m. 1 and m. 8 (see levels B and C). F is also always somehow linked with D♮ or D♭, while the D pitches often connect with B♭. From this connection of pitches, a primary motive results containing F–E♭–D–B♭ (shown on level B of the graph). The motive shows up in mm. 1 and 2. It further spans mm. 5, 6, and 7, whilst a compressed version occurs in mm. 7 and 8. Not coincidentally, the head tone of this motive is always F. At the end of m. 8, the final linking of F with D occurs, but at this location the link marks a change in structural importance. Here F is displaced as a structural tone by D. Note that on the surface of the music (level C), Parker emphasizes the importance of F5, by a second dramatic ascent to this high point. So, on the one hand, F5 in m. 1 initiates the importance of F generally as a structural pitch. On the other, F5 in m. 8 terminates this importance. This demonstrates that the link between the two high register F pitches as both registral and structural. Further, the second F5 marks the end of a section, because once replaced by D, the cadential process begins. This yielding of F to D really splits the chorus into two and not three.

III. Chorus 3

In many ways Parker's third improvised chorus (see Example 4) reprises material and approaches that have occurred in his previous two choruses. On the surface level, we hear the exact repetition of certain specific motives or subphrases used in the previous two choruses. For instance the introductory phrase of the chorus is similar to that found at the beginning of chorus 1. Certain structural similarities to chorus 1 turn up—the sixth is an important interval, and the structural melodic progression which spans the chorus is the same, namely a descent from the octave. Yet into each of these elements Parker injects variants, so that while it is apparent that there is a repetition of sorts, it is of a highly creative order.

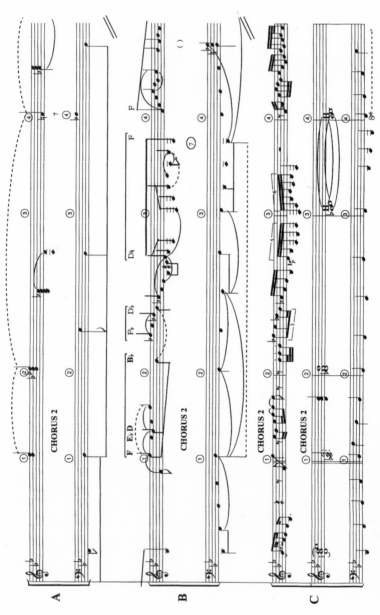

Example 3 (beginning): Parker's Mood solo, chorus 2, mm. 1—4

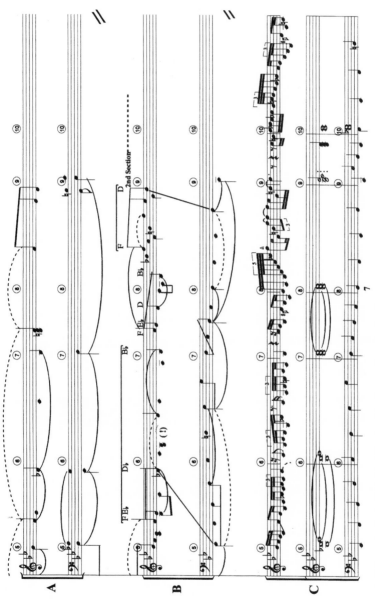

Example 3 (conclusion): Parker's Mood solo, chorus 2, mm. 5—9

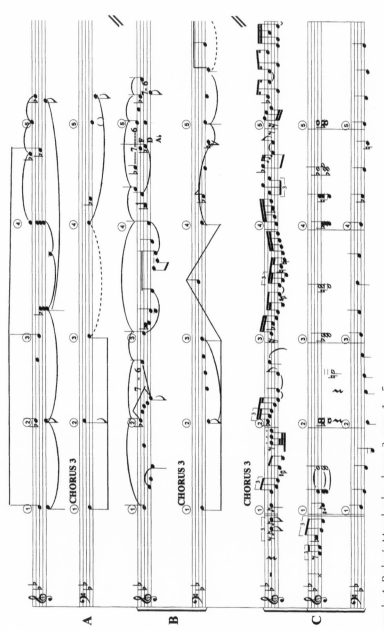

Example 4: Parker's Mood solo, chorus 3, mm. 1—5

An example of the contrast between the two choruses is highlighted by mm. 4 and 5 of chorus 3. In chorus 3, the sequence of structural pitches is identical to that found in chorus 1—B♭4 is replaced by A♭4. For this sequence, note, in m. 4 of chorus 3, the higher-register sequence, G♮5–G♭5–F5. Below the G♭ and F pitches in this sequence, A♭ has been established as the structural governing tone. As the stationary tone in the relationship, it enables the 7-6 interval succession in which G♭ resolves to F. But between these lower and higher notes, there is also a middle register, represented by D♮. In essence then, the B level of the graph shows, in m. 4 of both choruses 1 and 3, the same grouping of the following essential pitches, F–D–A♭, (see Example 2 for the analogous location in chorus 1). This sequence highlights contrasting aspects of choruses 1 and 3. Chorus 1 is introductory, thus the sixth, A♭/F receives no buildup. In chorus 3, the repeat of this sequence is more complex—the sixth is delayed and only appears after a resolution of the seventh, occurring between the structural tone A♭ and the tension tone above it—G♭.

IV. Codetta (Example 5)

In my reading of chorus 3, the structural tonic of the piece arrives on the downbeat of m. 11. Although the remaining measures of the chorus reinforce the arrival of this tonic, the final measure ends inconclusively on C. By preventing closure, this note prepares for the codetta, itself a curiosity, because it has nothing to do with the blues, and from this point of view, its nature is parenthetical. The first two chords evade an expected resoution to B♭ major. In these first two measures, Parker's mainly arpeggiated line is basically an elaboration on m. 12 of chorus 3, D–C. After the fermata, once the piano enters, an insistent F seems to take over as a structural tone. However, along with the pitch A♭5 that remains sustained at the fermata, these two notes occupy a subsidiary role, as does the whole codetta. Although we never hear it explicitly, C4 from m. 12 returns at the sustained chord under the fermata. Thus below the surface, a stepwise motion to the final B♭3 does take place.

CONCLUSION

For his interpretation of the slow-tempo blues analyzed here, Parker had various compositional means at his disposal—the blues scale, stock blues melodic figures, bebop-style scalar runs, arpeggiated figures derived from

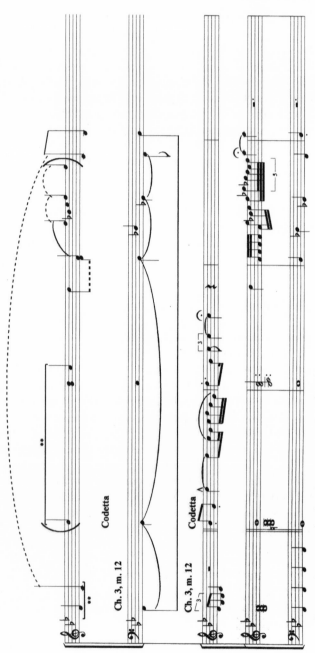

Example 5: Parker's Mood solo, chorus 3, m. 12 and codetta

substitute progressions, idiosyncratic articulation, and a historic tradition of improvisation. Such was his palette of resources. His application of these resources to the basic harmonic framework of the blues resulted in the three wonderful choruses heard on the recording. Essentially, each of these is a self-contained universe, yet Parker, to an extent, treated the three choruses of improvisation as one statement. The first is introductory, the second climactic, and the third, with its use of previous material, provides a summary of sorts.

In my view, the piece is best analyzed as a series of layers that progress in increasing complexity from the background to the foreground. To peel back these layers, so to speak, concepts drawn from Schenkerian theory seem considerable assets. Adapted to suit the harmonic context Parker dealt with, Schenkerian theory provides a means of delving below the surface of a seemingly simple genre, the blues. Parker's masterly achievement in this piece was the maintenance of the right balance between the folk traditions of the blues with the more sophisticated elements of the bebop style. This application of his unerring compositional skill has resulted in the legacy to us of this jazz classic.

NOTES

Acknowledgment: An earlier version of this paper was presented at the West Coast Music Theory Conference in April 1998. My thanks to Steven Strunk and Henry Martin for their invaluable suggestions.

1. This performance is also included on the *Smithsonian Collection of Classic Jazz*. Five takes were recorded. According to Carl Woideck (*Charlie Parker: His Music and Life* [Ann Arbor: University of Michigan Press, 1997], 154), takes 1 and 3 were false starts, take 4 was incomplete, and takes 2 and 5 were complete. Take 5 appears on the Savoy and Smithsonian issues.
2. Thomas Owens, "Charlie Parker's Techniques of Improvisation" (Ph.D. diss., University of California at Los Angeles, 1974), 84.
3. Remo Palmier, "Charlie Parker's Sax Solo on 'Parker's Mood'," *Downbeat* 62, no. 8 (August 1995): 62–63.
4. Henry Martin, *Charlie Parker and Thematic Improvisation* (Lanham, Maryland: Scarecrow Press, 1996), 107–109.
5. Lewis Porter, "The 'Blues Connotation' in Ornette Coleman's Music—and Some General Thoughts on the Relation of Blues to Jazz," *Annual Review of Jazz Studies* 7 (1996): 80.
6. Woideck, *Charlie Parker*, 153–59.
7. See Stephen Strunk, "Bebop Melodic Lines: Tonal Characteristics," *Annual Review of Jazz Studies* 3 (1985): 97–120. Strunk explains his theory on the function of tension tones.

USING e-COMMERCE MUSIC SITES FOR DISCOGRAPHICAL RESEARCH

Edward Berger

The Internet has added new dimensions to discographical research. For many years, database and desktop publishing software has facilitated the compilation and production of discographies. But over the past five years, the Internet has become a major source of discographical data itself. Vast amounts of information of interest to discographers is now readily available on a multitude of e-commerce sites maintained by commercial CD vendors, as well as on several extensive Internet databases which support them.

Although this survey concentrates on the use of commercial sites for discographical purposes, there are many other types of sites with major discographical components. For example, several websites devoted to individual artists have fairly extensive discographies. Other websites are specifically aimed at the jazz research community. Michael Fitzgerald maintains www.eclipse.net/~fitzgera as a clearinghouse for many research projects including several valuable discographical works. An example of a website devoted almost entirely to discographical research is the Red Saunders Research Foundation (hubcap.clemson.edu/~campber/rsrf.html), which traces the Chicago jazz, blues, doo-wop, and rhythm and blues scene through artist and label discographies. Record company websites may also prove useful, although many emphasize only new releases and have limited search capabilities.

Other Internet-based technologies have already had a profound effect on all types of jazz research and have the potential to completely change the way discographical information is disseminated. Discographical research has always been a cooperative undertaking, and news groups, forums, mailing lists, chat groups, and, of course, e-mail are ideally suited to the process of building research communities and the sharing of information. Already, several major discographical tools are beginning to appear in CD-ROM form (Lord, Bruyninckx). It is only a matter of time before researchers worldwide will be able to contribute to an online version of one of these comprehensive jazz discographies.

THE COMMERCIAL SITES

The commercial sites exist to sell music via the Internet. Many of these sites will be familiar to anyone who purchases CDs since they include vendors like Tower, Virgin, and Borders who maintain worldwide retail outlets. Others, like Amazon and CDNow, exist only on the Web and are accessible only online. Some of these e-businesses maintain no stock of their own but obtain requested product from other vendors or distributors as needed. Other sites represent joint listings of many vendors or individual sellers and may forward orders directly to the appropriate dealer for fulfillment.

While not intended for this purpose, these music sites offer a variety of search capabilities which can serve as a valuable source of discographical data (see Table 1). All offer an "artist" (leader) and "album title" search. Many also permit searches by song title and label. Several have "expert" or "advanced" search options which allow Boolean searches combining elements. The sites also vary widely in their ease of navigation, speed, format, and degree of detail.

In using these sites for discographical research, one must understand their purpose and limitations. They exist to sell CDs (or cassettes, videos, DVDs, laserdiscs, etc.), not to serve the jazz research community. Thus, with few exceptions, they list only currently available product (some sites do have limited "hard to find" or "out of print" sections). Furthermore, the information provided may not conform to standard discographical conventions. For example, some vendors no longer include issue or catalog numbers, a virtually indispensable element of almost every discography. Instead, CDs are identified by an in-house stock number—fine for filling orders but useless for discographical purposes. Record company names may also deviate from their commonly cited forms; recordings may be identified by distributors or parent companies rather than by the label name as it appears on the disc. Finally, there are inevitable name and title inconsistencies, but these can often be circumvented by judicious use of the usually forgiving search engines.

Given these caveats, how can these sites serve discographers? In updating our biodiscography, *Benny Carter: A Life in American Music* (Scarecrow Press, 1982), I have found these sites particularly useful in tracking reissue material. Less stringent European copyright laws, more active reissue programs by some of the major U.S. labels, and the seemingly unchecked importation and distribution of bootlegs, have all contributed to the unparalleled deluge of reissue CDs. Without the resources of the Internet, reasonably complete documentation of this material would be difficult if not impossible. Benny Carter's classic recordings of the 1920s and 1930s, as leader and sideman, have been reissued on literally hundreds of

CDs, from the systematic and carefully documented Classics and Masters of Jazz series to misidentified performances on slipshod anthologies.

For example, Carter's famous 1938 version of "I'm in the Mood for Swing," recorded with Lionel Hampton, appears to date on 29 CDs. Thirty-four CDs now contain "Crazy Rhythm" from the epic 1937 Paris collaboration with Coleman Hawkins. Even keeping up with legitimate reissues by major labels can be difficult. Billie Holiday's "Please Don't Talk About Me When I'm Gone" from the 1955 Clef session with Carter has been issued ten times on CD by Verve alone, not to mention issues by licensees or bootleggers.

While it is possible to locate many of these issues by visiting record stores or perusing catalogs, the commercial CD sites offer a much more expeditious method. Moreover, such retail outlets as Tower and Borders offer more extensive web listings than their stock on hand in any particular store, and continue to list items which may be available only intermittently. A search by artist or song title on the sites of the major vendors yields a surprising number of even the more ephemeral foreign and bootleg reissues.

Apart from reissue information, the commercial sites are valuable in finding recordings of particular songs. For example, in our Benny Carter project, we attempt to list all recorded versions of Carter's compositions and arrangements. Such standards as "When Lights Are Low," "Blues in My Heart," "Only Trust Your Heart," and even "Cow Cow Boogie" continue to be recorded by jazz and popular artists worldwide. The Internet is an indispensable tool in locating these recent recordings.

THE ALL MUSIC GUIDE

Perhaps the single most useful site for discographical purposes is the All Music Guide (allmusic.com). Early printed versions of the *All Music Guide to Jazz* were plagued by errors, inconsistencies, and idiosyncracies [see *ARJS 7*, 257-261]. (Recent editions, revised by Scott Yanow, are a vast improvement.) The on-line AMG is a different story and should be the first stop for anyone doing discographical research on the Internet. Although it is not a commercial vendor (one cannot purchase CDs through AMG), it licenses its content to many of the commercial vendors who integrate AMG data into their sites. The data can also be accessed directly by the public through AMG's own site.

AMG offers the standard search capabilities (artist, album title, song title, label) but provides additional information not available on any of the commercial sites. Most significantly, an artist search yields not only an artist's recordings as a leader but also work as a sideman, as well as appearances on anthologies. While some of the other sites may occasionally include access to featured sidemen, none approaches the AMG in consistent inclusion of this essential information. Moreover, AMG has included in its database producers, engineers, liner note writers, photographers, and other ancillary personnel.

The AMG also differs from the other sites in that it is not limited to in-print materials but contains many listings in such archaic formats as the LP. Other features include artist biographies (of varying usefulness depending upon the author), and a unique "songs by" section which locates recordings of compositions by the chosen artist.

In practice, a few clicks of the mouse will produce an instant and reasonably complete overview of an artist's career. For example, an AMG artist search on "Benny Carter" yields the following:

1. a brief but accurate biography by Scott Yanow
2. under "Discography (albums)": 70 CDs/LPs by Carter as leader
3. under "Discography (compilations, boxes)": 40 performances by Carter on anthologies
4. under "Appears on": 375 CDs/LPs on which Carter appears as sideman or arranger
5. under "Songs appear on": 87 CDs/LPs which contain Carter compositions
6. two videos
7. a short bibliography

Each of the album citations is linked to further information on that album, usually including personnel and recording dates, etc. AMG also includes many other features of more dubious value, including "musical maps" and lists of "related artists."

The commercial vendors' sites and related web databases like the All Music Guide will not replace Rust, Jepsen, Bruyninckx, Lord, Raben, or the vast array of specialized discographical works. Again, their purpose is to sell CDs, not to provide the kind of detail and accuracy required in serious discography. But the vast amounts of instantly accessible raw data can lead researchers to information they may not find elsewhere. For that reason these Internet resources are a valuable adjunct to traditional sources and methods of discographical research.

THE SURVEY

In order to judge the usefulness for discographical research of the major internet vendors' websites, some 16 sites were compared in several categories during December 1999.

TABLE 1: Search capabilities. Surveys the type of access provided by indicating which of the following search functions are provided (✓ = yes, blank = no):

1. *Leader search* (usually designated "artist" in the search dialog box)
2. *Sideman search*
3. *Album title search* (sometimes designated simply "title")
4. *Song title search*
5. *Label search*
6. *Finds artists in anthologies:* indicates whether an artist search will find performances included on anthology or compilation CDs
7. *Includes issue numbers:* indicates whether citations include issue or catalog numbers (some provide only an internal stock or order number)
8. *Includes out-of-print material*

TABLE 2A: Number of hits per site from CD sample list. Many of these sites claim huge inventories. This table attempts to give a practical sense of the extent of jazz coverage by indicating which CDs from a sample list of twenty were found on each site.

Numbers on the top of Table 2A correspond to the CDs listed in Table 2B. The following symbols are used in Table 2A:

✓ = the CD was found on the site;
– = the CD was found but only with minimal discographical data, e.g., lacks titles or personnel;
blank = the CD was not found.

The *total score* represents the total number of the twenty sample CDs found on a given site (– is counted as .5 in the calculation).

TABLE 2B: CD Sample list. The sample includes a wide variety of material: recent releases (including reissues) on major American labels; widely distributed independent labels; relatively obscure independent labels; imports from Europe and Japan, including reissue labels; bootlegs; specialist box sets and compilations.

TABLE 3: Recorded versions of sample tunes shows the effectiveness of a song title search by noting how many CDs containing three sample songs each site yielded. The songs searched were the often recorded standard "Body and Soul," and two jazz pieces recorded with less frequency: Lee Morgan's "Ceora," and John Coltrane's "Giant Steps." The *total* column indicates the combined number of hits for all three songs for each of the sites.

site	leader search	sideman search	album title search	song title search	label search	finds artists in anthologies	includes issue nos.	searches out of print	notes
allmusic.com	✓	✓		✓	✓	✓	✓	✓	
amazon.com	✓		✓	✓	✓	✓			
bn.com [barnes&noble]	✓		✓	✓	✓		✓		
borders.com	✓	some	✓	✓				see note	some out-of-print CDs under "hard to find"
cdconnection.com	✓		✓	✓			✓		
cdnow.com	✓		✓	✓	✓	✓			
cduniverse.com	✓		✓		✓		✓		
cdworld.com	✓		✓		✓	✓	✓		"show items featuring" yields anthologies
everycd.com	✓			✓	✓	✓	✓		requires annual membership fee of $39.95
gemm.com	✓		✓	✓	✓			see note	joint listing of some 2,000 vendors; includes some o.p.
jandr.com	✓	some	✓			✓*	see note**		*extensive sideman & anthology info. not accessible through search function--only through artist link and "appears on" in album list; **imbedded in local control # imports; "many song titles linked to wrong albums
musicxpress.com	✓		✓	✓*	✓		✓		
musicfile.com	✓		✓	✓			✓	see note	joint listing of commercial vendors & individuals; includes some used items
muze.com	✓			✓	✓		✓		not a vendor; database used in store kiosks
towerrecords.com	✓		✓		✓	✓*			*add "various artists" to artist name for anthology listings; "notes and reviews" field is also searchable
virginmega.com	✓		✓						search functions only from virginmega--not other virgin sites

Table 1: Search capabilities of each site

site	1	2	3	4	5	6	7	8	9	10	11	12	13	14	15	16	17	18	19	20	score
allmusic.com	✓	✓	✓	✓	✓	✓	-	✓	✓	✓	✓	✓	-	✓	✓	✓	-	-	✓	✓	18
towerrecords.com	✓	✓	✓	✓	✓	✓	✓	✓	✓	✓	✓	✓	-	✓	✓	✓	-		✓	✓	18
amazon.com	✓	✓	✓	✓	✓	✓	✓	✓		✓	✓	✓		✓	-	✓	-		✓	✓	15.5
cdnow.com	✓	✓	✓	✓	✓	✓	✓	✓		✓	-			✓	-	✓	✓		✓	✓	15.5
muze.com	✓	✓	✓	✓	✓	✓	✓	✓		✓	✓	✓		✓	✓	-	-		-	✓	15.5
borders.com	✓	✓	✓	✓	✓	✓	✓	✓	✓	✓	✓	✓		✓	✓	-	-		-	✓	15
cdconnection.com	✓	✓	✓	✓	✓	✓	✓	✓		✓	✓	✓		✓	✓	-	-			✓	15
jandr.com	✓	✓	✓	✓	✓	✓		✓		✓	✓	✓		✓	✓	✓			✓	✓	15
bn.com [barnes&noble]	✓	✓	✓	✓	✓	✓	-	✓		✓		✓		✓	✓	✓	-		✓	✓	14.5
cdworld.com	✓	✓	✓	✓	✓	✓	✓	✓		✓	✓	✓		✓	-	✓	✓				14.5
virginmega.com	✓	✓	✓	✓	✓	✓	✓	✓		✓	✓			✓	-	-	-		-	✓	14
cduniverse.com	✓	-	✓	✓	✓	✓	✓	✓		✓	✓	✓		✓	-	-				✓	13.5
gemm.com	-	-	-	-	-	-	✓	✓		✓	✓	✓	✓	✓	✓	✓			-	-	13.5
everycd.com	-	-	✓	✓	✓	✓	✓			✓	-	✓		-	-	-	-		-	✓	12.5
musicexpress.com	✓	✓	✓	-		-	✓			✓	✓	-	-	-	-	-	-				9.5
musicfile.com	-				-		-	-		-	-	-	-	-	-	-	-		-		8.5

Table 2A: Number of hits per site from CD sample list

1. Renee Rosnes, *Art and Soul* (Blue Note 99997)

2. Charlie Parker, *Big Band* (Verve 559835)

3. Brad Mehldau, *Art of the Trio* (WB 47463)

4. Louis Armstrong, *Satchmo the Great* (Columbia 53580)

5. Kenny Davern, *Breezin' Along* (Arbors 19170)

6. Billy Taylor, *Ten Fingers—One Voice* (Arkadia Jazz 71602)

7. *Soprano Summit* (Chiaroscuro 148)

8. Orange Then Blue, *While You Were Out* (GM 3028)[2CDs]

9. Benny Carter/Phil Woods, *Another Time, Another Place* (Evening Star 104)[2CDs]

10. Brian Lynch, *Keep Your Circle Small* (Sharp Nine 1001)

11. Greg Cohen, *Way Low* (DIW 918)

12. Zoot Sims, *Live in Copenhagen* (Storyville 8244)

13. Lucky Thompson, *Accent on Tenor Sax* (Fresh Sound 2001)

14. Bob Brookmeyer, *Paris Suite* (Challenge 70026)

15. Wardell Gray, *Vol. 1, 1944-1946* (Masters of Jazz 148)

16. Jimmie Noone, *1930-1934* (Classics 641)

17. Coleman Hawkins/Benny Carter, *Jammin' the Blues* (Moon 001)

18. Duke Ellington, *Live in Italy, 1967, v. 1* (Jazz Up 305)

19. *Nellie Lutcher & Her Rhythm* (Bear Family 15910)[4CDs]

20. *Big Band Renaissance: The Evolution of the Jazz Orchestra* (Smithsonian 108)[5CDs]

Table 2B: CD sample list

site	BODY & SOUL	CEORA	GIANT STEPS	total	notes
allmusic.com	200*	20	150	370	search claimed 999 items but showed only ca. 200
amazon.com	986	15	147	1,148	
bn.com [barnes&noble]	422	8	67	497	
borders.com	1,051	29	193	1,273	
cdconnection.com	96	13	85	194	
cdnow.com	523	6	73	602	
cduniverse.com	250*	9	148	407	*search limited to 250
cdworld.com	197	12	99	308	
everycd.com	na	na	na		search not available
gemm.com	na	na	na		search not available
jandr.com	na	na	na		search not available
musicexpress.com	98	10	80	188	
musicfile.com	na	na	na		
soundcity200.com	na	na	na		search not available
towerrecords.com	200*	20	148	368	*search limited to 200
virginmega.com	na	na	na		search not available
worldsrecords.com	350	3	27	380	

Table 3: Recorded versions of sample tunes

BUSTED: THE STORY OF GENE KRUPA'S ARREST, JANUARY 19, 1943

T. Dennis Brown

During the 1930s, the U.S. Government waged a war against a little-known plant called marijuana (*cannabis sativa*). Frequently used for medicinal purposes in the 1800s, it was introduced into America as a recreational drug during the first two decades of this century by Mexican immigrants. Better known by its many street names as "pot," "gage," "reefer," "Mary Jane," "hashish," "muggles," "grass," "weed," or "tea," marijuana became an alcohol substitute during and after Prohibition for lower class Americans for a number of reasons: it was cheap, could be produced practically anywhere, and needed considerably less preparation for consumption than alcohol.

The effects of marijuana were puzzling to most Americans, but it was generally understood that, when absorbed into the bloodstream by either ingestion or smoking, the drug might distort time and cause a mild sense of euphoria. In the 1920s, officials all but ignored the use of marijuana but when the drug became popular during the Great Depression, the government stepped up its attack.

Established in 1930, the Federal Bureau of Narcotics immediately began a decade-long campaign warning the American people against the dangers of marijuana. The Federal Marijuana Tax act of 1937 effectively curtailed the sale of the drug in the United States by imposing wide-sweeping restrictions on its distribution. Concurrently, marijuana was being demonized in local and national newspapers, magazines, and in popular scientific journals throughout the country. For example, in 1935, *American Mercury* published an article written by A. Perry titled, "The Menace of Marihuana."[1] This was followed by similar articles in *Literary Digest,* "Facts and Fancies About Marihuana,"[2] *Scientific America*, "Marihuana Menaces Youth,"[3] and *Christian Century,* "Youth Gone Loco; Villain is Marijuana."[4] The campaign was effective. In 1930, only sixteen states prohibited the use of marijuana. The following year twenty-nine states had antimarijuana laws and by the end of the decade, almost every state had passed stringent laws designed to eliminate the drug from society.

Armed with Federal and State regulations the government had, by the 1940s, a powerful weapon to use against the sale, production, possession, and use of marijuana. Still, most Americans knew little about the drug. This unfamiliarity enabled the government to paint a distorted picture of the effect of marijuana, as David Solomon, editor of *The Marijuana Papers,* explains:

> Deprived of the facts and primed on hysteria-provoking, apocryphal horror stories given to the press by the Federal Bureau of Narcotics, Americans were sold a mythological bill of goods. They were told that marijuana was a "killer drug" that triggered crimes of violence and acts of sexual excess; a toxic agent capable of driving normal persons into fits of madness and depraved behavior; a destroyer of the will; a satanically destructive drug which, employing lures of euphoria and heightened sensuality, visited physical degeneration and chronic psychosis upon the habitual user.[5]

The American public, fed by this steady stream of anti-marijuana propaganda, had reason to believe much of what it read. The evidence was right before them: swing music and its culture appeared to embody all of the dangers of the drug published in the press. One only had to listen to the "hot" tom-tom rhythms of Benny Goodman's "Sing, Sing, Sing" or watch the uncontrolled antics of a jitterbug trucking on the dance floor as proof that something had taken hold of American youth. It was easy to blame the "marijuana menace."

Jazz had long been associated with marijuana and reports of its use by some of America's best known performers occasionally appeared in newspaper and magazine articles in the 1920s and 1930s. During the latter decade, a number of song titles alluded to the drug: "Chant of the Weed," "Muggles," "Reefer Man," "Viper's Drag," and "Texas Tea Party," to name a few. This association was so well known that *Down Beat* was compelled to publish the following ominous warning in August 1938:

> One of these days, say those close to the situation, the Federal Bureau of Investigation will investigate the claim that the marijuana weed is promiscuously used and smoked by players of swing music.
>
> The idea that weed which is supposed to have first been taken hold of the low-down musicians playing in Harlem dives is now spreading to the bigger bands where instrumentalists now use it to emit the wild abandoned rhythms which comprise swing music is said to be arousing interest at J. Edgar Hoover's headquarters.
>
> Whether it is true or not, the FBI is convinced that there is a good deal to the rumors which they have heard and they are planning an investigation, allegedly, *which may one day treat the U.S. to an expose which will rock the music world* [emphasis added].[6]

Three years later national attention quickly focused on the connection between marijuana and swing music when two musicians from the Charlie Barnet band, guitarist Anthony (Bus) Etri and trumpeter Lloyd Hundling, were tragically killed in an automobile accident in California. Investigators blamed the accident on marijuana found at the scene. Labeled the "marijuana death ride," both *Metronome* and *Down Beat* condemned the tragedy and screamed in headlines for immediate action by the American Federation of Musicians. "'Tear Their Cards Up!' . . ." urged *Down Beat*,[7] quoting musicians, while *Metronome* urged the American Federation of Musicians (AFM) to expel tea-hounds!"[8]

An editorial published shortly after the accident condemned the use of drugs by musicians but stated that swing musicians were being unfairly stigmatized by the inference that they needed the drug for musical reasons. Referring to an article published in "one of America's best known and most widely circulated newspapers—a Los Angeles daily," *Down Beat* chastised the newspaper for the following comment about the accident: "The tragedy started an investigation to determine if a marijuana ring has been supplying musicians with poisonous 'reefer cigarets' to GIVE THEM THE WEIRD SENSE OF TIMING FOR THEIR HOT, BOOGIE WOOGIE RHYTHMS [original emphasis]."[9]

This latter assumption echoed the government's 1938 warning about the connection between "wild abandoned rhythms" and swing musicians, an idea that would be played out in nearly every subsequent media account of swing musicians and marijuana. After all, it seemed logical that swing musicians needed extra help to "send" their listeners or themselves "out of this world" during a heated musical performance. This might be especially true if one observed the superhuman performances of Gene Krupa, "America's Ace Drummer Man."

For Gene Krupa, the early 1940s had been good. Anita O'Day, Roy Eldridge, and Buddy DeFranco joined his band; he was the subject of a three-page photomontage in *Life;*[10] and he signed a film contract with MGM. In the summer of 1942, the Gene Krupa Orchestra headed for the West Coast as part of an extensive nationwide tour. In addition, it seemed that his personal life was coming together; he was reconciling with his ex-wife Ethel.

By December 1942, Krupa's band was breaking attendance records at the Palladium Ballroom in Hollywood, and this success seemed certain to continue during his return trip, which included performances in Nebraska, Wisconsin, Illinois, Ohio, Pennsylvania, and Boston. At 34, Gene Krupa was riding on a wave of popularity he had not experienced as a bandleader; he was a national figure, movie star, recording artist, and the most famous drummer in America. However, Gene Krupa was living in a powderkeg and sparks began flying the night of January 18, 1943.

Krupa's Palladium engagement ran from November 10 to December 28, 1942. The band then played a weekend job in Los Angeles before heading north for a week at the Golden Gate Hotel in San Francisco. While at the Palladium, Krupa replaced his long standing valet, Waverly Ivy, who had been drafted into the service, with John Pateakos, a twenty-year old "jitterbug" who played drums and idolized Krupa. Adventurous, excitable, and young, Pateakos had spent the previous year traveling across the country; shortly after graduating from high school in New Bedford, Massachusetts, he went to New York, then worked his way to Chicago and finally to Los Angeles. He stayed at local YMCAs and sought employment in hotels, ballrooms, and theaters—anywhere that would satisfy his craving for swing.

John Pateakos's first job in Los Angles was as a mail carrier for 20th Century Fox, where he encountered many movie stars. Later, as an usher at the Palladium Ballroom, he made friends with Waverly Ivy and asked Ivy to recommend him as his replacement. Krupa hired him in late December or early January, shortly before opening at the Golden Gate on January 17, 1943. His responsibilities included setting up Krupa's drums and band equipment and laying out his clothes for each engagement. He was also a "gofer" and was frequently found in Krupa's room on the twelfth floor of San Francisco's St. Francis Hotel. He was known to the band and Krupa as "Johnny."[11]

Remembering in 1997 the events that took place 54 years earlier, John Pateakos recalled two suspicious men backstage at the Golden Gate Hotel during opening day, Monday, January 18. He would later recognize the same men that night when they appeared backstage after Gene Krupa's last show. The men were agents from the Federal Bureau of Narcotics, Joseph V. Guibbini and O.W. Polcuch, who were there with another agent to speak with Krupa.

The following account of what happened that evening is taken from the Appellate Court records of May 29, 1944:

> On the night of January 18, 1943, three agents from the Federal Bureau of Narcotics, named Guibbini, Grady, and Polcuch, having been informed that appellant [Gene Krupa] was in the possession of marijuana cigarettes, called at appellant's dressing room in the theater in which he was playing, to interview him regarding the information they had received. Pateakos was present at the beginning of the interview, but the agents requested him to leave the room, which he did. After identifying themselves as federal narcotic agents, they asked appellant if he had any marijuana on his person or in his room, and

he denied having any. They told him they had been informed that he did have a quantity of marijuana in his possession, and he replied that there was nothing to the information.

They then asked him if they might search his dressing room, and he told them to "go ahead." While they were doing so Guibbini asked the appellant if he had ever used marijuana, and appellant stated that he had at one time, about 10 years ago, but that lately he had had nothing to do with it. While the search was going on, appellant asked permission to leave the room to go out and wash. He was allowed to do so, but as soon as he left Guibbini followed him and he observed the appellant about half way up the stairs leading to the second floor engaged in earnest conversation with Pateakos. Guibbini separated them, and brought appellant back to his dressing room, where he was further questioned.

Guibbini thereupon went to a phone and instructed the room clerk at the hotel where appellant was staying to allow no one except appellant to enter the latter's room. Guibbini then proceeded to the hotel, leaving Polcuch with appellant. As Guibbini got out of the elevator at the hall leading to appellant's room he saw Pateakos waiting to enter the elevator. He brought Pateakos back to the room adjoining appellant's, occupied by the manager of the band, who was there present and upon searching Pateakos found in his pocket two envelopes, one containing 37 marijuana cigarettes and the other containing two whole ones, and one-half of one partially smoked.

Shortly thereafter, Polcuch and Grady arrived with appellant, and Polcuch and Guibbini took him to his room, where the officers found some fragments of marijuana in a drawer of a writing desk. Appellant denied having anything to do with the marijuana cigarettes or the fragments found. He was then taken back to the adjoining room, and Pateakos was taken to appellant's room. Pateakos refused then to make a statement in explanation of his possession of the marijuana cigarettes. He admitted having them in his pocket, but denied knowing anything about marijuana. He was then returned to the room where appellant was, and appellant stated if the boy had the marijuana cigarettes on him, it was his worry and not his (appellant's); that he did not have anything to do with it. [12]

The federal agents then took Pateakos to their office in San Francisco, where he was interrogated for several hours. Eventually, he signed a statement implicating Krupa.

Krupa called San Francisco's most famous defense lawyer, J.W. "Jake" Ehrlich, then making headlines defending Madge Bellamy in one of San Francisco's most celebrated trials. Bellamy, an attractive but fading movie starlet, was accused of attempting to murder socialite and lumber tycoon A. Stanwood Murphy when she chased him through the streets of San Francisco, ricocheting slugs from a .38 pistol off cars and buildings.

Ehrlich had earlier defended a number of Hollywood celebrities, including Erroll Flynn, James Mason, and Howard Hughes. He would later help clear Billie Holiday of drug charges and in the 1960s, Ehrlich would be asked to represent Jack Ruby.

Federal agents and San Francisco police arrived at the Golden Gate Hotel after Krupa's last performance on January 19 and arrested him, charging him with violation of section 702 of the Welfare and Institutions Code— contributing to the delinquency of a minor—a misdemeanor. Ehrlich accompanied Krupa to the San Francisco Jail House, where he was released after posting $1,000 bail. The Federal Bureau of Narcotics had done what they said they would do five years earlier and "rocked the music world."

Headlines jolted swing fans across the country. Krupa, the handsome, electrifying swing-era idol, was brought to the level of the "low-down musicians playing in Harlem dives." National and local media announced the event to the world: "Gene Krupa Arrested Here In Juvenile Dope Case,"[13] exclaimed the *San Francisco Chronicle,* while the *San Francisco Examiner,* stated "Gene Krupa Linked to Dope Case: 'Swing' Drummer Seized by U.S. Agents."[14] *Variety,* erring on the amount of bail, explained: "Krupa, Free on 2G Bail, Continues Tour Pending Trial on Reefer Rap."[15]

Released on bail, Krupa rejoined his band, which was scheduled to play in Omaha, Nebraska. Two days later he returned to San Francisco to attend his preliminary hearing before Juvenile Court Judge Thomas M. Foley and to come face to face with his accuser, John Pateakos.

Pateakos's testimony given at the preliminary hearing described the events of the night of January 18, including his statement that Krupa told him to go back to the hotel and retrieve the envelope of marijuana cigarettes hidden in his overcoat pocket. As he did so, Pateakos could not look at Krupa sitting in the courtroom next to his lawyer. Serious damage had been done. The result of Pateakos's confession was an additional charge filed against Krupa; he was not only accused of contributing to the delinquency of a minor but was also charged with the more serious crime of using a minor to transport narcotics, a felony. Conviction meant a mandatory one to six years in San Quentin Prison without the possibility of parole. Further it would have effectively ended Krupa's career since the AMF prohibited convicted felons from obtaining a union card. Trial was set for April 19.

Undaunted and still believing the accusations against him would be proven untrue, Krupa returned to his band and continued the tour back to the East Coast. On January 29, the band stopped at the University of Wisconsin for the junior prom and a concert. On February 7, they began a two-week stay at the Panther Room at the Sherman Hotel, Chicago, where he drew nearly $6,000 during the first week. His next week was even more successful. *Variety* reported that the Panther Room was the "Hottest Spot in Town. Krupa Keeps 'em Clamoring for Admission. . . ."[16] Perhaps Krupa's notoriety increased attendance and bookings during his return trip. "Gene Krupa's ability to draw and to be booked apparently hasn't been deterred by the recent charges against him in San Francisco for contributing to the delinquency of a minor . . . in past couple months, Krupa has been booked for a string of eastern theaters that have played him in the past, and for Frank Dailey's Terrace Room, Newark, N.J."[17]

The band opened at the Terrace Room on April 16 for a four-week run. In California three days later, Ehrlich appeared before Judge Foley and entered a plea of guilty on Krupa's behalf to the original charge of contributing to the delinquency of a minor. Ehrlich also petitioned the court for probation. Foley took the petition under advisement and set sentencing for May 10.

Ehrlich and Krupa must have discussed this strategy. It was a difficult decision, but Ehrlich probably believed that the State had enough evidence to build a strong case against Krupa on the felony charge. Pleading guilty to the lesser count seemed less risky. Furthermore, Ehrlich felt that Krupa's guilty plea on a misdemeanor would likely result in a fine and probation, a common penalty for such a charge.

Ehrlich describes his earlier meeting with Judge Foley in his autobiography, *A Life In My Hands:*

> I discussed the matter with Tom Foley. I pointed out the obvious damage that the continuing publicity was doing to Krupa's professional career, as well as the human and social inequity of the penalties he was already paying—guilty or innocent—prior to any judicial determination of guilt or innocence. He agreed with me. I was also convinced that we were in agreement on another point: if Krupa would come back to San Francisco and plead guilty to the misdemeanor, he would be fined $500 and no further penalty, no prosecution on the felony rap.[18]

This was not the case; Krupa's guilty plea would have overwhelming consequences for the drummer, his band, and his career, as he and the world would find out during his sentencing before Judge Foley in May.

When Frank Daily heard of Krupa's guilty plea he immediately petitioned the AFM to "yank Krupa from the Terrace Room." After meeting with Krupa, Ehrlich (who flew in from California) and AFM officials convinced Daily to allow Krupa to complete his contract. However, other problems surfaced. Krupa's contract for the Coca Cola Company radio broadcast on April 26 was canceled, as was his May 26 opening at New York's Paramount Theater. The Paramount had received a warning from reform and religious "organizers" who threatened to picket the theater if Krupa should appear.[19]

Nevertheless, *Variety* reported that "Krupa's entanglement with the law in San Francisco has not harmed his b.o.[box office] since it occurred. In fact the picketing threats to the Par [Paramount Theater] are the first thus far. Everywhere his band has played it did better business than it had previously."[20]

Krupa followed his gig at the Terrace Room with a week at Boston's RKO Theater on May 7. Here, he was met by long lines and grossed over $9,000. After a three-day stint at the Metropolitan Theater in Providence, Rhode Island, Krupa boarded a plane to San Francisco for sentencing before Judge Foley on his misdemeanor guilty plea. Judge Foley had postponed sentencing from the original date of May 10 to the 18th, when Krupa would be available. Ehrlich was shocked by what occurred during sentencing:

> On the 18th of May, Krupa and I stood before Judge Foley. In my pocket were five $100 bills for the payment of the fine that Judge Foley and I had discussed. Foley levied the fine and then double-crossed me when he went on to sentence Krupa to ninety days in the county jail. At the end of the ninety days, less the usual five days from each month for good behavior, Krupa would be tried on the felony charge.[21]

Krupa was probably taken back by the jail term. Most likely he had been reassured by Ehrlich that he would have to pay the fine and would receive probation. If so, the sentence would have come as a total surprise.

But others saw another side to the issue. Having pleaded guilty to the misdemeanor charge Krupa might very well avoid conviction on the felony charge of using a minor to transport narcotics. According to the *San Francisco Examiner:*

> Net results of the sentence, court observers agreed, will be to assure Krupa's acquittal on the felony charge when it is called on June 8. They asserted that a jury verdict of "guilty" would be virtually impossible in view of the fact that Krupa has already been sentenced on the lesser charge.[22]

Variety agreed and ran the following headline: "Observers Foresee Krupa Freed on Felony Rap; Band to Remain Intact." The article then went on to explain what would happen to his band:

Gene Krupa's Orchestra will remain intact during the leader's absence. With a replacement at drums and possibly a w.k. [well-known] musician in front. The outfit will be billed as Gene Krupa's orchestra featuring _____. Neither replacements have been made yet but bookings have been setup for the outfit.[23]

Upon news of Krupa's 90-day jail term his orchestra was given a paid, two-week vacation and waited for the "well known leader" issue to be resolved. On May 18, Krupa began serving 90 days in the San Francisco County Jail and waiting for his felony trial scheduled for June 8.

There are conflicting reports about Krupa's treatment while he was in jail. These range from envy and retaliation to fair and compassionate treatment by jailers . The least plausible is the following description reminiscent of a scene from a Hollywood B movie:

> He [Krupa] remembered arriving in prison. "The one screw took me to the laundry, where I'd been assigned to work. . . . The screw and I stood there before all the convicts and he said. "I've got a guest for you fellas. The Great Gene Krupa.' Well not one of the convicts cracked a smile. Then he gives them a big smile, don'tcha see, and says, 'The first guy that gives 'im any help . . . gets the hole. You understan' me?' He meant solitary. Well . . . the minute he walks out, all of 'em gather aroun' me, shakin' my hand, and one of 'em, a spokesman, says to me, 'What is it we can do to help ya, Mr. Krupa?'"[24]

This account, written in 1985, conflicts with contemporaneous descriptions. In September 1943, *Metronome* indicated, "Gene says he was treated very well in the San Francisco jail," and that he was given time to write and study music.[25] But perhaps the most reliable source is a letter written from his cell in which Krupa explains, "The officials in and immediately about the prison here are most kind, and I'm given time each day to pursue my study of music."[26]

But, normally upbeat and optimistic, Krupa was shamed by the accusations made against him. One visitor indicated that he was so depressed that he belonged in a "sanitarium instead of a cell."[27] On June 7, the day before his felony trial, Krupa was taken ill. Some sources indicated that he had somehow obtained illegal drugs and had taken an overdose. The jail physician, Dr. Lee Hand, was called and Krupa was driven in an ambulance to San Francisco Hospital, then to the Harbor Emergency Hospital and examined by Dr. Thomas Fitzpatrick, an intern. Hospital records showed that he might have ingested an overdose of phenolbarbital, a prescriptive sedative, which, if taken in substantial quantity, could cause death. The *San Francisco Examiner* indicated that he took three tablets[28] and one account had him arriving at the hospital in a "semi-stupor."[29]

But it seems unlikely that Gene Krupa meant to cause himself harm. If he had taken an overdose of phenolbarbital, he did not take enough to cause serious injury. In fact, after he was examined at Harbor Emergency Hospital, he was not returned to San Francisco Hospital but sent back to the County Jail. Evidently he did not require hospital care. Later in the day Krupa declined to see visitors "explaining he wasn't feeling well and was a bit off the beat because of an attack of nausea." In all likelihood Krupa was, as one of his jailers said, "just sick—or it might have been something he ate."[30]

However, Krupa's image was even more tarnished by this event since the newspaper account implied that drugs were involved and that he might have obtained them surreptitiously while in jail. The event might confirm public suspicions of substance abuse, or an apparent attempted suicide, or an unbalanced mental state. Nothing could be further from the truth.

While Gene Krupa may have been despondent he most certainly was not suicidal. In response to one of what must have been numerous fan letters he received in jail, Krupa wrote: "Tell all the kids how-ever, those that care to know, I'm striving with all my will power to keep the proverbial chin up, and ultimately if I lose it shall be only after a hard fight."[31] Krupa's incarceration was a humbling experience, but he was not without hope.

On June 8, the day after his bout with nausea, Gene Krupa's trial was once again postponed but not because of the overdose issue. John Pateakos, the prosecution's main witness, had disappeared. Since he had been apprehended by federal agents, Pateakos had spent most of the next thirty days in custody as a material witness. He appeared at the preliminary hearing on January 26 but continued to be detained until his release in February. He then returned to the rooming house in Los Angeles, where he had lived prior to being hired by Krupa. But when the felony trial began he could not be found. Rumors circulated that he had been paid to leave California. Neither local police nor FBI agents, who were looking for him as a draft dodger, could locate him. In all likelihood it appeared that Pateakos would miss the trial. This would certainly not harm Gene Krupa's case.

Krupa's felony trial on the charge of using a minor to transport narcotics began on June 8, but the prosecution quickly asked for a continuance. Over strong objections by Ehrlich, Judge Foley continued the trial until June 29, when he was assured that Pateakos could be found. But Pateakos was still missing when the trial began on June 29.

Initially things went well for the defense. Assistant District Attorney Leslie Gillen requested another continuance since Pateakos could not be found and asked for more time to produce additional evidence. Judge Foley not only denied his request but found him in contempt after Gillen reproached the court for disallowing the extension. However, Judge Foley called for a recess until the next morning, when the trial would proceed without the prosecution's main witness and the "additional evidence of Krupa's guilt."[32]

On June 30 a jury of nine men and three women heard the prosecution's evidence, which included a transcript of Pateakos's statement made during the preliminary hearing in January. His affidavit asserted that Krupa had instructed him to go to the hotel and get the marijuana cigarettes from his coat pocket. His actions at the hotel were confirmed by the bellhop who let him into Krupa's hotel room and by testimony by federal narcotics agents.

After the prosecution presented its case, Krupa took the stand as the only witness for the defense. His testimony is described in the appellate court records:[33]

> [Gene Krupa] became a witness in his own behalf, and in contradiction of the denials he had made to the federal agents on the night of January 18th, he admitted that all of the marijuana cigarettes which had been taken from his clothes belonged to him. In this connection he testified that he brought them to San Francisco from Los Angeles in the clothing which Pateakos was required to take care of, and that he had smoked part of one of the cigarettes after coming to San Francisco. . . . He denied, however, that he had asked Pateakos on the night in question to remove them from the pockets of his clothes.

This last statement would remain consistent in almost every retelling of the event by Krupa.

He was also asked if it was true that most swing musicians used marijuana. Krupa replied: "It might be true of 'hot bands' playing in dives but that it would be impossible for members of a prominent band to habitually use marijuana in view of the split-second timing on radio, and the need for self-possession on the stage."

During the prosecution's presentation it had been brought out that the Federal Agents received a tip that Gene Krupa had purchased a "large amount" of marijuana when he was in Los Angeles. But Krupa's testimony contradicts this:

> Krupa testified that in the first place, he did not purchase marihuana in Los Angeles as charged by federal narcotics agents. He said somebody unknown to him—possibly one of his "fans"—admittedly a man who looked as if he might be a marihuana addict—had accosted him at the stage door of a Los Angeles theater and thrust an envelope in his hand. . . .

Krupa said he shoved the package into his coat pocket and later discovered that it contained marihuana cigarets. The entire matter was then forgotten, he said, until he happened to rummage through the coat pocket later in San Francisco and discovered the envelope. That was shortly before his arrest as he stepped from the stage of a local theater last January.

This account, or variations of it, is one of two Krupa supplied over the years. He also claimed that the illegal cigarettes were a gift from his departing valet, Westerly Ivy, as he explains in Burt Korall's *Drummin' Men:*

> We were closing at the Hollywood Palladium, prior to my going to San Francisco to play at the Golden Gate Theater. My valet [who had gotten his draft notice] wanted to give me a parting present. He shopped around L.A. and finally decided on grass. Apparently he had a rough time buying it and shot off his mouth a little: "This is for the greatest guy in the world—Gene Krupa," he said. Someone heard and fingered me for the narco police.[34]

But the most colorful narration is provided by his attorney Jake Ehrlich, who recounted Krupa's version in the hep vernacular of the day. According to Ehrlich, Krupa said:

> "I wouldn't con you, Master," he'd said. "I don't know a damn thing about this caper. The first time I pick up on the fact it's marijuana that's got them bugged is when the fuzz lay the story on me after they drop the net on Johnny [Pateakos]. They tell me he picked up the muggles in my suite, and I come all unzipped. That's a scene I don't dig, Jake; tea, goof balls, bennies—all that funny kind of quick energy. I don't need it! I got *me* [original emphasis]; that's plenty. If the kid had muggles, I sure don't know where he got it."[35]

Regardless of which story is to be believed Krupa's testimony rang hollow before the jury and "caused some embarrassment to listeners and which by its seeming lack of plausibility begged for rebuttal."[36] But Judge Foley, who at times seemed overwhelmingly in support of the defense, would not allow Assistant District Attorney Gillen time to gather his forces to rebut Krupa's explanation. He wanted to complete the trial that afternoon. Foley then declared a five-minute recess after which Gillen was told to proceed, but because Pateakos was absent and because he did not have time to produce "additional evidence," Gillen could not continue and rested his case.

At approximately 3:00 P.M. on June 30, the jury retired to ponder the fate of Gene Krupa. They returned to the courtroom two hours later and found him guilty as charged. Judge Foley would have no recourse: the law required that if found guilty of using a minor to transport narcotics, he would be sentenced to one to six years in San Quentin Prison without chance of parole. Formal sentencing would take place two days later.

On July 2, 1943 Gene Krupa received the mandatory sentence, to run concurrent with his present jail term. The local press had a field day at his expense. Assistant District Gillen's closing remarks to the jury found their way onto the front page of the *San Francisco Chronicle*: "It is a deadly, dreadful, unpredictable drug. . . . Can the jury condone his [Krupa's] persuading or allowing a minor to even come into contact with it?"[37] The *San Francisco Examiner* printed the following comment by District Attorney Matthew Brady:

> The conviction of Gene Krupa, it is to be hoped, will have a deterrent effect upon those who are careless regarding the welfare and morals of children and growing youth.
>
> I want it to serve as a warning that San Francisco will not tolerate exposing minors to immorality, liquor and narcotics, regardless of the social standing of the offenders.[38]

Even Judge Foley, whose position shifted frequently during the trial issued this condemnation:

> I hope this case will bring sharply to the attention of users of marihuana its vicious effects. It is ruinous to the morals and career and welfare of a person addicted, and above all, minors must be protected from contact with its vicious influence. I certainly trust that this case will bring to everyone's attention, especially to the attention of those who might use it for purposes of exhilaration, the consequences of its use.[39]

Ehrlich immediately filed an appeal which was granted by Judge Foley, and Krupa was returned to the San Francisco County Jail, where he continued to serve out his 90-day sentence.

After the two-week vacation given to them in May, Gene Krupa's band returned with trumpeter Roy Eldridge as leader and drummer Harry Jaeger filling in for Krupa. The band played a series of East Coast dates before returning to the Metropolitan Ballroom in Philadelphia for two weeks ending June 13. The ensemble then waited for the outcome of the trial. But one by one its members left; some were recruited by other bands, some returned home, others were drafted into the armed forces. When word came of Krupa's conviction and subsequent prison sentence, the band had effectively ceased to exist, and the likelihood of it ever being resurrected seemed doubtful.

Meanwhile the issue of John Pateakos took an interesting turn. A week after Gene Krupa was sentenced, John Pateakos was arrested in Los Angeles as a draft evader. Pateakos had received a draft notice in March 1943 and was ordered to take a physical that same month but failed to do so. The U.S. Government issued a warrant for his arrest for draft evasion, but FBI agents could not find him; neither could the San Francisco District Attorney's office, who sought him as a witness in the Krupa felony trial. In fact, the trial had been postponed three times in order for the prosecution to find their star witness. But did Pateakos disappear or did the D.A.'s office simply not want him found?

Jake Ehrlich contends that District Attorney Brady didn't want Pateakos to appear at the trial and that the prosecution knew where he was all the time. This was confirmed by Assistant District Attorney Gillen who revealed that Pateakos was "in Los Angeles during the time the State was looking for him as a State witness in Krupa's trial."[40] Just why did the D.A. not want Pateakos to appear at Krupa's trial? More importantly, why didn't Jake Ehrlich who also knew where Pateakos was, want him to appear at the trial? Presumably, Ehrlich would have welcomed a chance to discredit his previous testimony under cross-examination.

It would be several months before these questions would be answered. During the week of July 19 both lawyers would be battling each other in a Grand Jury investigation of bribery charges brought against Ehrlich. That investigation stemmed from a report that Pateakos was given $650 to leave California during Krupa's felony trial. Brady made the accusations against Ehrlich, his associate Roy Scharff, and two Hollywood agents who acted as middlemen between Pateakos and Ehrlich's office, Barney McDevitt and Jack Lavin. The Grand Jury convened at 8:00 P.M. on the evening of July 20 to hear testimony from Pateakos regarding his whereabouts before and during the trial and if he had been bribed by Ehrlich to leave town.

Pateakos testified that he did not hide from either FBI agents nor detectives sent by the San Francisco D.A.'s office. He may have gone to Chicago in April, but he was in Los Angeles at the time of the trial. But Pateakos did say that he was given $650 by Roy Sharff on April 29 with instructions to "get out of the State and stay out till the trial is over."[41]

Sharff admitted giving $500 to Pateakos but claimed that the money was for back pay, lost clothing, and other incidental expenses. He denied that he told Pateakos to leave California. Furthermore, Sharff produced a statement handwritten by Pateakos clearly stating that the money he received was not connected with any legal action taking place against Krupa.

On July 24 the Grand Jury, after a divisive vote, refused to indict any of those charged by District Attorney Brady. Ehrlich commented that he was in good company with a number of famous lawyers who had been brought before grand juries, including Clarence Darrow. John Pateakos was inducted into the Army three days later and served as a medical corpsman until his tour of duty ended May 25, 1946.

Gene Krupa was incarcerated for 84 days. He was never sent to San Quentin, as some sources have stipulated, but was released on $5,000 bail from the San Francisco County Jail August 9 pending the outcome of his appeal. The next few months were difficult for him, but he gradually began a slow and cautious reentry into the music business. Benny Goodman asked him to join his band for several USO appearances in November. In December he played with Goodman at the New Yorker Hotel. In early January he joined Tommy Dorsey at the Paramount Theater in New York and waited for the California Court of Appeals to make a decision.

Had "America's Ace Drummer Man" gone to sleep in January 1943 and awakened a year later he would have probably thought little had changed. True, he wasn't fronting his own band, but he was still getting standing ovations. He had won the 1943 *Down Beat* best drummer poll (beating Buddy Rich by over 2,500 votes), and critics who heard him with Goodman and Dorsey claimed he was playing better than ever. Yet a decision on his appeal had not been made, and it was still possible that he might have to return to jail to begin serving his sentence. The thought depressed him. At the end of the month, however, Krupa would have reason to be optimistic; John Pateakos recanted his earlier testimony which had implicated Krupa, caused his arrest, jail term, and felony conviction.

On January 14, 1944, a letter was sent to Gene Krupa, c/o Music Corporation of America. It contained $1 and a request for a photograph and had been written by Private John Pateakos, a corpsman stationed at the Letterman General Hospital in San Francisco. The letter was forwarded to the New York office of attorney John Gluskin, Krupa's new manager, who in turn called Pateakos to arrange a meeting. The two men met on January 26, at the Mark Hopkins Hotel in San Francisco.

The meeting between Gluskin and Pateakos was cordial; both men reminisced about the ordeal of the past year. Gluskin showed Pateakos a notebook of newspaper clippings and remarked that Krupa was anxious about his upcoming appeal and was depressed at the thought of returning to jail. Gluskin also said that Krupa continued to maintain that he never told Pateakos to go to his hotel room and get the marijuana cigarettes as alleged by the prosecution. In a startling revelation, Pateakos said that Krupa never told him to get the marijuana cigarettes from his hotel room. Then, Pateakos gave a different version of what happened the night of January 18, 1943:

> As Gene came off the stage, soaking wet as usual, these three men [agents Gubbini, Grady, and Polcuch] walked over to him and said they wanted to talk to him. They walked Gene into his dressing room and I walked right in after them. I felt something was wrong. [The agents] told me to leave the room. I looked at Gene who nodded approval but he had a very particular expression on his face. I felt then that something was going to happen. I waited outside the dressing room for quite a while. Gene finally came out, pale as a ghost and still soaking wet although he still had his robe on. He was all shaken up and excited. He motioned me to go with him and by now I was all excited myself. We started to walk toward the washroom. Gene seemed unable to talk at first but finally said to me " Johnny, I want you to do something for me," and before he could say another word, the [agent] broke up the conversation, walked Gene back to his dressing room and left me standing there alone. Right then and there, I thought I knew what Gene wanted me to do. He was a nice guy and I wanted to help him. So I ran as fast as I could back to the hotel and tried to get Frank Verniere [Krupa's manager] on the phone but it was busy. I finally got a bell-hop to let me in. I took an envelope of cigarettes out of the pocket of his coat in the closet and left the room. Then I remembered there were also a few cigarettes in a drawer of the writing desk. So I returned to the room and took those cigarettes out of the drawer, put them in an envelope and left the room.[42]

Gluskin interrupted him and asked if Gene Krupa had ever told him to go to Krupa's room and remove the marijuana cigarettes from his coat. Pateakos said: "Gene never asked me to remove the cigarettes from his coat in his room, he never had the chance to; but I was sure I knew what he wanted me to do and I wanted to help, so I did it."[43]

The remaining portion of Pateakos's story parallels the description cited in the appellate court records with the exception of what transpired when Pateakos was brought to the Federal Bureau of Narcotics office after leaving Krupa's room at the St. Francis Hotel. When he was taken into custody, Pateakos continued to remain silent and refused to say anything that would implicate Krupa. In fact, he denied that he even knew what marijuana cigarettes were or that he had ever seen them before. What happened next would certainly not have appeared in any official account of the evening:

> After quite a while trying to make me say something, the agents took me over to their office alone. There they really gave me the works. They pushed me

around and threatened to hit me with a black-jack and beat me up if I still refused to talk and furthermore, would put me in jail for possession of the cigarettes.

At this time it must have been well into the early hours of the morning, and he was tired and afraid. Eventually Pateakos told the agents what happened, but it was not what they wanted to hear. He reiterated that Krupa had not told him to get the dope from his room and that he had decided to go to the hotel and get the cigarettes because that's what he thought Krupa had wanted him to do. But the agents were not satisfied with his story. They continued to threaten him and then finally told him that whatever he said "wouldn't make any difference to Gene because he would be in exactly the same trouble anyway."[44] To an exhausted twenty-year old, threatened with physical harm and possibly jail, this might have made sense. Furthermore, he was alone. Without legal help or assistance of any kind, John Pateakos, believing that whatever he said could not hurt Gene Krupa anymore than he already had been hurt, agreed to sign a statement saying that Gene Krupa had asked him to go to his hotel and get the marijuana cigarettes in his overcoat.

Gluskin thanked Pateakos for his candor and the meeting ended. On January 29, Gluskin sent Pateakos a nine-page letter describing the events of their meeting and asked him to sign each page as verification that the details described in the letter were true. After making some minor corrections, Pateakos complied and returned the letter. Gluskin notified Attorney Ehrlich of Pateakos's statement, and Ehrlich brought it to the attention of the San Francisco Juvenile Court.

On February 10, the case was brought before Juvenile Court Judge Theresa Meikel. Pateakos admitted that he had lied during his previous testimony, and a deposition to this effect was entered into evidence by Ehrlich. Judge Meikel admonished Pateakos and told him that he could be charged with perjury for giving false testimony. But it also became clear that he had probably signed the original statement under threats made by federal agents and the D.A.'s office. Consequently, Pateakos was never charged with perjury.

Now it is understandable why the D.A.'s office chose not to find Pateakos during Gene Krupa's felony trial. They may have believed Pateakos would simply tell the truth: that he had been coerced into making a false statement. Regardless, the matter became moot when on May 29, 1944, Krupa won by a 2–1 decision by the Court of Appeal of California. The majority decision was based upon a finding that the felony and misdemeanor charges were founded on the same action and that punishment for both constituted double jeopardy. Although there were threats made by the D.A's office to bring the decision to the State Supreme Court, nothing was ever done. While Krupa was never really cleared of the charges brought against him, after the appellate court decision he was free.

Several stories have been perpetuated through the many tellings of Krupa's drug bust. Krupa frequently charged that he had been caught in a political maelstrom between two old adversaries, Ehrlich and Brady.[45] This is true. Ehrlich and Brady were fierce opponents in some of San Francisco's most notorious trials. But their squabbles had little or no direct impact on the outcome of Krupa's legal battles.

Krupa also stated that Brady was coming up for reelection in the fall of 1944 and needed a sensational trial in order to win.[46] If Brady was counting on Krupa's trial and subsequent conviction as a way to remain in office, he highly underestimated his constituents and Jake Ehrlich. In a resolute move to unseat Brady, Ehrlich resigned from his law firm and devoted himself to defeat Brady by campaigning for Edmund G. (Pat) Brown. Brady lost the election, and Brown would go on to become governor of California.

A number of preposterous ideas have filtered in and out of this story, including the notion concocted by Anita O'Day that John Pateakos was a "juvenile delinquent and a possible police plant,"[47] or the rumor that Krupa had been "set up" by an angry band member.[48] Neither of these is true.

What is true is that Gene Krupa's name would be forever connected with drugs and, by some, he would always be considered an addict. Later in life he would speak openly about marijuana and warn others against its use in lectures and interviews. Furthermore, whether on purpose or by coincidence, whenever an article about Krupa appeared in a trade magazine after this event, a drug-related story was frequently placed on the same page.

There remains one piece of unfinished business. During Krupa's trial, Assistant District Attorney Gillen unsuccessfully requested continuances in order to "obtain additional evidence of Krupa's guilt." It is quite possible that the information Gillen planned to bring into court was verification that Gene Krupa had purchased a large quantity of marijuana when he was in Los Angeles before going to San Francisco. The following appeared in the *San Francisco Examiner* five days before Krupa was freed:

> In repercussion of the Gene Krupa case, John Russo, 26, yesterday was sentenced to a term of from one to six years in San Quentin on a charge of using a minor to transport narcotics. . . .

Russo was apprehended in San Francisco after reports had been received by the district attorney's office [t]here that he had been suspected of furnishing narcotics to Gene Krupa in Los Angeles.[49]

Was John Russo the source of "additional evidence" against Gene Krupa? It appears he was, but his testimony would not have been detrimental to Krupa's case. Krupa admitted in court that he owned the marijuana cigarettes found in Pateakos's possession and that he had smoked marijuana. It seems Assistant District Attorney Gillen simply wanted the threat of possible further incriminating evidence to weigh heavily on the defense since Russo was never called to testify.

Several conclusions may be drawn from the events of 1943–44, including the fact that John Pateakos was most likely coerced or misled into making a false statement to federal narcotics agents. It is also probable that without that statement there simply was no case against Gene Krupa. His arrest, $500 fine, 90-day jail term, and felony sentence would not have happened.

Within a month of the Appellate Court decision Krupa began rehearsing what is generally called his second band ("The Band that Swings with Strings"), which opened at the RKO Theater in Boston, July 6, 1944. This group, which would later abandon the string section, would become a proving ground for several seminal bop musicians, including baritone saxophonist/arranger Gerry Mulligan, trumpeter Red Rodney, trumpeter Don Fagerquist, and vocalist Dave Lambert. The dissolution of the big bands by the 1950s found Krupa touring with Jazz at the Philharmonic, fronting his own small groups, and occasionally staging drum battles with Buddy Rich. Although declining health forced him into semiretirement in the 1960s, he occasionally played reunion concerts with the Benny Goodman Quartet. Ironically Gene Krupa made his last recording in April 1972 with fellow Chicagoan Eddie Condon, with whom he had made his first record 44 years earlier. Years after the San Francisco incident Krupa and Pateakos met after a concert. There was no animosity between to two men; Pateakos still revered Krupa, and the famous drummer had learned to accept the facts of his past. After Gene Krupa died in 1973, John Pateakos began a tradition that continues to this day; each year a Mass is said in honor of America's Ace Drummerman in his local Catholic Church.

NOTES

1. "The Menace of Marihuana," *American Mercury,* December 1935: 487–490.
2. "Facts and Fancies About Marihuana," *Literary Digest,* 24 October 1936: 7–8.

3. "Marihuana Menaces Youth," *Scientific America,* March 1936: 150.

4. W. Gard, "Youth Gone Loco; Villain is Marijuana," *Christian Century,* 29 June 1938, 812–13.

5. David Soloman, ed., *The Marijuana Papers* (New York: Mentor Book, 1966), xv.

6. "GMen to Expose Weed Hounds in Bands," *Down Beat,* August 1938: 2.

7. "'Tear Their Cards Up!' Musicians Cry," *Down Beat,* 15 September 1941: 2.

8. "AFM—Expel Tea-Hounds!!, *"Metronome,* September 1941: 50.

9. "One Jerk Writer Can Hurt All Musicians," editorial, *Down Beat,* 15 September 1941:10.

10. "Krupa Shows How to Play Drum In These Fantastic Sound Pictures, *"Life,* 9 June 1941: 81ff.

11. John Pateakos, personal interview, 27 January 1997.

12. The People, Respondent, v. Gene Krupa, Appellant Crim. No. 2281 Court of Appeal of California, First Appellate District, Division One, 64 Cal. App. 2d 592; 149 P.2d 416: 1944.

13. Gene Krupa Arrested Here In Juvenile Dope Case," *San Francisco Chronicle,* 20 January 1943: 1.

14. "Gene Krupa Linked to Dope Case: 'Swing' Drummer Seized by U.S. Agents," *San Francisco Examiner,* 20 January 1943: 1.

15. Krupa, Free on 2G Bail, Continues Tour Pending Trial on Reefer Rap," *Variety,* 27 January 1943: 3.

16. "Hottest Spot in Town. Krupa Keeps 'em Clamoring for Admission—$6,000 Last Week," *Variety,* 21 February 1943: 32.

17. "Inside Stuff—Orchestras," *Variety,* 10 March 1943: 35.

18. J.W. Ehrlich, *A Life in My Hands,* (New York: G.P. Putnam's Sons, 1965), 135.

19. "Report of 'Guilty' Plea Jams Krupa On Several Dates; N.Y. Par Looks Out," *Variety,* 28 April, 1943: 45.

20. "Krupa Defers Par, N.Y., Date Pending Outcome of Frisco Morals Charge," *Variety,* 5 May 1943: 41.

21. Ehrlich 136.

22. "Krupa Given Light Term and Fine," *San Francisco Examiner,* 19 May 1943: 1.

23. "Observers Forsee Krupa Freed on Felony Rap; Band to Remain Intact," *Variety,* 26 May 1943: 41.

24. Bobby Scott, "Gene Krupa: The World Is Not Enough," Gene Lees *Jazzletter,* 7 October 1985: 2.

25. "Gene in NY," *Metronome,* September 1943: 7.

26. Gene Krupa letter to Phil Ribner, n.d. online, *crash.simplenet.com,* Internet 20 September 1998.

27. Anita O'Day with George Eells, *High Times, Hard Times* (New York: Limelight Editions, 1989), 123.

28. *San Francisco Examiner,* 9 June 1943: B.

29. "Krupa Felony Trial Delayed By S.F. Court," *San Francisco Examiner,* 9 June 1943: B.

30. "Krupa Off the Beat: Skin Slugger is Mysteriously Ill in His Cell," *San Francisco Chronicle,* 8 June 1943: 15.

31. Gene Krupa letter to Phil Ribner.

32. "Foley Rejects Plea to Locate Krupa Witness,"*San Francisco Examiner* 30 June 1943: B.

33. The People, Respondent, v. Gene Krupa, Appellant (see note 12).

34. Burt Korall, *Drummin' Men* (New York: Schirmer Books, 1990), 76.

35. Ehrlich, 133.

36. "Foley Turns on Prosecutor in Krupa's Trial," *San Francisco Examiner,* 30 June 1943:1.

37. "Gene Krupa Guilty in Narcotics Case," *San Francisco Chronicle,*" 1 July 1943: 1.

38. "Krupa's Term Set Today," *San Francisco Examiner,* 2 July 1943: 2.

39. "Krupa Gets 1 to 6 Year Sentence," *San Francisco Examiner,* 3 July 1943: 1.

40. Grand Jurors Hear Pateakos in Krupa Case," *San Francisco Examiner,* 24 July 1943: 3.

41. "Grand Jury In Krupa Probe," *San Francisco Examiner,* 21 July 1943: 1.

42. John Gluskin, letter to John Pateakos, 29 January 1944: 3–4.

43. Gluskin, 4.

44. Gluskin, 6.

45. Korall, 76.

46. Bruce Klauber, *World of Gene Krupa* (Ventura, CA: Pathfinder Publishing, 1990) 54.

47. O'Day, 124.

48. John Pateakos personal interview.

49. "Krupa Suspect Gets Term," *San Francisco Examiner,* 4 August 1943: 3.

REVIEW ESSAYS

PRISM ON AN ERA:
SCOTT DEVEAUX'S THE BIRTH OF BEBOP

Scott DeVeaux, *The Birth of Bebop: A Social and Musical History* (Berkeley, Los Angeles and London: University of California Press, 1997, 572 + xv pp., $45.00 cloth, $18.95 paper)

Henry Martin

Scott DeVeaux's *The Birth of Bebop* combines social and music history alongside music analysis to present a sweeping panorama of the new jazz developing in the early 1940s. An ambitious volume that has deservedly received much attention since publication, *The Birth of Bebop* is in many ways a model for the kind of historical work much needed in the field. What in this book is new for jazz scholarship? Quite simply, it is comprehensive history, a full-scale study that seeks to integrate approaches usually considered distinct. Let us begin with a brief overview of the areas of jazz scholarship—fields DeVeaux's study hopes to unite.

1. AREAS OF JAZZ SCHOLARSHIP

As is well known, jazz is the subject of much biographical mythology and outright factual error. The recorded interview and its close cousin, the autobiographical memoir, are notoriously unreliable regarding fact, despite their immense value regarding the attitudes, perceptions, and cultural memories of the participants. Stories retold many times become embellished: errors creep in, fictions are repeated, legends grow.

During the last several years, we are fortunate that many scholars have devoted themselves to separating fact from fiction, particularly in the area of biography and discography. The appearance of such works has been a boon to jazz studies; we owe thanks to these scholars and the (largely) university presses that have supported such work. Nonetheless, the works themselves are properly concerned with individuals; as such, they often lack compelling interpretation of larger-scale culture and historical issues.

There are exceptions, of course. Among the finer biographical works that have helped illuminate the historical eras under investigation are Edward A. Berlin's *King of Ragtime: Scott Joplin and His Era*[1] and Scott E. Brown's *James P. Johnson: A Case of Mistaken Identity*.[2] These works bear the closest relationship to *The Birth of Bebop*. It is perhaps not remarkable that these two books are concerned with ragtime and older jazz, as the perceptions of pre-1940s jazz seem particularly complex, given the overlap between jazz and popular music more broadly considered.

In addition to growing biographical and discographical research, the 1990s witnessed an important trend in jazz scholarship, the rise of analytical studies dealing with a particular artist or "the act" of jazz itself. Among the latter are those with an ethnomusicological bent, such as Paul F. Berliner's *Thinking in Jazz: The Infinite Art of Improvisation*[3] and Ingrid Monson's *Saying Something: Jazz Improvisation and Interaction*.[4] For more traditional analytical studies, there is Ken Rattenbury's *Duke Ellington: Jazz Composer*[5] and my own *Charlie Parker and Thematic Improvisation*.[6]

Complementing analytical studies, there have been larger-scale overviews of particular musical eras Among these, the most important are Gunther Schuller's *Early Jazz*[7] and *The Swing Era*.[8] In Schuller's work, however, the emphasis is on the recorded musical works themselves as the "hard facts" of jazz history; there is fairly little in the way of intellectual, sociological, or even biographical study.[9]

Quite apart from biographical and analytical work, there have also been a growing number of social histories that have helped position jazz—especially earlier jazz—in a broader cultural context.[10] Despite their immense value, such studies usually avoid the music's history itself as well as the music-theoretical insights so essential to understanding the music from the inside.

With the types of studies described above dominating the field, one could argue that treatments of any given topic are usually incomplete, that because these areas are so disparate, a given book tends to engage its material in one way only. DeVeaux's large ambition is to combine all of these approaches in order to illuminate the birth of bebop from as many angles as possible. While it is not especially difficult in itself to touch upon all the facets of scholarship mentioned above, what is difficult is to integrate them convincingly, so that factors play off of and relate to one another. DeVeaux wants his study to function as a prism on bebop, that it should break down the era into different spectra and present an exhaustive and ultimately unified picture. In the following sections of this essay,

I shall focus on only some of DeVeaux's points, generally those that I found of particular interest. As a summation, I will consider his success in integrating the various facets of jazz scholarship into a comprehensive story of bebop's genesis.

2. ORGANICISM AND THE JAZZ TRADITION

DeVeaux sets the stage for his story of bebop origins by sympathetically recounting some of the criticisms of historical organicism, an issue that has recently occupied those academics of a postmodernist bent who feel that its often implicit assumptions are questionable. A brief consideration of DeVeaux's views here will help tell us what he hopes to achieve, how he hopes his history will correct approaches he considers deficient.

An important assumption of organicist musical history, in DeVeaux's view, is the practice of viewing music-stylistic evolution apart from the larger historical context. In the organicist view, musical styles have their own "essence" and can be viewed as a self-contained historical succession without necessarily considering nonmusical intrusions (except in the most general way). As a result, organicists can conceive of art forms as virtually living entities with their own essence maintained through any macro-historical "vicissitudes of change" (5). Among his many points, DeVeaux claims that considering only the musical qualities in which swing-style jazz evolved into bebop is a false path, albeit one commonly assumed in music-historical writing. DeVeaux is staking out an important ambition if he hopes that his own book will amend this historical commonplace by explicitly showing the effect of the larger historical context on the music itself.

Another of DeVeaux's important criticisms against organicism is a practice that has been common in jazz historiography: viewing earlier historical eras according to more recent standards—a form of historicism. For example, if historians detect "progress" in, say, the evolution of swing to bop, then they may find a comparable evolution in the transition of ragtime to jazz, or of 1920s jazz to swing (15). DeVeaux's protest against such forced interpretations is surely valid—and the tendency was indeed common among older jazz writers—but I think nowadays scholars are careful to avoid this fallacy. DeVeaux is particularly concerned with how jazz historians have viewed progress, an issue that is of paramount importance in his book as a whole. This critical theme will be considered further in the following section.

DeVeaux is also concerned with the idea of historical continuity itself. For example, something of a continuity can be seen by the persistence of the term "jazz" throughout the twentieth century; yet, interestingly, this word links musical worlds that are remarkably distinct. It has long been pointed out that jazz cannot be defined since the multitude of its formats precludes qualities common among all. Thus, the presumption of writing jazz history in the first place means seeking an apparent but unreal unity. According to DeVeaux, it is important to remember that the styles of the music called "jazz" are tremendously fragmented and have evolved through much complex give-and-take among all parties involved; history should reflect this: "The writing of jazz history is accordingly obsessed with continuity and consensus, even—perhaps *especially*—when the historical record suggests disruption and dissent" (6, DeVeaux's emphasis).

I would argue that there seems no credible alternative to the kind of history DeVeaux criticizes. For an historical reconstruction to make sense—for anyone to create a readable, linear narrative that *is* a book—that narrative will necessarily impose a continuity on past events that may have been discrete, disruptive, and confusing while taking place. DeVeaux wants to present a more complete, more nuanced reading of the birth of bebop, but he cannot transcend the narrative commonplace of telling a story, no matter how strongly he emphasizes controversies and ambiguities. He cannot make the history "disruptive," because history is how we impose order on the past. This is what we do as human beings to make sense of the staggering multiplicity of sensory and mental experience: the very act of existing through time forces us to credibly reinterpret the past in such a way as to make (narrative) sense of it.

3. HAWKINS, REVOLUTION/EVOLUTION, AND THE IDEA OF PROGRESS

With his principal historiographical viewpoints set, DeVeaux turns his attention to one of his most important themes: What accounts for the *perceived revolution* of bebop, in both its own time and ours, as well as a logical musical *evolution*, i.e., a natural next step? When viewed as a musical microcosm, bebop seems not much more than the natural outcome of the evolution of earlier jazz, in particular swing. Yet, among those who like to view bebop as representing an important cultural trend of the 1940s, bebop is persistently spoken of as a "revolution." How can both of these conflicting points of view be true? How can bebop be both a "revolution" and an "evolution"?

DeVeaux begins to resolve the revolution-evolution paradox by showing that twentieth-century modernism has critically influenced both the history and perception of jazz. What does DeVeaux assume to be modernism's most important traits? Among the items he mentions are (1) ongoing, radical innovation; (2) headlong pace of change; (3) the need to educate the audience; (4) a generally anti-commercial stance regarding marketing the art form, and (5) progress. After this general discussion regarding modernism and historiography, DeVeaux proceeds to introduce his book's central figure: not Charlie Parker, not Dizzy Gillespie, but Coleman Hawkins.

This is something of a shock: Coleman Hawkins? While Hawkins was surely one of the most important tenor players in jazz, his involvement with bebop is generally thought to be an oddity, as his style, which matured during the 1930s, was too well formed by the 1940s to undergo significant change. But DeVeaux takes Hawkins as an exemplar of the factors brought to bear on his analysis of the social factors of the time. His choice makes both practical and thematic sense. As a practical matter, Hawkins was the subject of DeVeaux's doctoral dissertation, which served as the basis for this book; thematically, Hawkins's story better serves the purposes of DeVeaux's themes of modernism and progress, which are more acutely embodied in Hawkins's age and temperament than in the younger Parker or Gillespie.

In particular, Hawkins, born in 1904, was the product of an era caught up in the spirit of progress, a hallmark of the new century as a whole. His own style—as heard, say, with the Fletcher Henderson band in the middle and late 1920s—was initially fairly stiff and "on the beat," his tone steely. In the early 1930s, his overall approach to the instrument changed into what is normally regarded as the mature Hawkins. Selections such as "It's the Talk of the Town" (with Fletcher Henderson in 1933) presaged the transformation that culminated in his famous 1939 recording, "Body and Soul." Hawkins's maturity from the early 1920s to about 1940 thus paralleled the evolution of jazz itself.

And Hawkins was a decided progressivist. As DeVeaux quotes Hawkins from an interview in 1946:

"It's like a man thinking back to when he couldn't walk, he had to crawl," he [Hawkins] complained after rehearing one of his solos twenty years later. That art, out of all areas of human endeavor, should be singled out and denied the possibility of systematic improvement made him indignant: "That's amazing to me, that so many people in music won't accept progress. It's the only field where advancement meets so much opposition. You take doctors—look what

medicine and science have accomplished in the last twenty or thirty years.
That's the way it should be in music—that's the way it has to be" (42).

From Hawkins's viewpoint, virtually everything in the jazz of the 1930s
was an improvement over the 1920s: musicians had a far greater technical
command of their instruments, rhythms were more sophisticated, intonation more secure, and so forth. And it is clear from such works as
Hawkins's composition "Queer Notions" (recorded with Fletcher Henderson in 1933) that he was interested in harmonic experimentation. Given his
stance, he would naturally have considered the innovations of the beboppers the "next step" in the maturing of jazz. Since Hawkins was fiercely
competitive, it is natural that he would want to be right at the cutting edge
of the action, making music with Parker and Gillespie and the other innovators who were some 10–20 years younger.[11]

The featuring of Hawkins's story over the more obvious Parker or Gillespie is a fascinating and, in my view, successful strategy on DeVeaux's part.
Hawkins then emerges as a cogent symbol of classic (pre-bebop) jazz and
the commercial power of swing coming to terms with the new music of the
early 1940s beboppers. Hawkins's fascination with harmonic experimentation surely influenced Gillespie, Monk, and Parker. His competitiveness fit
well into the cutting-contest atmosphere of the after-hours jam sessions at
Minton's and Monroe's. His celebrity and technical excellence were certainly an inspiration to the younger players.

But DeVeaux gets on thinner ice when he asserts that Hawkins was a major contributor to the music itself. The obvious objection is the standard
view that Hawkins's rhythmic conception was antithetical to the darting
quickness, the start-and-stop nervousness of the new style. While
Hawkins's vertical articulation of the harmonies was often echoed by Charlie Parker, who himself usually "made the changes," the rhythmic stolidity
of Hawkins (comparatively speaking) did not equate with the spirit of the
new music. DeVeaux certainly acknowledges this, and he demonstrates an-
alytically the difference between Hawkins and Lester Young in a brief comparative section of musical analysis (110–15). But recognition of
Hawkins's bebop deficiencies does not prevent DeVeaux from arguing:

> [T]he musician most involved in bringing experimental small-group jazz be-
> fore a paying public in 1944 was Coleman Hawkins. It was Hawkins, not
> Gillespie or Parker, who worked consistently on New York's 52nd Street with
> the likes of Thelonious Monk, Oscar Pettiford, and Howard McGhee; who
> made the first recordings of "Salt Peanuts" and who presided over Monk's
> commercial recording debut; and who in general was best positioned, artisti-

cally and professionally, to give the new music instant credibility. Had Hawkins been sufficiently motivated to exploit the situation, he could easily have become the public face of bebop (319).

Despite the important involvement of Hawkins with the bebop innovators and his presence on the scene, his style and comparatively advanced age make it difficult to conceive of him as the "public face of bebop."

In the course of equating Hawkins's temperament with the transition from swing to bebop, DeVeaux makes fascinating claims regarding the idea of progress in jazz history more generally. One of the most interesting concerns the old notion of jazz combining elements of the European and African musical traditions. Jazz, though obviously a part of Western culture, incorporates much of the spirit of African music: "The musical techniques that set jazz apart from European art music are precisely those that derive from black American musical folkways (and ultimately from Africa): swing, call-and-response patterns, vocalized timbre, 'blue notes', improvisation, and so forth" (17). This much is granted; but then DeVeaux goes on to claim that "[t]hese musical markers of ethnicity are usually treated as *essentials*: they are part of jazz's development but they are *not themselves subject to development*" (17, DeVeaux's emphasis).

Is it true that progress in jazz, insofar as it takes place at all, takes place within the *European* parameters of the art form? If true, this idea entails provocative implications. Let me digress for a moment to draw some of them out.

To make a case that progress (or perhaps better, "evolution," to use a term that does not imply continuing improvement) in jazz only takes place within Western parameters, the following points might be adduced as evidence:

1. Fluency on given instruments increased technique within the European desiderata of faster and cleaner, with better control of intonation within established Western parameters.

2. Harmonic change evolved through gradually increasing chromaticism and the incorporation of Western romantic and impressionistic harmonic practice.

3. Formal experimentation (in particular, the third stream music of the 1950s) reflected the Western penchant for structural complexity.

4. The modal practices of the 1950s reintroduced the medieval European church modes in a manner, again, not unlike the impressionists (and to a lesser extent the nineteenth-century romantics); Coltrane was himself studying Slonimsky's *Thesaurus of Scales and Melodic Patterns*.[12]

5. Rhythmic complexity drew from Stravinskian or Bartókian rhythmic experimentation with complex and/or changing meters.

6. The free jazz innovations of the late 1950s and 1960s were inspired by the parallel movement in the Western avant garde, in which increasing harmonic complexity finally yielded to atonality, most notably in the evolution of Schoenberg's compositional practice from the 1890s to his expressionist works of around 1910.

7. Many of the major jazz musicians before 1960 who were attracted to the concept of progress spoke of improving their art by studying the "classics," by which they meant European classical music. Here, numerous apposite quotations can be cited from Scott Joplin to Willie "The Lion" Smith to James P. Johnson, to Parker and Gillespie.

Since the 1960s, however, increasing Afrocentrism has considerably toned down connection with the European classical tradition. To many jazz musicians of the latter part of the century, too close an alliance seemed to underplay the importance of the African spirit of jazz. These newer musicians considered the older musicians' awe of Western classical music a nuanced version of Uncle Tomism. In its stead, newer points of view in the latter part of the twentieth century focused on the African and African-American spirit of jazz:

1. The seven examples of evidence cited above are at best only half the story: what is important are not the items themselves, but their manner of application, which in all instances was a jazz practice, not a European one.

2. The essence of swing, which is one of the essences of jazz, is not European. The evolution of jazz in the 1940s to bebop is particularly owing to African inspiration.

3. An essence of virtually all jazz is pervasive use of percussion, which is heard nowhere in previous European music.

4. Jazz since the 1960s has been highly influenced by African sources, especially rhythmic impulse and timbre.

5. DeVeaux's original premise is wrong: folk sensibilities can in fact evolve.[13]

6. Intonation practices that owe less to the European tradition became evident in the music of Ornette Coleman and the later avant garde players such as Archie Shepp and Albert Ayler.

The issue can be argued on both sides. Its elucidation can lead to insight on the machinery of evolution within music's own boundaries, without consideration of outside (societal) forces. Moreover, examining attitudes toward progress among the bebop pioneers might be a fruitful source of further study. For example, Parker, the most important bebop musician, was some sixteen years younger than Hawkins and benefited from the more conventional training of popular and jazz musicians taking place in the 1930s. Despite their age difference, Parker's interviews resonate deeply with the progressive outlook of Hawkins and are an important part of the intellectual environment surrounding early bebop.[14] DeVeaux's sensitive probing of this issue is a fascinating aspect of his study and greatly increases our appreciation of the intellectual currents of the time.

4. BEBOP AND CAPITALISM

A fresh addition to the field of bebop's origins is DeVeaux's analysis of the economic conditions of jazz, particularly swing. As he notes, ". . . the Swing Era was above all a *system* of economic interdependence in which the individual musicians played clearly defined roles" (118, DeVeaux's emphasis). Such economic interdependence was key in defining the direction of the music and the lives of the players.

The huge success of the swing bands was a largely capitalistic one, as record companies, musicians' managers, dancehall and club owners, and the players themselves (in some celebrated instances) reaped enormous economic rewards. Within this system, there gradually emerged the commercial dominance of New York (Tin Pan Alley, Broadway, the radio networks) and Los Angeles (Hollywood). This powerful and nationally integrated web of entertainment and broadcast media, through its sheer size and influence, transformed American popular culture.

DeVeaux cites numerous findings regarding the economic conditions of the times that resulted from the increased centralization and nationalization of popular music. His check of census data shows that the number of musicians actually declined from 1930 to 1940 (127). This fact alone raises many questions. Was it because the dominance of the national "name bands" diminished opportunities for local players? Did the impact result from the transition from silent film to talkies? Moreover, DeVeaux points out that a band made its "real money" on the road (129): the big hotel gigs and radio broadcasts were largely publicity for upcoming tours. This shows, too, the continuing importance of live performance at the time, despite the decline of sheet music sales in favor of recordings. Ironically, the swing boom *lessened* opportunities for black bands (146): there was room for only a few black bands at the top of the name band hierarchy (150).[15] Wartime rationing particularly hurt black bands who, typically denied gigs at the major urban hotels and the consequent broadcasts, were especially dependent on the road for their livelihood (151ff.); yet, the rationing of gasoline and shortages of rubber for tires led to severe restrictions on driving.

The impersonality of these market forces clash with the spirit of the jazz tradition, where, as DeVeaux points out, musicians' "authority"—literally—is celebrated, i.e., they are the "authors" of their own music (9). A common view presented in jazz history is that because the economic rewards were largely reaped by white musicians, the disillusioned, often bitter black players—the music's principal "authors"—innovated bebop for noncommercial purposes; in so doing, they created a music that was antipopular, largely undanceable, and more artistically inspired than big band swing. The result was what some would soon call "black music" as opposed to the diluted, white-influenced (implying less good) commercial pablum of the big-band era.

Among the interesting assumptions in this model of the "birth of bebop from anti-commercial forces" is one concerning black music itself. Is it correct to equate "real jazz" with black music and an anticommercial enterprise? To what extent is black music separate from American popular music more generally? An interesting paradox of bebop is that while it was surely innovated by black musicians, the style gradually lost the allegiance of the black mass audience. Indeed, as bebop metamorphosed and split into the various bebop-based substyles of the 1950s, the audience for jazz (in general) became increasingly white.[16]

In contrast to the idea of the growth of bebop from anticommercial forces, DeVeaux points out that the bop musicians did in fact wish to attract a mass audience. He documents this view at some length and further argues that the bebop musicians did not adopt a stance of anti-capitalism—like the leftist artists of the 1960s—but rather wished to be considered "professionals." As such, the beboppers wanted to be treated well: respected and requisitely rewarded for their musicianship; they rejected the identity of swing band "wage earners" cranking out a standard product. This view, which seems to ring true, is an important corrective to the prevailing jazz-historical cliché that associates bebop with a more simplistic "now-we-are-artists" rhetoric.

The anticommercial bias seems to have been instigated by the jazz writers of the era. In Leo Treitler's "crisis theory" of musical advancement (14), the mechanism of stylistic change is the sterility of the older music; further, according to the model, the pure interaction of artistic impulses is always impeded by commercialism (15). In the transition from swing to bop, one can argue that a crisis had arrived, that the big bands and swing in general had stagnated. Although the newly developing bebop style soon began to encounter resistance in the marketplace, the musical pioneers persisted in their revolution, ignoring the impeding commercial forces. Their campaign was endorsed by the pro-bebop jazz writers, who in support of the musicians were generally led to condemn commercial forces out of hand and apply similar assessments to previous periods of jazz. The pro-bebop writers' hostility to market forces was further inflamed by the rhetoric of the "moldy figs," the traditionalist camp, who, besides reviling the new music, also attacked its anticommercial spirit.

Consequently, commercialism quickly became the bogeyman of much jazz history. In early jazz, it was thought that commercialism stifled or diluted the folk basis of the music or the "natural" expressivity of the players. Folklorists like the Lomaxes, promoters such as John Hammond, early critics such as Goffin or Panassié, or romantically inclined writers such as Blesh often seemed to represent such a view. In later jazz, commercialism was seen to suppress the musical integrity of the players, who, if somehow freed from commercial constraints, would take wing in flights of artistic inspiration. Gunther Schuller is perhaps the most prominent of contemporary jazz scholars whose work explicitly tends to disparage commercial concerns.

It is to DeVeaux's credit that he works at defusing the commercial menace. If the bebop musicians were not necessarily trying to create art (16), what were they doing? Many of them indeed longed for commercial success. Parker's "with strings" recordings and many of his small-group Latin sessions reveal commercial intents. DeVeaux notes the importance for all bands, black and white, to have widely varying repertory, including waltzes and tangos (124). He quotes Earl Hines as saying, "I try to adapt myself to whatever the dancers demand" (125). Hines's "non-jazz" was apparently so successful that he received letters from listeners wanting to know his race. Rex Stewart is cited on how terrifically the Henderson band played waltzes. Louis Armstrong "like other black musicians of 1920s" used (in a sense) music to further the role of entertainer (74). Even Coleman Hawkins tried for success as a singer, an ambition that DeVeaux automatically equates with being an entertainer (75–76).[17]

Moreover, Gillespie himself is quoted as saying:

Bop is an interpretation of jazz. . . . It's all part of the same thing. . . . Bop is part of jazz and jazz music is to dance to. The trouble with bop as it's played now is that people can't dance to it. They don't hear those four beats. We'll never get bop across to a wide audience until they can dance to it. They're not particular about whether you're playing a flatted fifth or a ruptured 129th as people can understand where the beat is. . . . I'm not turning my back on bop. My band has a distinctive sound and I want to keep that. But I want to make bop bigger, get it to a wider audience. I think George Shearing is the greatest thing that's happened to bop in the past year. He's the only one who has helped it along. He plays bop so the average person can understand it. . . . Anybody can dance to Shearing's music. By doing that, he has made it easier for me and for everybody else who plays bop.[18]

DeVeaux also quotes Ralph Ellison as claiming that the original beboppers just wanted a "fresh entertainment" (24). Ellison goes so far as to claim that the beboppers were the "least revolutionary of men" (26). Thus, it can be argued that the beboppers were trying (in DeVeaux's felicitous phrase) to find "a new point of engagement" with commercialism, not denying it (17).

If the beboppers were not explicitly attempting to circumvent the commercialism of swing and the big bands, where was the social revolution in bebop? DeVeaux locates it principally in the rise of black consciousness. Among much complex argument, DeVeaux points out that during the Second World War respect was finally accorded black Americans as musicians; that is, black achievement was becoming accepted. "This explosive combination—the relatively successful and isolated world of the black musician, and the vulnerability of *any* black American to the slings of racial hatred—provided the unique and potent social subtext for bebop" (238, DeVeaux's emphasis). Further, war-year freedoms for black jazz musicians led to a potent combination of highly talented, individualistic, and forthright musicians hanging out in New York City and congregating at their own clubs. Thus, the jam session took on mythic significance as more than a place to play after hours; it became ". . . not simply a form of escape, but an act of defiance" (205). Further, ". . . dropping out was a visceral reaction to things as they were, unpremeditated and impervious to rational argument. This state of frustration, anger, and weariness was the necessary precondition for the emergence of bebop" (248).

Much of DeVeaux's argument is convincing, although the increase in ethnic consciousness among black musicians must be carefully qualified. While changes in attitude can be argued as occurring in the early 1940s, the contrast is typically heightened by comparison of the beboppers to such prototypical jazzmen/entertainers as Louis Armstrong or Cab Calloway. But this is not the complete picture. Consider, for example, Benny Carter or Duke Ellington, musicians who—not to mention numerous others—in no way could be accused of pandering to a white public. Many important leaders, including James Weldon Johnson and others associated with the Harlem Renaissance, had long been demanding justice and equal rights for blacks. So, again, are we justified in claiming the beboppers to be social revolutionaries?

In fact, I think that a case can be made that the attitudes of the beboppers were dramatically different in kind, as compared to the attitudes of an Ellington or Carter. Out of "frustration, anger, and weariness," the bebop generation exhibited an underlying demeanor that prefigured the emergence of black Islam and a more combative stance among blacks—both musicians and the population at large—who despaired of full and equal acceptance as American citizens. Thus, at the very foundation of bebop we can detect the militance and the roots of black separatism that underlay the upheavals of the 1960s.

5. THE MUSICAL ISSUES

Of the divides in the field of scholarly jazz studies, none is wider than that between music analysis and music history, especially when the latter emphasizes connection to relevant social history. DeVeaux's subtitle describes his volume as "a social and musical history," which I take to mean a history of the music rendered through the social context of the times. Intriguingly, "musical" comes after "social" in the subtitle, which suggests DeVeaux's overall slant. DeVeaux's music history itself mostly consists of the usual—important players, bands, and records, and who seemed to influence whom—while placing unusual emphasis on Hawkins.

The inclusion of analysis in music history has been controversial and even accounts for the divide between theorists and historians in the music-academic world at large. Just how much analysis is necessary to understand the history of music? Theorists and historians disagree, obviously. This is not the place to outline or take sides in these controversies, but it is generally agreed that the best music history always includes at least some analysis, as does DeVeaux's, although analysis is the least significant feature of his volume. Throughout, DeVeaux follows much standard jazz history in showing that the transition from swing to bebop was entirely reasonable—that this was not so much a revolution, but a natural "next step" after the swing era had in some sense played itself out.

DeVeaux's emphases on social contexts and broad historical narratives are obvious when scanning the relatively few musical examples to the many pages of straight text. The antianalytical slant is also apparent from DeVeaux's unnecessary definition of musical terms (e.g., tritones as intervals comprising three whole steps) that could have been relegated to footnotes, if included at all. Also, I was surprised by irrelevant, almost apologetic remarks for including any musical analysis at all (31). Despite these unpromising signs, DeVeaux makes effective points with the musical explication he chooses to include.

DeVeaux agrees with what has long been considered a key legend in the genesis of bebop: that the younger players looked more to Lester Young as a role model than to such players as Coleman Hawkins. Despite the common opinion that Young's style led to Parker's, it must be pointed out that Parker never claimed Young as his role model any more than, say, Hawkins. Parker even went so far as to insist, "I was crazy about Lester. . . He played so clean and beautifully. But I wasn't influenced by Lester. Our ideas ran on differently."[19] Alternatively, a strong case can be made for Parker's being dazzled by Art Tatum's virtuosity in the development of his style. Is it not possible that the startling rhythmic angularities in Parker did not derive from Young, but instead were his most important and original contribution to the genre? Surely nothing of their edgy nervousness can be heard in the work of the older master.

Nevertheless, the linear, off-the-beat qualities of Young's style certainly did portend the general rhythmic future of bebop. If we assume that the Young-over-Hawkins myth is reasonably defensible in the larger sense that Young was one of the most celebrated melodic stylists of the time, what was his attraction to the bebop pioneers? For an answer, DeVeaux returns to his overarching theme that it was Young's use of the principles of "ambiguity and discontinuity" rather than the "continuity and certainty" (111) of the older players. These more modern principles conform to DeVeaux's views on modernism more generally, as is made explicit in the following:

It is this open-ended quality—the open-endedness of ambiguity—that Parker shared with Lester Young, and that made both of them devastatingly effective in a cutting contest. If Hawkins's art is monologic, . . . the art of Charlie Parker, and the bebop idiom he helped call into being, is dialogic. So too, one might add, is much of jazz and the blues. But bebop managed to *absorb* Hawkins's specialized "progressive" brand of virtuosity and bring it into a new relationship with other kinds of rhetoric, especially the blues, and into a new rhythmic configuration that undermined its tendency toward sameness and continuity (268; emphasis DeVeaux's).

Throughout the discussion, DeVeaux continues to argue for the relevance of Hawkins's musical style to bebop's genesis, in particular by stressing his virtuosity and his interest in harmonic exploration. As noted earlier, DeVeaux's brief discussion of Young (as a contrast to Hawkins) is effective (110–15), though it could have profited from more musical examples.

Also musically germane to the genesis of bebop is DeVeaux's discussion of Parker's and Gillespie's Redcross recordings from February 15, 1943 (260–69). As is well known, because of the 1942 recording ban by the American Federation of Musicians, seminal swing-to-bop groups, such as the Earl Hines big band, went unrecorded commercially. The private Redcross recordings from a jam session at Chicago's Savoy Hotel are rare examples of the new style in transition. Unfortunately, I found it frustrating to deal with the musical examples in this section. DeVeaux does not provide the CD timings for his excerpts, and the descriptions of chorus and measure numbers are too vague to be helpful. Since Parker and Gillespie alternate solos, it is unclear what chorus DeVeaux is referring to.[20]

In the analysis of the Redcross "Sweet Georgia Brown," the basic swing idiom can be heard as stretched, loosened, and ultimately transformed. Parker is on tenor, too, which provides the interesting perspective of Parker coming to grips with the preeminence of Hawkins and Young on their own turf. DeVeaux describes the difference between Parker's new approach to the style and Hawkins's rhythmic directness: "Hawkins is expansive, saturating the sonic space. Parker, for all the profusion of notes, is concise and streamlined" (267). DeVeaux asks us to compare a Hawkins line on "Sweet Georgia" (Example 7 [96]) with one of Parker's (Example 50 [268]) to show how similar they are if we overlook "accentual nuances" (267). I think his example only serves to heighten the dissimilarity between Hawkins and Parker: even though the lines are atypically close, Parker's eighth-note groupings are slightly more irregular as heard against the grain of the beat.

I also question DeVeaux's characterizing early Parker as "more conservative" harmonically than Gillespie at this stage (261), as if to imply this would soon change: Parker's care in resolving the extended-chord dissonances in his lines would persist throughout his career (except for experimental jam-session playing). Gillespie always enjoyed "ostentacious" (262) dissonances, which I think he intended to be at least partly humorous.

DeVeaux's key analytical section on "Sweet Georgia Brown" would have been more striking if he had found some way of characterizing the differences between Parker's and Gillespie's styles (or even between bebop and swing), perhaps through some theoretical innovation or graphic charts that probed the rhythmic qualities of the lines. Nevertheless, DeVeaux makes several good points, for example how Gillespie was ghosting less effectively than Parker by under-playing notes on the weaker parts of the beat rather than on the stronger (269). Of course, Gillespie would soon master elements of Parker's rhythmic innovations and make them his own.

Despite the importance of the Redcross jam sessions (not to mention earlier transitional recordings that are not discussed), the story line inevitably returns to Hawkins. DeVeaux's best case for connecting him to the birth of bebop comes from his club work on 52nd Street and on his Apollo recordings of late 1943 and 1944, where, ironically, Hawkins became the first leading saxophonist to record proto-bebop with Gillespie rather than Parker. Probably the most significant pieces from the Apollo sessions are "Woody'n You" and "Disorder at the Border," both from February 1944. Yet, in these recordings, as DeVeaux notes, Gillespie was virtually the sole modernist in the all-important matter of rhythmic conception; Hawkins was present, as well as the 20-year-old Max Roach in his first recording session[21] on drums, but except for Gillespie, the group sound remained defined by the basic swing paradigm.

Hawkins's work on 52nd Street in late 1943 and1944 continued to raise interest in the new bebop genre, and thus provides further evidence, in DeVeaux's view, for the elevation of Hawkins to a greater role in bebop's evolution.[22] But it is Charlie Parker who, in his absence from the scene, truly whets the imagination. In the summer of 1943, Parker left the Earl Hines band and returned home to Kansas City, where he continued to work locally. For the next year—a crucial time in the birth of bebop—Parker's life and activities are virtually unknown.[23] He resurfaced in the spring of 1944 for a short-lived, yet mythic stint in the Billy Eckstine big band, which included Gillespie, Wardell Gray, Oscar Pettiford, Art Blakey, Sarah Vaughan, and other notable innovators.[24] Parker left the Eckstine band around August of 1944. Soon after, on September 15, he recorded his first small-group session, for Savoy, with the Tiny Grimes group. Since these recordings provide the first commercially recorded Parker solos in the new style, DeVeaux rightly devotes his most extended section of musical analysis to them.[25]

DeVeaux describes the early Parker style well in this analytical section. Perhaps the best moment is the illustration of the jazz improviser's use of formula (378-9),[26] particularly how an improviser might approach both rhythm changes and that all-important move to the subdominant on measure 5 of a blues. (I should clarify a confusing error on DeVeaux's transcriptions of 379: the chord at measure 5 should be $E\flat7$, not $B\flat7$.) DeVeaux also compares the two takes of "Red Cross" (375–6) and relates them to the well-known "Shaw 'Nuff," later to be recorded with Gillespie on May 11, 1945. (There are two noteworthy errors in the transcriptions of "Red Cross": in the A section of the theme (373), the eighth notes in measure 6 should be B-F$\sharp$-G$\sharp$-C$\sharp$, not B-D$\sharp$-F$\sharp$-C$\sharp$;[27] in measure 19 of the solos (376), the important eighth note on the third beat should be B$\flat$, not B-natural.)[28]

In addition to DeVeaux's work on Parker and Gillespie, there is considerable transcription of Hawkins, of course, throughout the volume, but it seems best taken as counterexample: this is how *not* to play bebop. Despite Hawkins's virtuosity and interest in harmonic exploration, his rhythmic concept was not readily adaptable to the new music. Further, Hawkins was around 40 years old at the time—far too late in his career to rhythmically retool his basic melodic style.

Although DeVeaux's discussion of early bebop, as seen particularly in the work of Parker and Gillespie, is effective, his book could have benefited from a more imaginative use of music-theoretical tools. His decision to characterize portions of transcriptions verbally, but not to avail himself of other techniques, may derive from his wanting to emphasize the social and broad musical aspects of his topic. Surely DeVeaux wished to preserve a nontechnical tone to a book aimed at a broad market of jazz scholars, but the music-analytical portions of the volume were the only moments where I found myself wishing for fresh insights on the material.

6. UNIFYING THEMES

One of my graduate students once remarked that DeVeaux's presentation of history in *The Birth of Bebop* was very relaxed. I was struck by this statement, for DeVeaux's presentation seemed to me very dense. Upon further discussion, it became clear that what my student meant was that much of the jazz history he was studying dealt principally with the establishment and presentation of biographical and discographical fact. DeVeaux, interestingly, could be faulted—in a huge book, no less!—for attending to fairly little in the way of this more conventional material. For example, Hawkins is the figure given by far the most personal coverage, yet salient details of his life are ignored: his childhood, family background, even his date of birth! The same biographical thinness is even truer of Parker and Gillespie. Still, such a skewing is part of DeVeaux's larger strategy and ultimately does not detract from the overall impact of his study: as he is presenting an interpretation of an era, detailed biographical chronology is unnecessary. Further, for his purposes, the relatively ignored Hawkins is more significant than the legendary Parker.

DeVeaux's multivalent interpretation of the birth of bebop throws considerable new light on the era. At the same time, it raises the issue of the relationship between a group of historical forces properly seen as social versus the musical unfolding of a style succession that has traditionally been viewed as self-contained. Just how and at what point do these forces for change intersect and influence the other? This is a difficult issue, reminiscent of the levels of organization seen in scientific investigation: a biologist, even one working at the cellular level, rarely must apply the tools of the physicist working at the atomic and subatomic levels. Who is to say how the systems of subatomic organization influence the workings of, say, consciousness? That there is a connection seems plausible, but the difficulty is specification of hypothesis and consequent investigation.

Something of the same can be said of *The Birth of Bebop*. How does one even hypothesize a correlation between nationwide pressures on black bands through wartime shortages of gasoline and rubber and the jittery, fragmented melodic line of the new music being innovated in Harlem? These are among the facts of life at the time, but on vastly different qualitative and quantitative levels of reality; they may correlate in some way, but precisely how?

One might argue that a weakness of *The Birth of Bebop* lies in its lack of convincing correlation between musical detail and the broader levels. Such correlations are unusually difficult, and, when made, can be forced or trite. This is an error sometimes seen in the work of the "new musicologists" who have been an important academic presence for the last several years. For example, writers such as Susan McClary have tried to correlate close analytical readings of musical pieces with the sociological and intellectual climate of the times in which they were produced, resulting in an all-too-modern focus on race, gender, and sexuality.[29]

On the other hand, scholars such as Scott Burnham have demonstrated considerable skill in reconciling the intellectual life of an era with detailed musical interpretation.[30] Now, the dynamics of intellectual culture are certainly closer to artistic creation than, say, economic and sociological forces, so successfully interrelating levels of intellectual influence may not be too much of a stretch. But DeVeaux's ambition is greater still: he seeks to deal not only with an era's *Zeitgeist*, but also with the more fundamental, "material" (to invoke a Marxist slant) forces. The fundamental divide may be between the material and the intellectual, which has traditionally been difficult to bridge in historical writing. For example, there may be no particular problem in showing that the concept of progress influenced musical direction: if the music is fast, progress dictates that the newer music must be faster. But how did the lack of broadcast opportunities for black bands or their generally lower pay structure influence attitudes toward artistic progress in the first place? Perhaps this may be likened to the divide between the atomic and the biological: the relationship may be there, but can it be fathomed precisely?

Thus, DeVeaux may be faulted for lack of overall integration of the musical issues of bebop—the notes closely considered—with the broader music-historical, cultural, and economic factors. But such problems arise from the scope of DeVeaux's ambition; they are minor—rather like the idiosyncratic overemphasis on Coleman Hawkins—and do not at all detract from the study's overall impact. By virtually any measure, *The Birth of Bebop* is first-rate. Of any historical study of jazz, it is easily the broadest in its ambitions and subtlest in its insights. DeVeaux's cogent writing shows that history begins only after the facts have been established; it best marshals and explains the multitude of factors leading to the key transition between classic and modern jazz. Scott DeVeaux's work on bebop is certain to have lasting influence on all subsequent jazz-historical writing that aims to tackle the whys and wherefores of music-stylistic succession. Anyone seriously interested in jazz history cannot afford to miss it.

NOTES

I wish to acknowledge and thank David Cayer for thoughtful comments on an earlier draft of this article.

1. New York and Oxford: Oxford University Press, 1994.
2. Lanham, Maryland: Scarecrow Press, 1986.
3. Chicago and London: University of Chicago Press, 1994.
4. Chicago and London: University of Chicago Press, 1996.
5. New Haven and London: Yale University Press, 1990.
6. Lanham, Maryland: Scarecrow Press, 1996.
7. New York and Oxford: Oxford University Press, 1968.
8. New York and Oxford: Oxford University Press, 1989.
9. Single-volume studies and texts on jazz history generally have too much music to consider, which means less opportunity for a more comprehensive approach. Our soon-to-be-published jazz history text, *Jazz: The First 100 Years* (Henry Martin and Keith Waters, Belmont, CA: Wadsworth, 2002) is typical: we focus on the music necessarily while trying to provide a concomitant overview of the times.
10. For recent social histories, there are Kathy Ogren, *The Jazz Revolution: Twenties America and the Meaning of Jazz* (New York and Oxford: Oxford

University Press, 1989); William Howland Kenney, *Chicago Jazz: A Cultural History 1904–1930* (New York and Oxford: Oxford University Press, 1993); Lewis A. Erenberg, *Swingin' the Dream: Big Band Jazz and the Rebirth of American Culture* (Chicago and London: University of Chicago Press, 1998); and David W. Stowe, *Swing Changes: Big-Band Jazz in New Deal America* (Cambridge, Mass. and London: Harvard University Press, 1994).

11. Hawkins's concern with progress extends to formal music education. DeVeaux quotes the story of the young Miles Davis asking Hawkins where to find Charlie Parker in late 1944. Hawkins replies by telling him to finish up his studies at Juilliard and forget Bird! The remark enrages Davis (368).

12. New York: Scribner, 1947.

13. DeVeaux later qualifies the idea of the stability of jazz folkways by pointing out that "Although folk sensibility certainly did evolve (the blues of Charlie Parker could not be mistaken for the blues of Bessie Smith or Charlie Patton), the continuity and stability it provided were perhaps more important" (62).

14. For example, consider Parker's only blindfold test, where he says, "music graduates, it goes from ragtime to jazz and from jazz to swing and from swing to . . . rebop." Leonard Feather, "A Bird's-Ear View of Music," *Metronome* 64 (no. 8, August 1948): 14, 21–22. Reprinted in Carl Woideck, *The Charlie Parker Companion: Six Decades of Commentary* (New York: Schirmer Books, 1998), 67.

15. DeVeaux argues that Calloway "made it" because of personality; the same was largely true for Armstrong (plus his unsurpassable technique); Ellington was *sui generis*. Thus, the market could only support one Basie-style swing band; all the other fine black bands were "out of the picture" as far as the general public was concerned.

16. In discussing the issue of bebop and its impact on the black masses, DeVeaux cites a provocative point made by Gerald Early: ". . . to the black masses, the concept of the artist and of art as it is generally fixed by Euro-American standards is, quite frankly, incomprehensible" (26, footnote). This alone raises many issues: Do the black masses only identify with the performer as entertainer? Did this place them outside the stream of Western "progress," unable to participate in the meaning of twentieth-century modernism? If so, it would account for the jazz audience gradually becoming more white. (Note also the contrast with the acceptance of jazz by Asians, an ethnic group that embraces the tenets of progress.) Lastly, it is significant that avant garde jazz in our own time continues to flourish in Europe, cradle of Western progressive values.

17. In discussing the commercial menace, I must include DeVeaux's controversial comment about the major black band leaders being usually men of relatively modest instrumental talent: Fletcher Henderson, Jimmie Lunceford, Andy Kirk, even perhaps Basie and Ellington. It could be argued that their real virtuosity was as organizers or as channels for others' talents. In some

sense, this was a commercial talent as opposed to the Charlie Parker archetype of the musician concerned about just music and nothing else.

18. John S. Wilson, "Bird Wrong; Bop Must Get a Beat: Diz," *Down Beat* 16 (no. 19, October 7, 1949): 1. Reprinted in *Down Beat* 61 (no. 2, February 1994): 26.

19. Michael Levin and John S. Wilson, "No Bop Roots in Jazz: Parker." *Down Beat*, September 9, 1949. Reprinted in Woideck, *The Charlie Parker Companion*, 74.

20. For example, DeVeaux's Example 44 is labeled as "chorus 1" (265), but since Parker solos twice in the recording, it is unclear which solo is intended. The excerpt in Example 44 can be found in Parker's second chorus at 4:03. Does by "chorus 1" DeVeaux mean that it is Parker's first time through the changes, despite it being his second time soloing? No, because Parker's second solo enters in mid-chorus, so Example 44 is actually from Parker's second chorus of his second solo. Probably, DeVeaux means second complete chorus, but this designation is confusing. Similarly, with the Gillespie examples (261), DeVeaux's labelings of "chorus 1" and "chorus 2" are confusing; they in fact refer to Gillespie's second solo (third solo, really, if you consider his partial statement of the head) which begins at 5:56. Thus, Example 34 (261), which is called "chorus 1," can be found at 6:23. These CD timings are from the Redcross "Sweet Georgia Brown," *Charlie Parker: Volumes 1 & 2, Young Bird, 1940–1944*, Média 7 Masters of Jazz MJCD 78/79.

21. According to Martin Williams, liner notes to *Dizzy Gillespie: The Development of an American Artist, 1940–1946*. Smithsonian Records P2 13455.

22. For example, the appearance of the Gillespie-Pettiford band at the Onyx in November, 1943, "is generally regarded, with good reason, as the first bop combo to appear in a public venue — 'the birth of the bebop era,' as Gillespie has put it" (291).

23. Apparently, a wire to Parker inviting him to join the Gillespie-Pettiford band was never received.

24. The Eckstine band invited the 18-year-old Miles Davis to sit in during a gig in St. Louis in August 1944. Later, Davis remembered: "The greatest feeling I ever had in my life — with my clothes on — was when I first heard Diz and Bird together in St. Louis, Missouri, back in 1944." Davis with Quincey Troupe, *Miles: The Autobiography* (New York: Simon and Schuster, 1989), 7.

25. Returning again to his theme of the unfortunate anticommercial bias of standard jazz history, DeVeaux notes that the entertainment aspects of the Grimes sessions have often "discomfited" bebop enthusiasts (371).

26. Explored at length in Thomas Owens's "Charlie Parker: Techniques of Improvisation" (2 vols.), Ph. D. dissertation, UCLA, 1974. In my *Charlie Parker and Thematic Improvisation* (Scarecrow Press, 1996), I argue that Parker's use of formula does not rule out brilliant thematic connection to the principal melodic material.

27. I also make an error at precisely the same point in the melodic line, as given in *Charlie Parker and Thematic Improvisation* (43). Since I spell the chord in C♭, my incorrect notes are C♭-E♭-A♭-D♭; the correct melody is C♭-G♭-A♭-D♭. Thanks to João Moreira for pointing this out.

28. There are other transcription errors that I noticed. In Example 28, Parker's well-known "Hootie Blues" solo, m. 5 should have an A♭7 chord and m. 7 an E♭ chord (193). In Example 60, the fourth chorus of Hawkins's "Disorder at the Border" solo, there should be a B♭ chord at m. 11 (313). There is an important harmonic error in DeVeaux's transcription of the tune "Little Benny" (a. k. a. "Crazeology") in Example 88 (383): the second chord in m. 5 should be C#7, not C7.

29. See, for example, Susan McClary's *Feminine Endings: Music, Gender, and Sexuality*. Minneapolis: University of Minnesota Press, 1991.

30. See, for example, Burnham's *Beethoven Hero*. Princeton: Princeton University Press, 1995.

SAYING SOMETHING

Ingrid Monson, *Saying Something: Jazz Improvisation and Interaction* (Chicago: University of Chicago Press, 1996, 253 pp., $39.95; paperback: $14.95)

Evan Spring

Despite its furtive conquest of world culture, jazz is usually ignored by the cultural studies departments of academia. This situation is slowly changing, but jazz largely remains a self-contained world of craftsmen, fans, and critics, usually claimed at a young age. Ingrid Monson, an assistant professor of music at Washington University, has ventured gamely into the wilderness between jazz and other disciplines. She aims for nothing less than to reconcile jazz studies with recent advances in ethnomusicology, cultural history, anthropology, linguistics, and post-structuralism. *Saying Something* strives to understand "the reciprocal and multilayered relationships among sound, social settings, and cultural politics that affect the meaning of jazz improvisation in twentieth-century American cultural life." (2) The likes of W.E.B. Du Bois, Michel Foucault, and Jaki Byard agreeably commingle on the page, amid elaborate musical notation. Monson is especially interested in the jazz rhythm section. This "view from the bottom of the band" abets her larger purpose, which is to portray jazz as an interactive, face-to-face, consociating form of expression, with a fundamental interdependence of musical roles, and a discursive, allusional, "signifying" sensibility.

Monson is an interdisciplinarian by temperament, but an ethnomusicologist by training. True to fieldwork principles, she studied with the masters (orchestration with Jaki Byard, history and ensemble with Richard Davis, and drums with Michael Carvin), gigged on trumpet, and interviewed leading practitioners, including clarinetist Don Byron; pianists Joanne Brackeen, Sir Roland Hanna, and Michael Weiss; bassists Phil Bowler and Cecil McBee; guitarist/bassist Jerome Harris; and drummers Roy Haynes, Billy Higgins, Ralph Peterson, Jr., and Kenny

Washington. She earnestly discloses how she sat at the bar writing "field notes." She includes a long disclaimer on the potential misrepresentations of interview transcriptions, and tactfully employs nonstandard spellings "when they seem to be used purposefully to signal ethnicity and when failure to include them would detract from intelligibility." (23) One quibble: reflecting her ethnomusicological training, Monson disparages phone interviews, which in my experience can translate relatively well to written form. Telephones, like books, cannot convey body language, so "informants" (as they say in ethnomusicology) are more alert to making words stand on their own.

An ethnomusicological account of the jazz world has few predecessors, and the most inescapable is Paul Berliner's massive 1994 study *Thinking in Jazz*, which Monson calls "the most comprehensive and detailed account of jazz improvisation currently in existence, as well as the most detailed exposition of ethnotheory in ethnomusicology." (4) Both books are grounded in the voice of the musician, and both have an excellent feel for the musician's practical and figurative use of language. Monson, however, is much more in step with intellectual vogue, while Berliner is more the old-fashioned "social scientist," doggedly compiling every scrap of firsthand observation into empirically sound, verifiable generalizations. Sometimes Berliner sounds as if he is explaining jazz to a classroom of extraterrestrials:

> Among all the challenges a group faces, one that is extremely subtle yet fundamental to its travels is a feature of group interaction that requires the negotiation of a shared sense of the beat, known, in its most successful realization, as striking a groove. (Berliner, 349)

Monson, in a delicate and indirect critique of her colleague, implies that Berliner relied too heavily on methods "formed from an ethnographic practice centered in relatively homogeneous, nonurban cultural situations, in which a general presumption of cultural coherence and the transparency of representation went unquestioned." (5) This may be a discreet reference to Berliner's acclaimed 1978 study, *The Soul of Mbira: Music and Traditions of the Shona People of Zimbabwe*. In any case, while *Thinking in Jazz* is an indispensable compendium of ethnographic observations, it left the field wide open for Monson to culturally situate jazz within urban, multiethnic, postmodern America.

Fortunately, despite her wariness of traditional musicological techniques, Monson unapologetically makes ample use of music transcriptions. (The layman can skim the hard parts without undue panic or resentment, though it would certainly help to understand some basic terms like "interval" or "pedal point.") The transcriptions are intricate yet easy to parse, deftly situated within the text, and well annotated, including record label, catalog number, date, location, and personnel. (Gunther Schuller's publisher and others have avoided such details, fearing copyright fees.) A practical and succinct notation key includes symbols for shakes, scoops, slides, "ghost notes," and notes played ahead or behind the beat. Since the focus is on group interaction, multiple instruments are lined up on parallel staffs, with clear drum notation sometimes placed *between* the bassist and soloist.

In the second chapter, we hear straight from the musicians on the inner workings of the jazz rhythm section. They switch from technical shoptalk to images of waves, gravy, and bathtub soaking, and Monson keeps jauntily apace with hardly a whiff of academic slumming. She is especially interested in their most linguistic, social, and interactive metaphors. Musicians stress the importance of listening, responding, and learning to anticipate each other's actions. Terms like "grooving" are applied interrelationally, rather than to individuals. Monson's focus on interaction is meant to counter the influence of certain classically oriented jazz theorists, particularly Gunther Schuller. As she warns, "musicians' discussions of the higher levels of improvisational achievement frequently emphasize time and ensemble responsiveness as the relevant framework rather than, for example, large-scale tonal organization." (29) Certainly Schuller in particular has judged jazz by classical standards, decontextualizing jazz pieces into autonomous works of Art, and overemphasizing thematic continuity, execution, and large-scale structural organicism at the expense of interactive and emergent aesthetic virtues. Schuller even exults in declaring that his armchair record rankings are based purely on "objective" criteria.

Reading this chapter, I often found myself nodding or murmuring in recognition as some aurally familiar aspect of rhythm section work was formulated on the page. Examples include the way bassists drop down an octave before leaving the bridge, or how piano comping would make rhythmic sense even without the soloist. Piano comping is linked both to big band orchestrations and the drummer's left hand; Michael Carvin then brings it full circle, commenting "I really feel my left hand is more brass . . . like in a big band, the brass section is playing the shout parts." (58) Monson elicits one pithy quote after another, like Carvin's advice to drummers: produce "something floating and something solid," and "give the band one limb." (55) The following excerpt demonstrates her own knowledge as a working musician:

> The basic harmonic function of the pedal point is fundamentally the same as that articulated by theorists of Western classical music: prolongation of a principal chord, often for purposes of emphasizing an impending cadence or new section of a work. . . . In jazz improvisation, however, pedal points also have interactional and rhythmic implications that contrast greatly with those of their classical counterparts. When a bass player initiates a pedal point, he or she signals a range of musical possibilities to the rest of the ensemble. The pianist and soloist can deviate more freely from the written harmonic progression while playing over a pedal. The drummer is temporarily freed from coordinating with the walking bass and may choose to play in a more active, soloistic manner. . . the pedal point can also support the rhythm section in a much wider variety of musical situations. Pedal points can be used to differentiate the B section in an AABA form, for example. They may be played in rhythmic ostinatos that set up temporary metric modulations, such as those achieved by the legendary Miles Davis rhythm section, which included Ron Carter, Tony Williams, and Herbie Hancock. They may help cue the top of a chorus to musicians who have lost their place in the time cycle. Pedal points have also been an important resource for jazz composers interested in extending structural frameworks for improvisation beyond the traditional chorus-structured form. (35–37)

(More quibbles. Stressing the commonalities of African-American musics, Monson implies that jazz has a 12/8 feel with quarter notes subdivided into thirds of equal duration, when, as she knows, quarter-note subdivisions in jazz are highly varied, flexible, and asymmetric. She may also exaggerate the timekeeping responsibility of the drummer at the expense of the bassist.)

Monson states, hyperbolically, that "The drummer is generally the member of the band most underrated by the audience and least discussed in the jazz historical and analytical literature." (51) Of all the instrumentalists, the drummer is perhaps the most important focal point for the interactive ideals which she believes jazz scholars have overlooked. A little too convenient, then, for the jazz drummer to seem so unappreciated, contrary to my concertgoing experience. A little too convenient, also, that the section on the "The Soloist" is so undeveloped. This sense of selective convenience in service to her thesis becomes more pronounced as the book progresses.

Saying Something gently dismantles a comforting, intuitive notion: that music has a direct line to emotion, bypassing the reductive and profaning medium of speech. In our subliminal shorthand, words are referential and music is emotional. Jazz musicians themselves claim music is uniquely uninterpretable through a filter of language ("if you gotta ask, you'll never know"). Yet the same musicians, describing their own work, call most frequently on metaphors of conversation and storytelling: having something to "say," developing a "voice," or identifying a player by his "phrasing" or a "signature" lick. They also compare jazz to a "language," with its native and nonnative speakers. Monson skillfully unravels these perplexities, describing how jazz is analogous to language, even when verbal renderings of the music can only seem puny and frail. Her analysis is less syntactic than sociocultural; that is, she is less concerned with the jazz idiom as an integrated system (as if we were studying a foreign language), than with how jazz is like talking, listening, responding, managing relationships, and sharing experiences. Monson is not saying jazz always sounds like people conversing. Even the most intense, nonverbal emotions expressed in jazz can be "discursive," or language-like, in the sense of being not just amorphous globs of sentiment, but culturally situated performative gestures, with their own intrinsic power of metaphor, allusion, and commentary.

Monson looks at black speech patterns and their musical analogues, including conversational turn-taking, verbal jousting ("From an African American perspective, the essence of a 'cool' or 'hip' response includes reacting with poise and balance to these potentially unsettling verbal teases and challenges" [88]), call-and-response patterns, the alternation of fixed and variable phrases, and the function of repetition in "creating a participatory musical framework against which highly idiosyncratic and innovative improvisation can take place." (89) She also examines the historic affinity of African Americans for "indirect modes of discourse" and "cultural codeswitching," drawing parallels in the work of W.E.B. DuBois ("double consciousness"), Henry Louis Gates, Jr. ("signifying"), and Mikhail Bakhtin ("internal dialogism").

"Signifying" is the most useful term here, referring broadly to the performative, dialogic production of multiple meanings through gesture, allusion, improvisation, and signalings of ethnicity (in contrast to strictly transparent, denotative meanings abstracted from the people producing them and the circumstances of exchange). The individual jazz soloist can harbor many voices, since "signifying as an aesthetic developed from interactive, participatory, turn-taking games and genres that are multiply authored." (87) Alert to the potential misuse of these ideas, Monson insists that an African-American signifying aesthetic need not imply an insincere, conflicted, superficial, unoriginal, or otherwise inauthentic self. Rather, signifying entails social insight and relatedness; a healthy respect for complexity, contingency, incongruity, and ambiguity; a transformative sense of identity; and a talent for improvisation, plasticity of expression, irony, distortion, parody, playfulness, witty repartee, quotation, appropriation, and recontextualization. If signifying is in itself an art, questions like "Is bebop's transformation of Tin Pan Alley songs ironic or sincere?" seem beside the point. In relation to standard tunes, jazz players transcend the tension between critical distance and complicity. Since jazz is in many ways a self-contained, running commentary on itself, signifying always connects players past and present. A trumpeter who picks up a Harmon mute has no choice but to signify on Miles Davis, consciously or not, and Davis's ghost signifies right back.

Folding several of her themes together, Monson proposes a new addition to academic dialect: "intermusicality," meaning, "how music functions in a relational or discursive rather than an absolute manner." Its literary analogue, "intertextuality," has been applied to music, with limited success.

Though her premise—emphasizing the discursive, interrelational, signifying and emergent nature of jazz—is sound, Monson has a tendency to overinflate her thesis, selectively pruning the most convenient evidence available. Often all that's needed is a dash of restraint in light of varying interpretations.

First of all, Monson tries too hard to make jazz into a subset of sociable, face-to-face communication: "Good jazz improvisation is sociable and interactive just like a conversation; a good player communicates with the other players in the band. If this doesn't happen, it's not good jazz." (84) With sleight of hand, Monson has conflated an essential operating guideline (practitioners should listen carefully to their bandmates) with abstract criteria for artistic success (jazz is good to the degree that it is sociable and interactive). Of course these things can't be neatly autonomized, but, to the extent they can, neither should be strictly limited to the sociable and interactive. Aspiring musicians are well advised to listen carefully to their bandmates, but if Charlie Parker charges ahead, oblivious to his desperate accompanists, that in itself can be artistically compelling. Conversely, a soloist can respond intimately to other bandmembers while expressing a feeling of social remoteness. With Sonny Rollins, for example, I sometimes perceive an independent, introspective, or solitary quality, expressed with an aura of soliloquy rather than face-to-face interaction, even when he is extremely responsive to accompaniment.

Monson is missing a common intuitive feeling that the jazz soloist is— well, alone. Jazz has an undeniable individualist streak. When it comes time to solo, the spotlight is on you to stand or fall, no matter how good your accompanists are. This is hardly mentioned in the book, which hews to rhythm section work and contains only a cursory account of the soloist's unique role. Monson also conveniently ignores jazz's long and valued history of solo performance.

The individualism of jazz is even quite compatible with Western images of the artist as an obsessive, socially marginal, genius figure. Monson, criticizing Gunther Schuller, writes:

> The values [Schuller] cites—expressive fervor, artistic commitment, structural logic, virtuosity—are all criteria derived from ideas of German romanticism and modernism about absolute and autonomous music and the artist as genius. Ethnomusicologists have long remarked that these supposedly "timeless" artistic values actually articulate a culturally specific notion of musical art, not an objective, universal framework. (134)

Fair enough, but it sounds as if jazz, German romanticism, and modernism may have something in common. Monson drops the subject, however, so the insinuation is that "expressive fervor, artistic commitment, structural logic, and virtuosity" are not highly prized among jazz musicians. As she knows, this is hardly the case.

Even within the parameters of sociability and interaction, Monson can be too selective. For example, metaphors of "conversation" are emphasized much more than "storytelling," even though both are equally invoked by musicians. Perhaps this is an inadvertent byproduct of her focus on the rhythm section, rather than the soloist. However, I suspect she just prefers the more interactive metaphor. Titling the book "Telling a Story," an equally apt description of jazz improvisation, might have seemed too individualistic to be of service to her thesis. Another example is her selective emphasis on the verb "groove," as opposed to the more common term "swing." Again, "grooving" better reflects the imperatives of the rhythm section, but references to "swinging" might have been ignored only because they applied more to individuals.

Monson's general presentation of jazz is, for the most part, historically static. Given time and space constraints, Monson cannot be expected to add a historical dimension to every generalization made in the book. The problem is not the ahistorical mode of presentation itself, but the ways it can be tacitly manipulated. All the musicians interviewed (except for Byard) are currently active, and are thus more likely to emphasize current standards. For example, Monson's subjects aspire to "never playing what you practiced," whereas a player from an older generation might see nothing wrong with playing variations on the same solo night after night. Monson only mentions the modern ideal, perhaps because "never playing what you practiced" better reinforces her chosen models of interaction and conversation. When convenient, the ahistoric mode allows current axioms to surreptitiously represent all jazz.

Similarly, saying what jazz "is" always runs the risk of tacitly implying what other musics "aren't." As Gates himself made clear, the concept of "signifying" can be more a distinction of degree than kind. Monson is usually on top of this problem, noting for instance that eighteenth-century European observers frequently discussed the conversational and rhetorical aspects of classical music. However, some of her broader formulations of the jazz aesthetic—e.g., "the crucial point is that the iconic moment is not simply resemblance but a transformation of the thing resembled" (127)—could apply to just about anyone's artistic methods.

This problem is compounded when literary terms are transplanted into the realm of music. For instance, Monson borrows the phrase "repetition with a signal difference" from Gates, who was writing primarily about black literature and speech patterns. However, music in general may simply embody the principle of "repetition with a signal difference" more than language does. Music is always repeating things with signal differences. Thus the term probably distinguishes "black" from "white" speech patterns better than it does Louis Armstrong from Bach, whose "Inventions" are a brilliant realization of the general principle.

In fact, Monson might be highlighting the socially interactive aspects of jazz simply because in some ways they are easier to write about. Jazz at its most conversational and signifying is relatively compatible with written language, and written language is the medium of books, and books are what professors have to write. Berliner noticed a wider range of metaphors used by musicians to describe jazz performance, perhaps because his aim was to document jazz culture more than theorize about it. Many of these metaphors—notably journeying, exploration, channeling, trance, grace, soul, and heroism—can't be be grouped neatly under the heading of "signifying" or "sociable, face-to-face interaction." I don't, however, envy the jazz theorist who first tries to tackle these concepts. Many emotional and sensory comparisons—such as Carvin's rather self-contained image of soaking in the bathtub—also cannot be subsumed within the social and allusional.

As for ethnotheory, Monson never makes jazz a simple expression of "blackness." She takes an admirable stand against "an essentialized notion of cultural identity or racial experience," noting that "ethnic identities, skin colors, class stratification, and musical identities do not map neatly onto one another." (8) (Or, as Henry Threadgill once said, "It's a mutt world, and I'm going for the big mutt.") Jazz musicians are not culturally isolated, but rather, tied to "transnational webs of economics, politics, media, travel, and musical exchange." (192–93) At the same time, Monson stresses the fundamental black leadership role in jazz, as well as the underlying commonalities of African-American and African diasporic musics. Jazz and Yoruba music, for example, share "a simultaneous articulation of social and musical space, and the emergent musical shapes and social events have an intensely interpersonal quality." (194) On the whole, Monson strikes a judicious balance on these touchy issues, as in this look at "color-blind" rhetoric and its uses:

> Universalist and ethnically assertive points of view, it must be emphasized, often coexist in the same person and are best conceived as discourses upon which musicians draw in particular interactive contexts. An individual speaking to an interlocutor who underplays the role of African American culture in the music, for example, might choose to respond with ethnically assertive comments. In a context in which something closer to racial harmony prevails, a musician might choose to invoke a more universalistic rhetoric. . . . Since whiteness tends to be a sign of inauthenticity within the world of jazz, the appeals of white musicians to universalistic rhetoric can be perceived as power plays rather than genuine expressions of universal brotherhood. If jazz is one of the few cultural activities in which being African American is evaluated as "better" or more "authentic" than being non-African American, a white musician's appeal to a colorblind rhetoric might cloak a move to minimize the black cultural advantage by "lowering" an assertive African American musician from his or her pedestal to a more "equal" playing field. It is this use of colorblind rhetoric that often provokes African Americans to take more extreme positions on ethnic particularity. (202–203)

Still, Monson's ethnic distinctions are sometimes a little too crude, as in this suggestion that whites are uncomfortable with playfulness and ambiguity:

> The presumption that indirect, multisided, and metaphorical modes of speaking require less development of the mind reflects a Western cultural ideology about language that prefers the nonambiguous and non-playful delineation of ideas in intellectual discourse as well as the separation of these ideas from emotions. (92)

This is especially ironic because she herself sometimes sounds like Chris Rock parodying a nerdy white anthropologist:

> Interjections from congregants such as "Tell it," "That's right!," "Uh-huh," and "So true!" have direct counterparts in the frequently heard responses of jazz audience members to memorable passages of improvisation: "Yeah!," "Um-huh," and "Right." Composer Olly Wilson (1990) has suggested calling such passages *soul focal points*, a term that underscores the connection between musical climaxes and African American ideas of spirituality. These soul focal points somehow manage to project attitude and feeling in a way that set them apart from less inspired moments. (95–96)

Monson also makes the mistake of dichotomizing African American community and white egotism. She does acknowledge that the jazz life is "fiercely competitive," but also has a weakness for homilies in praise of togetherness, e.g., "The importance of human personality and individuality is conveyed through metaphors that unify sound and the human beings who make the sound through collaborative musical activity." (93) In isolation, this kind of feel-good boosterism is perfectly harmless. The problem is that it is situated within a passage distinguishing African American and "Western" aesthetic sensibilities. The bland insinuation is that African Americans care more about "the importance of human personality."

Sometimes her tone becomes too labored and defensive, to the point of sounding patronizing:

> "I always speak in parables," Carvin added, because it "helps for people to understand" (Carvin 1992). There is nothing inarticulate or analytically vague about these statements; metaphorical images are in many cases more communicative than ordinary analytical language. (93)

> The appreciation of humor in the African American tradition often conflicts with the preference in Western classical music for more "serious" means of musical expression. In jazz, humor and artistic seriousness are not incompatible. (124)

or cloying:

> The relationships between interactive performance and intermusical associations are not merely "in the head" but also in the heart and the body. They are part of the process by which communities grow out of the social activities and emotions of real people. (180)

If Monson's readers don't already know that metaphor can be communicative, humor is not antithetical to art, and jazz musicians are not fake people, there's no helping them.

Monson can also be too lax in equating "white" with the American "mainstream," as in this sentence:

> I explore musical references and allusions . . . for their use of transformative resources in African American musical practices to invert, challenge, and often triumph over the ordinary hegemony of mainstream white aesthetic values. [8]

Monson should keep in mind Albert Murray's 1970 axiom that "the mainstream is not white but mulatto." Or, as Ralph Ellison wrote in his 1964 review of "Blues People," by Leroi Jones (Amiri Baraka):

> . . . the most authoritative rendering of America in music is that of American Negroes. For as I see it, from the days of their introduction into the colonies, Negroes have taken, with the ruthlessness of those without articulate investments in cultural styles, whatever they could of European music, making of it that which would, when blended with the cultural tendencies inherited from Africa, express their own sense of life, while rejecting the rest. . . . white Americans have been walking Negro walks, talking Negro-flavored talk (and prizing it when spoken by Southern belles), dancing Negro dances and singing Negro melodies far too long to talk of a "mainstream" of American culture to which they're alien. (Ellison, 285–6)

Monson, however, is not particularly interested in broadening ethnic categories to demonstrate how jazz expresses Americanness. To Africans or Europeans, jazz can seem like the very embodiment of the American strut, or the American ideals of democracy and personal reinvention, as partially defined by African Americans. A foreigner might even, in a way, hear what is distinctly "American" about African-American particularism. To give an esoteric example, Americans historically have been particularly fond of defining tradition through pantheons of male icons. Thus for jazz musicians and fans, Armstrong and Parker in some way occupy the same mental compartments that Americans use to store Washington and Lincoln. However, exploring common national folkways is not fashionable these days, and such speculations are not to be found here.

Despite all these drawbacks, Monson, by example rather than exhortation, affirms an important principle: any scholar of jazz history should have a decent understanding of how African Americans interact. This understanding is almost impossible without extensive social contact. Though she doesn't mention it directly, *Saying Something* holds an important integrative message.

Monson spotlights four musical examples, all of which "employ musical allusion in one form or another to communicate the ironic play of difference." (127) Her concept of "allusion" is broad: "almost any musical detail or composite thereof, could convey a reference, as long as a community of interpreters can recognize the continuity." (127) Still, Monson has already focused too narrowly on "the ironic play of difference." This problem reaches its nadir in her analysis of John Coltrane's 1960 studio recording of "My Favorite Things."

Apparently Monson was tipped by Henry Louis Gates, Jr., whom she quotes:

> Repeating a form and then inverting it through a process of variation is central to jazz—a stellar example is John Coltrane's rendition of "My Favorite Things," compared to Julie Andrews's vapid version. Resemblance thus can be evoked cleverly by dissemblance. (Gates 1984, 291) (107)

Monson first clarifies that Julie Andrews's alleged vapidity took place five years *after* Coltrane's recording. Coltrane was given the sheet music by a song plugger for the Broadway version of *The Sound of Music*, which had been in production for about a year, with Mary Martin in the lead role. When Coltrane made the recording, he almost certainly hadn't heard any previous performance of the song.

Monson thoroughly details Coltrane's structural transformation of the song. The original has an AAAB chorus structure, with 16 bars per section. The lyrics of the A sections list pleasant things to think about ("Raindrops on roses and whiskers on kittens," etc.), and the lyrics of the B section advise the listener to recount such things when times are rough. Coltrane stretches the performance into one huge 13:41-minute chorus, waiting almost to the end before arriving at the B section. The solos are built not on the tune's original chord structure, as is customary, but on long polyrhythmic vamps, with a 6/8 feel and a bass tonic pedal point.

Monson diplomatically states that the original version of "My Favorite Things" is "appropriate to the musical theater context for which it is intended" (115) and that African-American versions of show tunes "are not 'better' inherently but relative to a particular aesthetic." (115) She also says she cannot speak for Coltrane or impute his intentions, adding that the degree of irony perceived in Coltrane's rendition will depend on the listener's frame of reference. This is disingenuous. With no evidence whatsoever, Monson clearly infers throughout that Coltrane's version is a conscious, ironic reversal of a corny tune. She never even mentions that in the musical, the "sentimental" lyrics are sung to children.

In his 1998 Coltrane biography (published after Monson's book), Lewis Porter writes of "My Favorite Things":

> People often make the mistake of assuming that Coltrane wanted to dress this song up because he must have thought it was silly. Quite the opposite; Coltrane was under no pressure to record such a song. In fact, he told [Francois] Postif, "Lots of people imagine wrongly that 'My Favorite Things' is one of my compositions; I would have loved to have written it, but it's by Rodgers and Hammerstein." (Porter, 182)

In fairness to Monson, Coltrane didn't say much on the subject, and the Postif interview was available only in French (Coltrane's exact words are unknown, since Porter is translating a translation). She continues:

> Since the lyrics would have been on the sheet music the song plugger brought to the quartet, Coltrane would have been well aware of the emphasis on white things in the lyric—girls in white dress, snowflakes on eyelashes, silver white winters, cream-colored ponies. In 1960—a year of tremendous escalation in the Civil Rights movement and a time of growing politicization of the jazz community—there was certainly the possibility that Coltrane looked upon the lyrics with an ironic eye. Even if he didn't, however, the potential for an ironic interpretation on the part of his listeners and fellow musicians is clearly present. (118)

Monson forgot to include "schnitzel with *noodles,*" which are clearly of a white hue. She also fails to mention the possibility that Julie Andrews, in the movie version of "My Favorite Things," is signifying on John Coltrane's 25-minute live renditions. Andrews may have been troubled by the way Coltrane dwells so long on the A sections, thus overemphasizing pleasant things. Even if she was not, however, the potential for an ironic interpretation on the part of her listeners and fellow musicians is clearly present.

Monson then states:

> Another possible inversion has to do with Coltrane's version beating the European American musical standards at their own game, and this is where the

idea of irony at a cultural level becomes important. Coltrane's quartet turns a musical theater tune upside down by playing with it, transforming it, and turning it into a vehicle for the expression of an African American-based sensibility that even many non-African Americans prefer to the original. In so doing, it invokes some of the standards of European classical music against European American musical theater songs. The simple setting of the Broadway version of "My Favorite Things" works well within the context for which it was intended. . . . Under the evaluative standards of Western classical music, however, the tune and arrangement would perhaps be described as "unsophisticated," "simple," or "too obvious." By contrast, the four-part contrapuntal texture generated by the musicians in the Coltrane quartet is certainly "more complex" than that of the Broadway version when measured by these standards. . . . Jazz musicians, in this sense, are able to invoke selectively some of the hegemonic standards of Western classical music in their favor. (119–120)

Let's break this down. Classical people think classical music is more sophisticated, thus better, than Broadway show tunes. Jazz players transform Broadway show tunes into more sophisticated music. Thus jazz musicians are "beating the European American musical standards at their own game." There's a good point in there somewhere, but Coltrane's "My Favorite Things" is not the place for it. Maybe Coltrane just liked the song. Besides, if he was interested in upstaging classical music, a better example would be his composition "Giant Steps," with its frenetic chord changes, multiple tonal resolutions, and unrelenting virtuosic demands—especially given the recent finding that Coltrane adopted the theme from the preface of a classical exercise book. Long, harmonically static vamps are hardly "beating the European American musical standards at their own game."

In short, portraying Coltrane's "My Favorite Things" as a kind of knowing, ironic commentary on hegemonic "Western" standards has much more to do with scholarship in the 1990s than anything Coltrane actually played.

Monson's other musical examples are much more insightful and relevant. Eric Dolphy and Jaki Byard's performance of "Parkeriana" with the Charles Mingus group (1964) has a demonstrable sense of "intertextual irony"; Dolphy ventures "out there" over rhythm changes, while Byard provides mock big band riffs. Rahsaan Roland Kirk's "Rip, Rig and Panic" (1965) signifies humorously on the French-American composer Edgar Varèse.

Monson's exposition of the Jaki Byard Quartet's "Bass-ment Blues" alone consumes 37 pages, and anyone looking for fresh approaches to jazz theory and analysis should examine it. (The recording is from 1965, with George Tucker, bass, Alan Dawson, drums, and Joe Farrell, flute. The composition, by Byard and Tucker, was originally released on *The Jaki Byard Quartet Live! Vol. 2*, Prestige PR-7477.) All instruments are transcribed for the first thirteen choruses, and through patient, line-by-line analysis, Monson brings the emergent, "intermusical" virtues of jazz wonderfully to life. Byard alludes all over the jazz map, including dissonant parodies of big band orchestration and a quote from Mingus's "Fables of Faubus." When Tucker gets lost in the form, Monson explains precisely how Byard and Dawson cue him back in. Interaction among all players is stressed, not just the binary relationships between the soloist and accompanists.

Once again, however, Monson's emphasis on Byard (who appears on three of her four musical examples) is too selective and convenient in advancing her broader claims. Byard's playing is particularly allusional, pan-historic, parodying, and dialogic; you might say he was "postmodern" before the word was coined. Other jazz musicians are different. Dolphy, Kirk and Byard have a well-developed sense of "intertextual irony." Others don't. Even within her analysis of "Bass-ment Blues," dialogism in itself tacitly becomes a proxy for "groove"—hardly an airtight correlation. Monson is quite candid about her agenda, admitting she picked "Bass-ment Blues" because it "embodied so well the interactive musical playfulness that I was interested in getting musicians to talk about." (138) She should also have chosen less ready-made targets.

Monson detours extensively into the arcane world of linguistic anthropology, drawing mostly on the theories of Michael Silverstein. (Readers put off by terms like "metapragmatic indexicals" can safely skim the hard parts.) Traditional linguistics were "designed to describe only the referential function of language," but meanings are also conveyed in context-dependent, or "pragmatic" ways, so that listeners will interpret the same referential statements quite differently. Silverstein is not saying simply that the social context of language is important. These "pragmatic" elements socially cohere over time, becoming systematized in ways analogous to grammatical structures themselves. These higher-order pragmatic functions are termed "metapragmatic." We tend to see the referential function of language as structural, and the pragmatic function as contextual—but these functions are in fact reciprocally foundational. A grammatical speech pattern, for example, could just as easily be viewed as the "context" of a metapragmatic social "structure." Monson then returns to music:

> In music, the traditional objects of analysis have been the parameters of musical sound most amenable to Western notation—pitch, rhythm, counterpoint, harmony—and their combinations, relations of inclusion, structural properties, and architectonic shapes. These features of musical structure and the categories in which they have been analyzed in the most widely known schools of music theory, I would argue, are epistemologically analogous to the referential function about which Silverstein speaks. They are those features of a musical text that lend themselves most readily to segmental formalization, analytic systematization, abstraction from context, and structural analysis. (187–88)

> Improvisational modes of music making highlight the pragmatic aspects of music most visibly, for what is crucial in the creative process is that improvisers in differentiated musical roles continuously monitor and react to the metapragmatic, pragmatic, and formal aspects of performance. While music theory has bequeathed to us extremely complicated means of approaching the resultant musical scores and work-internal relationships, including the measurement and mapping of all kinds of musical spaces . . . this essential interactive component of improvisation, with its emergent musical shapes and historical as well as socially constructive dimensions, has not been an object of theoretical inquiry. (190)

This subject alone could fill several books, and Monson admits that "Silverstein's terminology would not be necessary if we had a vocabulary in music that recognized the complexity and simultaneity of contextual issues in music." (190–91) Sometimes Monson seems to be floundering in interdisciplinary no-man's land, heroically attempting to reconcile specialized vocabularies. Still, someone at least has made a good beginning, and these necessarily speculative and exploratory passages are highly recommended to anyone willing to risk a severe case of intellectual vertigo.

Monson's tangle with poststructuralism is on firmer ground, because she has a relatively straightforward point to make. The first principles of poststructuralism and ethnography, it seems, are fundamentally at odds. In the teachings of Michel Foucault and Jacques Derrida, "The biggest 'sin' . . . is to suppose that some 'originary,' undivided, essential self (or objective reality) exists outside of . . . systems of signification or discourse." (206) Poststructuralists distrust the speaking subject and vernacular belief; ethnographers document little else. Ethnomusicologists should be especially miffed, since poststructuralists have made language the "general model of relationality," barring music from any chance to constitute or precede "discourse." Monson admirably transcends this duel altogether:

> . . . there is simply no reason to imagine that engaging with what someone says (or plays) is any less significant from a social constructionist (and representational) point of view than engaging with the theoretical and ideological speculations of Foucault or Derrida. In other words, I question the opposition between social constructionism and lived experience that is frequently drawn (or presumed) in deconstructionist cultural interpretation. . . . Interdisciplinary work on music and popular culture cannot afford to pretend that sound is not an active participant in the shaping of cultural meaning and human subjectivities, however peculiar its phenomenological discursivity might be and however much music is simultaneously involved with other overlapping discourses, such as those of gender, race, and class. (210–11)

In the end, *Saying Something* considerably broadens our perspectives on jazz—no small achievement. In a much-needed counterweight to the formalist bias of Gunther Schuller and others, Monson has illuminated the comparatively neglected aesthetics of conversation, social interaction, interdependence, allusion, metaphor, irony, signifying, emergence, and gesture. *Saying Something* should be widely discussed among jazz theorists. They should simply be warned not to let their range of responses to the music be constricted. Too often Monson, openly or backhandedly, tries to stuff jazz into her own theoretical suitcase. Jazz is about "sociable, face-to-face interaction" and many other things. Jazz can express the "ironic play of difference," or, "I have a toothache." Jazz musicians value large-scale structure and spontaneous signifying, technical virtuosity and distortive plasticity, posterity and the bathtub. The jazz artist is socially intertwined, on the African model, and socially marginal, on the Western model, and neither. Jazz represents ego and selflessness, irony and earnestness, highbrow culture and ephemeral entertainment, autonomous art and emanations of life in progress. Jazz is huge, and jazz has once again run circles around its analysts.

TEXTS QUOTED

Berliner, Paul F. *Thinking in Jazz: The Infinite Art of Improvisation*. Chicago: University of Chicago Press, 1994.

Ellison, Ralph. *The Collected Essays of Ralph Ellison*. New York: The Modern Library, 1995. The essay quoted was originally published in *The New York Review*, February 6, 1964.

Gates, Henry Louis, Jr. "The Blackness of Blackness: A Critique of the Sign and the Signifying Monkey." In *Black Literature & Literary Theory*, edited by Henry Louis Gates, Jr., 285–321. New York: Methuen, 1984.

Porter, Lewis. *John Coltrane: His Life and Music*. Ann Arbor: The University of Michigan Press, 1998.

BOOK REVIEWS

Peter Pettinger, *Bill Evans: How My Heart Sings* (New Haven and London: Yale University Press, 1998, 320 pp., $35; paperback: $15.95)

Reviewed by Robert W. Wason

Where were you, and what were you doing, when you first heard Bill Evans? Evans's friend Gene Lees has written that "it is a commonplace of psychology that people remember very precisely the circumstances in which they learned of certain historic events—for Americans, the death of John F. Kennedy. . . . A great many musicians . . . recall with comparable vividness their discovery of Bill Evans."[1] To those of a certain age—old enough to have heard, and to remember, jazz piano-playing before Bill Evans's arrival on the scene (and before his style was quickly taken up by legions of Bill Evans impersonators)—these words have great resonance. The late Peter Pettinger, author of the book under review, was certainly one of them.[2]

My first reaction to Evans was disquiet: as a young high-school jazz pianist at the beginning of the 1960s, I was one of the many that found his playing on *Kind of Blue* too understated and "unswinging." But his unique approach to the instrument drew me in nevertheless, and I quickly went on to steep myself in his playing. I must admit, however, that *Sunday at the Village Vanguard* was the highpoint for me;[3] though it is one of the touchstones of my career (and is no less moving to me now in its CD reissue), when Bill Evans moved on to Verve, I moved on to different musical interests, only to return occasionally to the fold. On the other side of the Atlantic, Pettinger, a classical pianist of my age, reacted more strongly, and, to judge from this book, remained an Evans-devotee to the end: "[Evans] sounded like a classical pianist, and yet he was playing jazz. I was captured there and then—the archetypal pivotal moment. The concept of the 'Bill Evans sound' instantly enshrined and distilled what I had always hoped to hear." (ix)

The years of our discovery were years when jazz changed rapidly, continually, and profoundly. In the summer of 1963, fresh out of high school, I was doing a steady quartet gig on the Cape, and my young colleagues and

I would debate during breaks whether both Evans and Coltrane had not already gone beyond acceptable (to us) jazz practice on *Kind of Blue*. Of course, this was a mere taste of what was to come. The modernist tendencies that emerged in jazz at the end of the 1940s and worked their way through during the 1950s were by now spinning out of control (we thought), creating a virtually "new" music with each recording by Coltrane (not to mention Dolphy and Coleman)—as though the modernist evolution of twentieth-century "classical" music was being recapitulated at a dizzying rate in jazz. Ultimately, Bill Evans's contribution fell somewhere in the middle of the development from the early 1950s on. Thus he would quickly be "outdistanced" by the evolution of jazz, while at the same time alienated from a new world of popular music—the core of the Evans dilemma, I would maintain, and certainly something to consider in evaluating a career that had its problems along with its great successes. But the high moral tone of Pettinger's reading is open-and-shut: "after [Kennedy] was assassinated, in November 1963, the floodgates were opened onto the vulgarity and excess of a musically permissive era." (97) However, our hero would remain aloof from all of that: "as a trio leader over two decades [Evans] had thrilled a dedicated band of enthusiasts, and their consistent following gave the lie to the value of fashion, a commodity that never touched him." (273)

I've reminisced enough to set the scene for Pettinger's book, a heartfelt, if uncritical, response to the impact that Bill Evans's music had on our lives, and on the lives of many others of our generation.[4] Therein lies both its strengths and its weaknesses. His generational view and respect—indeed, awe—of his subject (whom he never actually talked to, except to request a single tune [xi]) color all aspects of the book: the tone of the prose, the nature of the coverage—what you'll find there, and what you won't. Look neither for a searching, dispassionate analysis of Evans the person, nor a critical treatment of his playing in the larger context of jazz.

Still, there is much more than hero-worship here: in a project that must have taken many years and much energy, Pettinger has painstakingly filled in the chronological details of Evans's performance career by collating printed accounts and conducting many interviews with the key figures involved. After the preprofessional biography, the book largely follows the discography presented at the end (287–335), though the author fills in with much detail on unrecorded performances along the way (often calling upon *The Secret Sessions* compilation to provide that richer context).[5] The result is a kind of extended "liner notes" that, in tandem with the recent Bill Evans compilation reissues on CD,[6] will provide new generations of listener/readers with a complete survey of Bill Evans's career. We need only add "The Universal Mind," a video from the early 1960s, and "Jazz at the Maintainance Shop," made at Iowa State University with the last trio in 1979, to fill out the picture.[7] Thanks to Pettinger, it is now possible to say that few jazz careers have been so well documented.

Pettinger's "liner-note style" is literate, urbane, and often given to wonderful cross-cultural metaphors, as when Bill Evans "ring[s] the changes on familiar patterns" (216) during a less-than-inspired performance. The British perspective adds much detail that would have been unavailable to an American author: e.g., Brian Hennessey's efforts to preserve Evans (and now Evansiana, in his museum), or Evans's appearances at Ronnie Scott's in London; even the wonderfully tweedy (and smoky) picture of Evans on the dust cover was taken during a rehearsal for a BBC appearance in 1965. Pettinger also has much of interest and value to say about Evans's music; interspersed, in the course of the chronological flow of his prose, are brief, but often apposite, analytical remarks on Evans's playing, illustrated at important juctures by four transcribed examples (none by the author). Those wishing to deal with Evans's music in greater analytical detail will certainly want to read Pettinger in this regard, but the scattering of analysis through the book will not make that job an easy one. The book includes quite a good index, but there is considerably more analysis than shows up under "Evans . . . jazz technique of."

Perhaps the most original single contribution of the book is an entirely different sort of analysis: Pettinger's remarks on Evans's piano-playing technique, most of which are accessible through the index-entry, "Evans . . . , piano technique of." This topic was important enough to the author that he has made it the subtitle of his book: "How My Heart Sings" is, of course, the title of a tune by Earl Zindars that Evans played through much of his career; but to Pettinger, the classical pianist, that title certainly evoked the "how" of producing a sustained, "singing" tone on the instrument, for which Bill Evans was justly famous. Pettinger shows, to lapse momentarily into piano-technical prose, that the "Bill Evans sound" demands a playing technique close to the key, and close to the point of escapement. Through most of his career, Evans played consciously with arm weight (as is promoted by a significant faction of classical pianists) to assure that singing tone, rather than finger strokes, whether flat fingered (earlier in his career) of with curled fingers (later). The quote in which Evans himself addresses this issue, from near the end of his career, is tantalizingly incomplete, however:

> Bach changed my hand approach to playing the piano. I used to use a lot of finger technique when I was younger, and I changed over to a weight technique. Actually, if you play Bach and the voices sing at all, and sustain the way they should, you can't really play it with the wrong approach." (39).

Though Evans fails to tell us exactly when this occurred, I think we can presume that he would likely have made the change during his college years (there is no documented piano study with a teacher after this point).[8] Moreover, this may well have been one of the techniques that he worked on during the year of practice in which he lived with his parents, after his release from the Army in January 1954. In July 1955, he moved to a small apartment on West 83rd St., and that fall enrolled in theory courses at the Mannes College of Music—an event passed over in a paragraph by Pettinger (24).[9]

In its effort to document Evans's life punctiliously, Pettinger's book is a "scholarly" work, but in its interaction with other published sources on Evans, it remains at the level of liner notes, unfortunately. Up to now, the best accout that we have had was Hanns E. Petrik's book *Bill Evans; Sein Leben, Seine Musik, Seine Schallplatten* (1989) from the Oreos "Collection Jazz," which Pettinger cites (xiii).[10] The traditional German musicological "life and works" genre would end with the obligatory *Werkverzeichnis* (work-list); in the Oreos format, each book takes the format of life, musical analysis (since the "works" are not fully notated, and their discussion is not unproblematic), and discography (the "work-list"). Petrik begins by lamenting the biographical lacunae that are unfillable by a German writer unable to get to crucial American sources first-hand, and certainly his biography is a mere sketch compared to Pettinger's. But the second section of Petrik's book is a substantial attempt to deal with Evans's musical contribution—something that the present book cannot claim to be. Moreover, Petrik's discography, which is based on Peter H. Larsen's discography *Turn on the Stars* (Copenhagen, 1984) as Pettinger's is (295), reproduces the cover art in color—an extremely important feature of the original recordings that is in danger of disappearing as we move to small-format CD collections (the Riverside and Fantasy reissues are packaged in LP-sized boxes, and preserve cover art in the enclosed booklets, but the Verve reissue is CD-sized). Finally, Petrik includes the covers of European-issued recordings that many Americans have never seen. This is sufficient to indicate that his book is still of use; indeed, one wishes that an English-language publisher would adopt a similar design for a series of jazz biographies (or that these would appear in translation).

Aside from Petrik, a number of American dissertations on Bill Evans have appeared in the last twenty years. Gregory Smith started the analytical discussion with an application of Perry and Lord's work on oral transmission of poetry (applied by Treitler to chant) to the analysis of Evans's jazz solos.[11] More recently, Steve Larson has used Schenkerian analytical technique in his discussion of Evans's improvisation in his dissertation,[12] and in subsequent work (including a talk on his transcription of Evans's playing on Marian McPartland's "Piano Jazz" at the Third International Schenker Symposium given at The Mannes College of Music in 1999). Although LaRue's notion of "style analysis" has been the object of considerable criticism, Paula Berardinelli's dissertation (which adopts this approach) contains much useful material nevertheless;[13] even the first trio as a whole has been the subject of a study.[14] None of these sources has had any impact on Pettinger's study, however.

But, as I stated earlier, we should not look to this book for a critical assessment of Evans or his playing, lest we come away disappointed. Let us be thankful instead for what the book does contribute: the most complete documentary account of Evans's professional activities available, from which we can begin to build that critical assessment of one of the most important postwar jazz pianists.

NOTES

1. Gene Lees, *Meet Me at Jim and Andy's* (New York and Oxford: Oxford University Press, 1988), 142.
2. Peter Pettinger, a distinguished concert pianist, died in August 1998, shortly before this book was published.
3. Pettinger seems no less impressed; of the Vanguard sessions in general he writes: "For depth of feeling, in-group affinity, and beauty of conception with a pliant touch, these records will be forever peerless." (113)
4. Many were—or became—"classical" composers, a connection that would be interesting to pursue in greater detail.
5. *Bill Evans: The Secret Sessions.* 8-CD collection (Milestone 4421–2, 1996); recorded surreptitiously by Mike Harris, a loyal fan, this compilation documents Evans's (otherwise unrecorded) playing at the Village Vanguard from 1966 to 1975.
6. *Bill Evans; The Complete Riverside Recordings*, 12-CD edition (Riverside 018, 1987); *Bill Evans: The Complete Verve Recordings*, 18-CD collection (Verve 527 953, 1997); *Bill Evans: The Complete Fantasy Recordings*. 9 CDs; (Fantasy, 1012, 1989); *Turn Out the Stars: The Final Village Vanguard Recordings, June 1980* (Warner Brothers 45925, 1996) 6-CD collection.
7. *The Universal Mind of Bill Evans* (Rhapsody Films 9034, 1966); *Jazz at the Maintenance Shop* (Shanachie Video 6306, 1979)
8. This would have provoked interesting discussion in a seminar on Bill Evans that I gave two years ago at the Eastman School, if I had had the benefit of Pettinger's analysis then. Chopin recommended the study of Bach to his pupils, in part for the same reason that Evans does in this quote. Indeed, Bill

Evans is an excellent point of entry into jazz for classical pianists, as I found in this course (witness also the recent CD of transcriptions of Bill Evans's playing "Conversations with Bill Evans" by the classical pianist, Jean-Yves Thibaudet [Decca 455 512–2, 1997]). A detailed study and comparison of the early and late Bill Evans videos might offer a way to study the evolution of Evan's playing technique.

9. Thanks to research of Henry Martin I was able to find that Evans studied with Felix Salzer in at least one course.

10. This series, from Oreos Verlag (D-8176, Schaftlach, Germany) is an important source for jazz scholarship. (Ironically, the Germans have always taken "America's classical music" more seriously than we sometimes seem to.) My 1995/96 catalogue lists books on Armstrong, Baker, Basie, Beiderbecke, Braxton, Blakey, Coleman, Coltrane, Davis, Ellington, Fitzgerald, Getz, Gillespie, Mingus, Monk (apparently out of print), Parker, Reinhardt, Rollins; among books on jazz not in the series is a provocatively titled collection of essays (newly issued at that time): *Der Marsalis-Faktor*.

11. Gregory Eugene Smith, "Homer, Gregory and Bill Evans? The Theory of Formulaic Composition in the Context of Jazz Piano Improvisation" (Ph.D. diss.: Harvard, 1983).

12. Steven Leroy Larson, "Schenkerian Analysis of Modern Jazz" (Ph.D. diss., University of Michigan, 1987).

13. Paula Berardinelli, "Bill Evans: His Contributions as a Jazz Pianist and an Analysis of His Musical Style" (Ph.D. diss., New York University, 1992).

14. Donald L. Wilner, "Interactive Jazz Improvisation in the Bill Evans Trio (1959–1961): A Stylistic Study for Advanced Double Bass Performance" (DMA diss., University of Miami, 1995).

Laurent DeWilde, *Monk* (New York: Marlowe, 1997, discography, 1998, 218 pp. $13.95)
Thomas Fitterling, *Thelonious Monk: His Life and Music* (Berkeley: Berkeley Hills Books, 1997, 238 pp., appendices, 28 photographs, with a forward by Steve Lacy, $15.95)
Leslie Gourse, *Straight, No Chaser: The Life and Genius of Thelonious Monk* (New York: Schirmer Books, 1997, 340 + *xvi* pages, appendices, 42 photographs, $15.00)

Reviewed by David Baise

We are now living in a unique end-of-cycle when the "modal-chromatic" explorations of the Miles Davis quintet are about thirty-five years old, while the developments of bebop at Minton's Playhouse are even older, at about fifty-five. Closer study of the music and its context—in the forms of participant interviews, fact gathering, hard musical research, and personal celebration—all appear to be welcome and growing with the inevitable passing of time. Currently available are three books in English on pianist Thelonious Monk, two as translations. Each is notable and different, with *Monk*, by DeWilde being the shortest and least scholarly of the three.

Author Laurent DeWilde is a jazz pianist and writer, dividing his time between Paris and New York. *Monk* was written in French and translated into English, for the edition considered here. The writing is very impressionistic and colorful, using images and metaphors to tell Monk's story and to describe the music. While granting that translations can become highly idiomatic, the book has a relaxed, artistic flavor that is well in keeping with the spirit of Monk's music. On the name for New York City (the "Big Apple"), DeWilde explains that the jazz musicians claim to have come up with the nickname, because when you perform there "You better be sure you're ready, or you'll feel a lump in your throat you can't swallow, a big Adam's apple." The author also points out the background of the Monk's title for "Evidence." He tells us that the Monk tune uses the form and chord changes of the standard, "Just You, Just Me." "Just you, just me" means "just us"—(Justice)—DeWilde writes, and in order to have justice, one needs the requisite evidence. hence the song's title.

This is a very enthusiastic and thoughtful book. Thelonious Monk is portrayed as quite a ero and character; the possessor of one of the most individually expressive voices in jazz. The author also provides short biographical details on key people within Monk's immediate circle. Art Blakey, Charlie Rouse, Pannonica, and others, are included. A reader less familiar with this world will enjoy these digressions. Women were very important to Thelonious Monk, as nurturing protectors, as companions, and as inspirational muses. There is an early chapter devoted to Monk's women, which has an imagined (and very funny) list of distaff grievances from Thelonious's patient wife Nellie. The portrait of the pianist painted by the author throughout this book lends credence to this imaginary and very human exchange.

This is a subjective book, but the only book of the three to make a connection between Monk's experiences performing on the organ at church as a youngster and the later wild motion of Monk's feet during jazz performances on the piano. DeWilde's *Monk* has many interesting points and quotations (e.g., Steve Lacy, Johnny Griffin) throughout, but these are unattributed and hard to trace. There are no photographs, no bibliography, or index, but included is a selected discography of essential recordings. If we remember that this is a highly personal book, it is easier to forgive the lack of scholarship. *Monk* is best read, perhaps, as a quick study.

Thelonious Monk: His Life and Music by Thomas Fetterling is divided into three major sections: Monk's Life, Monk's Music, and Monk's Catalog. The biography section is fairly short and is divided in terms of record label associations. It includes many obscure photographs of musicians and family. The music is discussed in four headings: the sound, the ensemble pianist, the composer, and a close look at the "Bag's Groove—The Man I Love" recordings made on Christmas Eve, 1954, with Miles Davis as leader. Although the book is not a work of musicology in a strict sense, Fetterling begins to hint at these very concerns, citing an unnamed European musicologist. He also includes a quotation from pianist Bill Evans, discussing "external forms" as a vehicle for "deeper structures." It is not elaborated, however. It would have been helpful to have included a short paragraph or two as explanation for those readers not familiar with "forms" and "structures" as relative to Monk's compositions. As readers we do not know if Fetterling chose to leave these tantalizing threads alone, or if a more expansive section and actual analysis were editorially omitted.

The longest section of the book is the last third, dealing with Monk's catalog. This has black and white reproductions of album covers and puts the recordings in context with the pianist's life. Each is discussed as a minireview — personnel, strengths and weaknesses (very subjective) — and serves as a good introduction to the music for someone with little knowledge of the subject. Again, regretfully as with the DeWilde, Fetterling's volume has no index. The recordings *are* indexed — where they appear in the book — but this is pretty unnecessary. Other appendices include a list of films and videos, a short discussion of available boxed-set recordings, a musical glossary, and a list of sources used. The Fetterling is a translation of the original German. Like the DeWilde, it is a neither a serious biography nor discography, but something in between, and as such, is a good introduction to Thelonious Monk's world and music.

The book by Leslie Gourse, *Straight, No Chaser*, is intended as a much more definitive and scholarly work, with much of the research gathered from interviews with those closest to Monk, most notably his sister, Marion Monk White. Moreover, these quotations and interviews are all attributed. The painstaking care of detail is here in this book. Gourse has interviewed many jazz musicians for this, and the reader gets a good picture of Monk's regard by peers. There is an overall reliance on and balance toward fact in this book, lacking in the others. Where the other two volumes concentrate on Monk in terms of recordings for specific record labels, the biography by Gourse seems more like true biography: that is, objectively focussing on the man, his family, and circle of musicians. By collecting previous print sources and expanding them to include new interviews, Gourse has gathered the most information on Monk available in one volume. Gourse is very sympathetic towrd the subject. If Monk is celebrated as a *jazz hero* in the volume by Laurent DeWilde, Gourse's *Straight, No Chaser*, by comparison, ultimately portrays the pianist as victim and genius. What emerges from these details of Monk's pampered family life, nurtured musical explorations, the early disappointments and triumphs, is a portrait of Monk as the ultimate survivor, confident in his own music, stoic in the face of indifference and sometimes outright unfavorable criticism. Early on, Gourse quotes sister Marion, on Monk's later fame: "I knew he was that good. It didn't surprise him, either. He always said he was good, anyway. . . . He was a perfectionist. He demanded a lot of himself."

Born the middle child in 1917 in Rocky Mount, North Carolina, Thelonious, sister Marion, and brother Thomas were brought to New York City in 1922 by Barbara, their mother, where they settled in the San Juan Hill section of Manhattan. It was the elder Marion who began piano lessons, later to be pursued by Thelonious. Gourse has consulted school records from Junior High School 69, finding Thelonious's grades in music superior to other subjects. It was during this time and a little later that Monk was set up in the small apartment in an area of the kitchen-family room where he had his piano, a narrow bed, and a dresser. Along with the piano Monk studied and played organ at the Union Baptist Church in his teens. This was possibly the connection enabling Monk to go on the road with evangelist Reverend Graham, a faith healer who had a traveling road show. It was in Kansas City that Mary Lou Williams first heard Monk, saying "He was one of the original modernists, playing pretty much the same harmonies then that he's playing now."

Back home Monk began writing and playing all the time. James P. Johnson influenced the younger pianist. It was not long before the pianist became a member of the Minton's house band, recorded by Columbia student Jerry Newman on a Wilcox Gay disc cutter.

The role of Monk in the then modern jazz scene is interestingly detailed by the author. Mary Lou Williams identifies Monk, Charlie Christian, Kenny Clarke, Art Blakey, and Idrees (sic) Sulieman as the "first wave." Later came Gillespie and Parker. Monk did not work very much with either Bird or Diz. Gillespie tells of hiring Monk for his big band and subsequently having to let him go because of unreliability. Monk himself downplays the collective notion of "bop," saying "it's my music." Charlie Parker has also emphasized in radio interviews the idea of "bop" being "just a title." While hindsight affords us the ability to ascribe definite characteristics to the modern jazz of the 1940s, we also begin to realize how large the bigger picture and musical composite really was.

From primary interviews Gourse relates many interesting stories about Monk's piano style(s). Billy Taylor relates how he was sitting in during a trip to New York, running into Clarence Profit, composer of "Lullaby in Rhythm." Profit then took him to a piano session around the corner where they found Willie the Lion Smith, James P. Johnson, "and there was one other my age, who played like Art Tatum. . . . That was Monk. He later told me that the older guys encouraged him. Especially Willie the Lion Smith was encouraging to him." Another story from Walter Bishop, Jr., demonstrates Monk's affinity toward Tatum-like chops when Bishop found Monk playing and sounding exactly like Bud Powell. "Don't tell anybody," was Monk's admonishment.

Many pages detail Monk's particular performance practices and rehearsal techniques. Gourse relates how saxophonist Charlie Rouse would learn tunes by ear first, playing along with the pianist. If a song was particularly challenging, Monk would then either write it down or get the chart. We find, to little surprise, that Monk was interested in his musicians soloing as they heard the music. "You'd play the chords as such and he didn't want to hear that. He wanted you to experiment. He wanted you to be as free as possible and not be boxed in by playing from the chords," said Rouse. Steve Lacy corroborates Rouse when he says, "He didn't believe in showing paper to musicians. He would play the songs over and over until we learned them." The primary interview with drummer Ben Riley is particularly interesting, revealing Monk's ideas of time, playing melodically, and directing group dynamics. Riley's affection for the pianist is unmistakable.

There are many such reminiscences, anecdotes, and stories, along with biographical detail. Beginning in the late 1950s, Monk began having episodic bouts of strange behavior that were unpredictable and widely spaced apart. These are corroborated by family members, band members, and club owners. Gourse gives special thanks to Dr. Edward Holtzman, a "psychiatrist, whose uncanny understanding of Monk's musical genius and mental condition guided me." If the subject of Monk's mental health, as addressed in *Straight, No Chaser*, seem inchoate or inconclusive, the reason rests perhaps on limited documentation and the privacy of the pianist's medical records. The author relies on information from secondary doctors who, we are told, are familiar with the circumstances of Monk's condition. That Gourse should include this information, much of it speculative, must be a matter of a biographer's sense of completeness.

Overall, this is a fine addition to Gourse's other jazz writings. Little has been written of Thelonious Monk recently except for the brief conversation with Orrin Keepnews as included in *The View From Within* (New York: Oxford University Press, 1987). Notes to *Straight, No Chaser* are found at the end of each of the fifteen chapters, with the personal interviews listed first. This arrangement is very helpful to readers, who more often than not must vexingly wade through notes collated by page number at the end of a book. *Straight, No Chaser* also has some very useful appendices: a list of 91 registered compositions, a videography, a sessionography, a bibliography, and an index. There is the curious use of a Monk silhouette as an icon throughout the book, at chapter beginnings, and other places that is somewhat unnecessary.

Gourse writes at the outset that "much of the analysis of individual pieces comes from historical critical appraisals and explanations by musicians who play the music." The concern of the author is primarily to document Monk's biography. She adds that the music "awaits augmentation by a musicologist or musician devoted to writing a note-for-note dissertation." Several works are forthcoming. Currently in preparation are books by Chris Sheridan (Greenwood), a *Thelonious Monk Reader* by Bob van der Bliek (Oxford), a study by the late musicologist Mark Tucker, and a biography by Peter Keepnews.

Barbara J. Kukla, *Swing City: Newark Nightlife, 1925-1950* (Philadelphia: Temple University Press, 1991, 269 pp., $29.95)

Reviewed by Javier González

There is a tendency in writings on jazz to focus on the "great men." There is a wealth of material on Charlie Parker, Miles Davis, John Coltrane, Duke Ellington, etc. Similarly, there is a tendency to focus on the jazz scenes that existed in New York, New Orleans, Kansas City, Chicago, and even Los Angeles, often ignoring other significant locales like Baltimore, Philadelphia, and Newark. *Swing City* is a departure from that tendency and offers a glimpse into what was happening in entertainment in Newark over a span of 25 years. Author Barbara J. Kukla's focus is on some of the lesser known artists, their way of life, the clubs in which they worked, and the other socioeconomic factors that affected their lives. "The theme is entertainment and music, but *Swing City* is just as much about the vicissitudes of life in urban Black America"(1).

Kukla, editor of the *Newark This Week* portion of Newark's *Star-Ledger* newspaper at the time she wrote the book, sets the stage with a brief history of Newark from its beginnings as a Puritan village in 1666. In 1746, Newark became the site of the first college in New Jersey, the College Of New Jersey, which predated Princeton. Newark's prime geographic location for distribution of goods made it an early manufacturing center, and by the late 1800s products as diverse as books, clocks, paint, and steam engines, were being produced in Newark. By 1925, the city housed 1,668 factories. This concentration of businesses also helped to make Newark the financial hub of New Jersey from the beginning of the twentieth century.

These factors were important in attracting numerous immigrants, creating "the mosaic of ethnic groups and neighborhoods [which were] dominated by enclaves of Irish, Germans, Jews, Italians, middle-Europeans, and Blacks who emigrated from southern states"(1). Her description of their distribution throughout the city is particularly vivid when one has some familiarity with Newark. The Third Ward was the poor and working class Black neighborhood during the time covered by the book. Details like the location of the Barbary Coast, the red-light district, further help to contextualize the information. The information on the performers themselves, drawn mostly from extensive oral histories, is thus placed in a tangible context. Naturally, much of the scenery has changed, particularly since the riots of 1967. Given the number of exact addresses and locations included in the book, a map with a legend of the clubs and neighborhoods would have been helpful.

Newark's location also aided its rise to prominence as an entertainment center; "Shows headed for New York played Newark on the way in or out"(3). Names like Ella Fitzgerald, Billy Eckstine, Duke Ellington, Count Basie, Jimmie Lunceford, and Louis Jordan were a common sight on the marquees of the city's theatres. The population itself also made it a logical stop for travelling acts. The Black population in Newark grew from 16,977 in 1920, to 38,880 in 1930, to 45,760 in 1940 (over 10% of a total of 429,760).

Furthermore, Kukla points out that Newark was a beer town, even during Prohibition; its many speakeasies were easily accessible for the price of a membership. A post-Prohibition tally showed Newark with the nation's highest per capita number of saloons in 1938, roughly 1 per 429 residents (roughly 1,000 saloons). All of these factors worked together to make Newark a lively entertainment center.

The city's importance was not limited to music. Comedians Redd Foxx and Jackie Gleason got their starts in clubs in Newark. Larger venues like the Nest and Dodger's featured full-scale revues, with dancers, singers, chorus girls, comedians, skits, and emcees.

Legalized segregation in Newark prevailed until 1949, making most of downtown Newark off limits to Blacks (with the notable exception of the Coleman Hotel, owned from 1944 by the Coleman Brothers, a Black gospel singing group). This gave rise to Black-only theatres and an abundance of clubs in Black neighborhoods in the Third Ward. As Kukla points out, nightlife became an important source of jobs for the Black community, as other avenues were not available to Blacks because of racism and segregation.

After setting the stage set with this historical overview, Kukla turns to the people and places of the music scene. She dedicates a chapter to a social phenomenon that was important for Black entertainers and the Black community: the rent party. The rent party was an essential aspect of survival in many neighborhoods in Black America during the height of the Depression. Tenants would host these parties, charging admission at the door, to raise money to pay their rent.

For the man or woman who worked all day as a factory worker or "in service" as a domestic and was struggling to make ends meet, the rent party was a painless way to meet expenses. The motive was economic, but the byproduct was fun, a major venue of Black socialization.

More often than not, music was an essential ingredient of the parties. In the
homes of the working class, they were relatively simple affairs, offering food,
drink, and a bit of music for the price of admission, generally a quarter (20).

The musical aspect helped launch the careers of pianists like Fats Waller,
and James P. Johnson, among others. In Newark, the main pianists of note
were the legendary Willie the Lion Smith and Donald Lambert, although
Lambert reportedly eschewed rent parties. As rent parties typically ran all
night, musicians could leave their earlier engagements and continue to play
until dawn at one of these affairs. One of the many lesser-known figures introduced in the book is pianist Duke Anderson, a pianist from Orange, New
Jersey, who made his living playing these parties. His anecdotes underscore
the regional rivalry between pianists from different towns. Anderson speaks
of having to lie and say he was from Newark to get hired to play at Newark
rent parties. The modern phenomenon of the DJ also has its roots in the rent
party. Among Newark's earliest was Jesse Jones, a mechanic who invented
a portable record player to play 78 rpm disks and charged $5 to play par-
ties where there were no musicians.

As she does throughout the book, Kukla evokes the imagery of the scene
with the warmth and factuality derived from numerous first-hand oral histories of the people who hosted the parties. Rent parties diminished in
economic importance with the advent of World War II and the greater
economic possibilities available in wartime industry.

Swing City devotes sections to clubs, bands, singers, dancers, comedians,
and individual musicians. Chapters begin with background information and
then present specific anecdotes drawn from the many hours of Kukla's interviews. The story of trumpeter Hal Mitchell, an icon in the Newark scene and
member of Tiny Bradshaw's and Benny Carter's bands of the 1940s, shows
the importance of what oral histories can tell us. Mitchell started in music
thanks to one Miss Corprew "who ran the neighborhood house." She bought
him his first trumpet after seeing the young boy's enthusiasm while watching
the house band. Kukla does not specify what kind of "house" Miss Corprew
was running, nor does Mitchell. Mitchell relates the ways many musicians
went about learning to play, even the piano players. His anecdote about his
six-month stint playing duets with Newark stride man Donald Lambert illu-
minates both how the combination came together and the typical image of
stride pianists as solo performers. There is no recorded evidence of this collaboration, which survives only in the memories of those who witnessed it.

Chapter Four focuses on the two leading stride pianists based in Newark,
Willie the Lion Smith and Donald Lambert. The section on Smith is

based more on others' research than Kukla's, a logical choice given the ample (relative to the more obscure Lambert) amount of published material available on Smith, including an autobiography. As such, Kukla's picture of Smith is consistent with other works depicting him as a bombastic personality (musically and personally), who shied away from nothing and savored the "cutting contests" by which pianists of the time were measured. William Henry Bonaparte Bertholoff Smith was not a Newark native, having been born in Goshen, New York. He acquired his last names from his mother's marriages, the last of which landed the family in Newark. As a teenager, Smith was already a figure in the clubs of Newark's Barbary Coast. Smith worked his way into New York clubs before being drafted to serve in the First World War. He acquired the nickname of "the Lion," for his exploits in the 350th Field Artillery Division. Upon his return, Smith became a fixture at Leroy Wilkins's cabaret in Harlem, where he furthered his well-deserved reputation.

Lambert, also known as "The Lamb" or "Muffin," was not a native of Newark either, but hailed from Princeton, where he was born in 1904. Lambert's mother, a piano teacher and bandleader, gave Lambert his initial instruction. Despite this early grounding, Lambert never learned to read or write music. By age ten, Lambert was playing in a movie pit accompanying silent films. Kukla builds her account of Lambert from accounts by some of the other prominent figures in her book. Viola Wells, better known by her stage name of Miss Rhapsody, worked with him regularly at Angeline's, an after-hours joint on Washington Street in Newark:

> Donald played entirely by ear. As a child, he told me he sat under the piano while his mother gave lessons. He absorbed everything he heard. He could play anything—stride, classical, anything you ever heard. If you'd hum it he'd play it. And he could play stone drunk or sober (35).

Lambert, in Kukla's words, "dominated the stride scene in Newark," "could play two songs at once," and, "by all accounts, had one of the hottest left hands in the business." Lambert's relative obscurity, like that of other artists mentioned by Kukla, was partially his own doing. Stricken by grief over his wife's death in 1936, Lambert settled back in Newark after a period in New York and rarely left. When he did return, only once or twice a year, he was faced with the lack of respect of being an out-of-towner. By the account of many of his peers, including Ellington and Waller, Lambert would "cut anybody" and "astound everyone" and then return to New Jersey. Kukla thus offers a portrait of a complex, often difficult, man brimming with talent. By eschewing New York, he undoubtedly contributed to his small discography (Lambert did not record initially until 1941 and only a handful of times after that), but also made himself an important influence on many Newark musicians, like pianist June Cole, who "would hang around Donald all night to try to learn something new"(37). This is one of many stories of this type that Kukla includes in the book.

Other figures mentioned include the aforementioned Duke Anderson, who was perhaps best known for subbing for Count Basie in the 1960s and 1970s and for his work in Dizzy Gillespie's first big band. Anderson, a notorious gambler known to lose thousands of dollars at a time, also led a band in Newark with his brother Billy and spent time on the road with blues singer Ida Cox. Anderson's stories of traveling with Cox, although not about Newark per se, are graphic in their detail and suggest what life on the road was during the Depression for the Black musician.

There were local singing legends in Newark during this period. Many of them—including Miss Rhapsody, Grace Smith, Geneva Turman, and Billie Sermond—would fare better with their audiences than better-known artists from out of town. Sarah Vaughan is the most famous singer to emerge from Newark during this era. Others had chances at stardom, but passed it up. Kukla tells the story of Billie Sermond, a light-skinned beauty who was the first Black woman to sing in the previously all-White Broad Street clubs. Sermond reputedly turned down an offer from Hollywood because she was fearful and, in her own words, "too stupid to go" (48). Others, like Miss Rhapsody (Viola Wells) were recorded and worked long careers in show business without reaching the level of national celebrity of Sarah Vaughan, while remaining local staples in the Newark scene.

The plethora of clubs in Newark gave ample opportunities for the diverse entertainers based in the city during the period covered by the book. The Kinney, the Nest, and Dodger's, among others, catered to different clienteles, and were always attempting to outdo each other. The Kinney was one of Newark's first Black nightclubs. The big revues staged by many of these clubs gave a forum for dancers like Doryce Bradley (famous for her striptease routine in the 1930s), Gertrude Turman (who had several talented siblings who also performed in different capacities during this era), and the multitalented Joe Gregory, who also sang, played piano, emceed, and led bands from time to time.

Tenor saxophonist Ike Quebec (born Isaac Abrams in Newark on August 17, 1918) got his start as a dancer in one of these revues before getting his first break as a musician. Quebec got his start playing piano, accompanying singer/dancer Sadie Matthews. Quebec went on to have a successful career first in some of Newark's big bands, then with Cab Calloway, then as one of the first beboppers to play in Newark. Drug problems slowed his career and eventually killed him in 1963, as he was making a comeback as an A & R man and musician for Blue Note Records.

Of course, the dancers on the stage were not the only ones dancing during the swing era. A fierce competitiveness developed between two of Newark's big bands, the Savoy Sultans and the Savoy Dictators. According to Kukla, the Sultans enjoyed the most fame, playing as the intermission band at New York's Savoy Ballroom in the late 1930s and early 1940s, where they held their own with the likes of the Ellington, Basie, and Lunceford bands. These two bands, along with the mainly teen-aged Barons of Rhythm, at one time or another, employed most of Newark's best jazz musicians of the era. The Sultans even hit the road on national tours. The talent level was so high in these bands that Tiny Bradshaw recruited half of the Sultans at one time to join his band on the road. These, of course, are only two of the many bands that Kukla mentions. As was the case with many of these local figures, they did not record prolifically like the "name" bands and most of their legacy rests on word-of-mouth legend.

Newark musicians were often recorded by the local label, Savoy Records, and its notorious owner, Herman Lubinsky. Lubinsky, who owned the Radio Record Shop in downtown Newark, started his label in 1942 by releasing four sides by the Savoy Dictators. The story surrounding the making and release of this recording typifies the bottom line mentality of Lubinsky's dealings with his musicians: he didn't pay them. And yet, Lubinsky was an important figure in the Newark scene and beyond, having recorded some of the early bebop bands like those of Charlie Parker, Dexter Gordon, and Miles Davis, as well as some of the local talent that possibly would not have otherwise made it to disc. Kukla's account abounds with stories of animosity toward Lubinsky; although many musicians saw recording for Savoy as their only opportunity, she notes: "To this day, many of those who didn't record when he came calling consider it a badge of honor" (158).

Newark also boasted an important bebop club in the 1940s, Lloyd's Manor. Lloyd's was an important launching point for a number of musicians who went on to greater fame, such as tenor saxophonists Hank Mobley and James Moody, singer/pianist Babs Gonzales (Lee Brown), and (later) guitarist George Benson. Of course, there is the usual group of local legends like pianist Larue Jordan. Newark's first Black mayor, Ken Gibson, also played there as a teenager. It was also a stop for travelling acts and the scene of jam sessions, which, in the case of Moody, helped to get him recruited into Gillespie's band.

Kukla's collection of stories is thoroughly enhanced by the numerous photographs that help put faces to the names of the people and places whose stories she tells. The stories present vivid figurative and literal snapshots of the era that are supported with solid research. Appendixes of clubs, bands, and entertainers not only supplement her topic but lay a solid foundation for further research. *Swing City* emphasizes the importance of oral history, presenting much information that would otherwise be completely lost. It also emphasizes the importance of undertaking such historical research, while the figures who formed the history are still alive.

BOOKS RECEIVED

Starting with this volume of *ARJS,* Vincent Pelote, librarian at the Rutgers Institute of Jazz Studies, will compile a list of recently published or re-published books added to the IJS archives. This list below includes books published in 1999 and 2000. On the assumption that readers will seek volumes by subject matter rather than author, these lists will be alphabetized by title, with the primary title in all capitals.

AFRICA AND THE BLUES, by Gerhard Kubik (Jackson: University of Mississippi Press, 1999)

ALL ROOTS LEAD TO ROCK: Legends of Early Rock'n'Roll, edited by Colin Escott (New York: Schirmer Books, 1999)

THE BEST OF JACKSON PAYNE, a novel by Jack Fuller (New York, Alfred A. Knopf, 2000)

BLACK GYPSY: The Recordings of Eddie South, by Anthony Barnett (Lewes [U.K.]: Allardyce Barnett, 1999)

BLUTOPIA: Visions of the Future and Revisions of the Past in the Work of Sun Ra, Duke Ellington, and Anthony Braxton, by Graham Lock (Durham and London: Duke University Press, 1999)

BRIGHT MOMENTS: The Life and Legacy of Rahsaan Roland Kirk, by John Kruth (New York: Welcome Rain Publisher, 2000)

BROTHERHOOD IN RHYTHM: The Jazz Tap Dancing of the Nicholas Brothers, by Constance Valis Hill (New York: Oxford University Press, 2000)

CHICAGO BLUES: As Seen from the Inside—The Photographs of Raeburn Flerlage, edited by Lisa Day (Toronto: ECW, 2000)

CHICAGO BLUES: DOWN AT THERESA'S . . .: The Photographs of Marc Pokempner, by Marc Pokempner and Wolfgang Schorlau (Munich & New York: Prestel Verlag, 2000)

CLIFFORD BROWN: The Life and Art of the Legendary Jazz Trumpeter, by Nick Catalano (New York: Oxford University Press, 2000)

DUKE ELLINGTON: A Spiritual Biography, by Janna Tull Steed (New York: Crossroad Publishing Company, 1999)

THE ESSENTIAL JAZZ RECORDS, Volume 1: Ragtime to Swing, by Max Harrison, Charles Fox, and Eric Thacker (London: Mansell Publishing, 2000)

THE ESSENTIAL JAZZ RECORDS, Volume 2: Modernism To Postmodernism, by Max Harrison, Eric Thacker, and Stuart Nicholson (London: Mansell Publishing, 2000)

EUGENE BULLARD: Black Expatriate in Jazz-Age Paris, by Craig Lloyd (Athens: University of Georgia Press, 2000)

GIRL SINGER: An Autobiography, by Rosemary Clooney with Joan Barthel (New York: Doubleday, 1999)

GIANT STEPS: Bebop and the Creators of Modern Jazz 1945–65, by Kenny Mathieson (Edinburgh: Payback Press, 1999)

GIANT STRIDES: The Legacy of Dick Wellstood, by Edward N. Meyer (Lanham, Maryland, and London: Scarecrow Press, 1999)

GRANT GREEN: Rediscovering The Forgotten Genius of Jazz Guitar, by Sharony Andrews Green (San Francisco: Miller Freeman Books, 1999)

THE GREAT JAZZ DAY, by Charles Graham, Dan Morgenstern, et al. (New York: Woodford Press, 2000)

GROOVIN' HIGH: The Life of Dizzy Gillespie, by Alyn Shipton (New York: Oxford University Press, 1999)

JAZZ: A Visual Journey, by Herb Snitzer (Florida: Notables, 1999)

JAZZ: The First Century, edited by John Edward Hasse (New York: William Morrow, 2000)

JAZZ 101: A Complete Guide to Learning and Loving Jazz, by John F. Seward (New York: Hyperion, 2000)

JAZZ BY MAIL: Record Clubs and Record Labels 1936-1958, by Geoffrey Wheeler (Manassas, Virginia: Hillbrook Press, 1999)

JAZZ MAN'S JOURNEY: A Biography of Ellis Louis Marsalis, Jr., by D. Antoinette Handy (Lanham, Maryland, and London: Scarecrow Press, 1999)

JAZZ PARTY: A Photo Gallery of Great Jazz Musicians, by Al White, text edited by Jim Shacter (Little Rock, Arkansas: August House Publishers, 2000)

JAZZ SINGERS: The Great Song Stylists in Their Own Words, edited by Mike Evans (London: Hamlyn, 1999)

JIMMY DORSEY: A Study in Contrasts, by Robert L. Stockdale (Lanham, Maryland, and London: Scarecrow Press, 1999)

LATIN JAZZ: The First of the Fusions,1880s to Today, by John Storm Roberts (New York: Schirmer Books, 1999)

LATIN TINGE: The Impact of Latin American Music of the United States, second edition, by John Storm Roberts (New York: Oxford University Press, 1999)

LET'S GO SEE SOME JAZZ, photographs by Michael T. Solomon (Sacramento, California: Solomon Dubnick, 2000)

LITTLE LABELS—BIG SOUND: Small Record Companies and the Rise of American Music, by Rick Kennedy and Randy McNutt (Bloomington: Indiana University Press, 1999)

LOST CHORDS: White Musicians and Their Contribution to Jazz, 1915–1945, by Richard M. Sudhalter (New York: Oxford University Press, 1999)

LOUIS ARMSTRONG: In His Own Words, by Louis Armstrong (New York: Oxford University Press, 1999)

MIDNIGHT AT MABEL'S: The Mabel Mercer Story, by Margaret Cheney (Washington, DC: New Voyage Publishing, 2000)

MORNING GLORY: A Biography of Mary Lou Williams, by Linda Dahl (New York: Pantheon Books, 1999)

THE MUSICAL WORLD OF J. J. JOHNSON, by Joshua Berrett and Louis G. Bourgois (Lanham, Maryland, and London: Scarecrow Press, 1999)

MYSELF WHEN I AM REAL: The Life and Music of Charles Mingus, by Gene Santoro (New York: Oxford University Press, 2000)

NAT KING COLE, by Daniel Mark Epstein (New York: Farrar, Straus and Giroux, 1999)

NO EYES: Lester Young, by David Meltzer (Santa Rosa, California: Black Sparrow Press, 2000)

NOW IT'S JAZZ: Writings on Kerouac & the Sounds, by Clark Coolidge (Albuquerque: Living Batch Press, 1999)

"OH, MISTER JELLY": A Jelly Roll Morton Scrapbook, compiled by William Russell (Copenhagen: Jazz Media Aps, 1999)

OPEN SKY: Sonny Rollins and His World of Improvisation, by Eric Nisenson (New York: St. Martin's Press, 2000)

RECORDED MUSIC IN AMERICAN LIFE: The Phonograph and Popular Memory, 1890–1945, by William Howland Kenney (New York: Oxford University Press, 1999)

REFERENCE BACK: Philip Larkin's Uncollected Jazz Writings, 1940–84, edited by Richard Palmer and John White (Hull: University of Hull Press, 1999)

RIDE RED RIDE: The Life of Henry "Red" Allen, by John Chilton (London and New York: Cassell, 1999)

ROLLIN' AND TUMBLIN': The Postwar Blues Guitarists, by Jas Obrecht (San Francisco: Miller Freeman Books, 2000)

SESSIONS WITH SINATRA: Frank Sinatra and the Art of Recording, by Charles L. Granata (Chicago: A Cappella Books, 1999)

SPINNING BLUES INTO GOLD: The Chess Brothers and the Legendary Chess Records, by Nadine Cohodas (New York: St. Martin's Press, 2000)

A SPIRAL WAY: How the Phonograph Changed Ethnography, by Erika Brady (Jackson: University Press of Mississippi, 1999)

STRANGE FRUIT: Billie Holiday, Café Society, and an Early Cry for Civil Rights, by David Margolick (Philadelphia: Running Press, 2000)

STRIDE!: Fats, Jimmy, Lion, Lamb, and All the Other Ticklers, by John L. Fell and Terkid Vinding (Lanham, Maryland, and London: Scarecrow Press, 1999)

SWING IT!: The Andrews Sisters Story, by John Sforza (Lexington: University of Kentucky Press, 2000)

SWING SHIFT: "All-Girl" Bands of the 1940s, by Sherrie Tucker (Durham, North Carolina: Duke University Press, 2000)

TRUMPET BLUES: The Life of Harry James, by Peter J. Levinson (New York: Oxford University Press, 1999

ABOUT THE EDITORS

EDWARD BERGER, associate director of the Institute of Jazz Studies, is coauthor of *Benny Carter: A Life in American Music, Reminiscing in Tempo,* and *Basically Speaking: An Oral History of George Duvivier,* all published by Scarecrow Press. He frequently serves as road manager for Benny Carter and has produced and annotated most of Carter's recent recordings, including the Grammy-winning *Harlem Renaissance* and *Elegy in Blue* CDs.

DAVID A. CAYER was a founding coeditor of *Journal of Jazz Studies,* the predecessor of *Annual Review of Jazz Studies* in 1973 and has been affiliated with the Institute of Jazz Studies since 1965. In 1991 he retired from Rutgers University as associate vice president of Academic Affairs.

HENRY MARTIN, associate professor of music at Rutgers University–Newark, is a composer and music theorist. He has recently completed commissions from the Barlow Endowment of Brigham Young University (whose composition competition he won in 1998), the University of North Carolina–Greensboro, and the San Antonio International Piano Competition. Wadsworth is publishing his jazz history text (coauthored with Keith Waters) in 2001.

DAN MORGENSTERN, director of the Institute of Jazz Studies, is a jazz historian and former editor of *Down Beat.* His many publications include *Jazz People,* and he has won six Grammy awards for album notes. He has been a vice president of the National Academy of Recording Arts and Sciences, a jazz panelist for the Music Program of the National Endowment for the Arts, and a teacher of jazz history at Brooklyn College, New York University, the Peabody Institute, and Rutgers.

ABOUT THE CONTRIBUTORS

DAVID BAISE is a guitarist and composer. A recent graduate of the Master of Arts program in jazz history and research at Rutgers, he has performed with saxophonist James Spaulding, vibraphonist Steve Nelson, and organist Big John Patton, among others.

T. DENNIS BROWN, Ph.D., is associate professor of music at the University of Massachusetts at Amherst and has written extensively about jazz drummers and drumming. He is currently writing a biography of Gene Krupa.

MICHELE CANIATO is a composer and saxophonist. He received the Bachelor of Music degree in saxophone performance and jazz composition from Berklee College and the Master of Music and Doctor of Musical Arts in composition from Boston University. His works have been performed by Alan Dawson, Bill Pierce, Andy McGee, Berklee Faculty Big Band, on National Italian Radio, and at festivals in Italy by Stefan Thut and Alessandra Trentin. He is currently director of jazz ensembles at Boston University, where he coaches the jazz ensembles and teaches jazz history. He has been an artist-in-residence at the Adria Conservatory in Italy.

TIM DEAN-LEWIS is currently completing his Ph.D. in music at City University, London, England. This work concerns strategies used by musicians when playing "outside" the conventional tonality. He is a jazz pianist, organist (with "The Dorgan Trio"), and theorist, and has lectured in jazz history, jazz piano, composition, and theory at the University of Brighton, England, for a number of years. This is his second article for *ARJS*.

JAVIER GONZÁLEZ was born in San Juan, Argentina, but has lived in the U.S. most of his life. A student and player of different forms of black music since 1991, he has recently completed a Masters' degree in jazz history and research at Rutgers–Newark.

MARK S. HAYWOOD lives in England, holds a Ph.D. in classics from Liverpool University, and currently coordinates staff training at a college of Further Education in Birmingham. He has had two books of popular piano music and various jazz research papers published, and has a particular interest in the sonnet form as a means of expression.

KWATEI JONES-QUARTEY is a doctoral student at the City University of New York Graduate Center. He is currently working on a dissertation that focuses on aspects of Dizzy Gillespie's improvising style.

BARRY KENNY is currently completing his Ph.D. at the University of New South Wales (Sydney, Australia), where he is employed as a tutor and part-time lecturer. He has also been actively involved in the local jazz scene as a pianist, teacher, and accompanist. Other journals to which he has contributed include the *Journal of Research in Music Education*.

CLIFFORD KORMAN is a pianist who received his M.A. in 1996 from the City College of New York, specializing in jazz performance. He was awarded a 1999 Fulbright Lecture/Research grant; in Brazil, he taught courses in improvisation, repertoire, and piano, and studied similarities between the development of jazz and the Brazilian instrumental genre of *choro*. His CD *Mood Ingênuo: Pixinguinha Meets Duke Ellington,* a document of his duo with Brazilian clarinetist/saxophonist Paulo Moura, was released in June 1999. He presented an earlier version of this article at the 1998 conference of the Society for American Music (formerly the Sonneck Society).

BRIAN PRIESTLEY has written several books on jazz, including biographies of Charles Mingus, Charlie Parker, and John Coltrane. He is a contributor to the *New Grove Dictionary of Jazz* and coauthor of the encyclopedia *Jazz: The Rough Guide*. An influential jazz radio presenter in London, he is active as a pianist and arranger, and teaches jazz history at various colleges.

DAVID RIFE holds the John P. Graham Chair in Teaching at Lycoming College in Williamsport, Pennsylvania, where he teaches in the English Department. His essays have appeared in *The Dictionary of Literary Biography, American Literary Realism, Journal of Modern Literature,* and *The Oxford Companion to Crime and Mystery Writing,* among other places. He is working on an annotated bibliography of jazz fiction.

PAUL RINZLER is director of jazz studies at California Polytechnic State University in San Luis Obispo. His previous article on McCoy Tyner appeared in *ARJS 2* (1983).

EVAN SPRING graduated from the Master of Arts program in jazz history and research at the Newark Campus of Rutgers, The State University. For thirteen years, he has hosted a jazz program at WKCR-FM in New York and has interviewed more than 150 musicians.

ROBERT W. WASON is professor of music theory, cochair of the Department of Music Theory, and affiliate faculty member in the Department of Jazz and Contemporary Media at the Eastman School of Music, Rochester, New York. A recipient of grants from the Guggenheim Foundation, National Endowment for the Humanities, Paul Sacher Foundation, and the German Academic Exchange (DAAD), he has taught at the Hartt School, Trinity College (Hartford), Clark University, the University of North Texas, and has been guest professor at the University of Basel (Switzerland), the University of British Columbia (Vancouver), and SUNY–Buffalo.

ABOUT THE INSTITUTE OF JAZZ STUDIES

The Institute of Jazz Studies of Rutgers, the State University of New Jersey, is a unique research facility and archival collection, the foremost of its kind. IJS was founded in 1952 by Marshall Stearns (1908–1966), a pioneer jazz scholar, professor of medieval English literature at Hunter College, and the author of two essential jazz books: *The Story of Jazz* and *Jazz Dance*. In 1966, Rutgers was chosen as the collection's permanent academic home. IJS is located on the Newark campus of Rutgers and is a branch of the John Cotton Dana Library of the Rutgers University Libraries.

IJS carries on a comprehensive program to preserve and further jazz in al its facets. The archival collection, which has quadrupled its holdings since coming to Rutgers, as of 1991 consists of more than 100,000 sound recordings in all formats, from phonograph cylinders and piano rolls to video cassettes and laser discs; more than 5,000 books on jazz and related subjects, including discographies, bibliographies, and dissertations; and comprehensive holdings in jazz periodicals from throughout the world. In addition, there are extensive vertical files on individuals and selected topics, a large collection of photographs, sheet music, big band arrangements, realia, and memorabilia.

IJS serves a broad range of users, from students to seasoned scholars, authors, and collectors. The facilities are open to the public on weekdays by appointment. In order to allow the widest possible access, there is no charge for routine use of reference materials. Researchers requiring extensive staff assistance, however, are assessed a charge. Due to limited audio facilities, as well as to preserve the record collection, listening and taping are limited to serious research projects.

In addition to students, scholars, and other researchers, IJS routinely assists teachers, musicians, the media, record companies and producers, libraries and archives, arts agencies, and jazz organizations.

For further information on IJS programs and activities, write to:
Institute of Jazz Studies
Dana Library
Rutgers, The State University
Newark, New Jersey 07102